SAS® Programming 2: Data Manipulation Techniques

Course Notes

SAS® Programming 2: Data Manipulation Techniques Course Notes was developed by Davetta Dunlap, Susan Farmer, Karen Feldman, and Johnny Johnson. Additional contributions were made by Mark Jordan, Marjorie Lampton, Rob McAfee, Linda Mitterling, and Kathy Passarella. Editing and production support was provided by the Curriculum Development and Support Department.

SAS® Programming 2: Data Manipulation Techniques Course Notes

Book code E2139, course code LWPRG2/PRG2, prepared date 21Feb2013. LWPRG2_004

ISBN 978-1-61290-528-0

Table of Contents

Course Description viii

Prerequisites ix

Chapter 1 Introduction 1-1

1.1 An Overview of SAS Foundation 1-3

1.2 Course Logistics 1-6

1.3 Course Data Files 1-12

Demonstration: Creating Course Data Flies 1-13

Exercises 1-14

Chapter 2 Controlling Input and Output 2-1

2.1 Writing Observations Explicitly 2-3

Exercises 2-14

2.2 Writing to Multiple SAS Data Sets 2-17

Demonstration: Creating Multiple Data Sets 2-21

Exercises 2-26

2.3 Selecting Variables and Observations 2-29

Exercises 2-43

2.4 Solutions 2-46

Solutions to Exercises 2-46

Solutions to Student Activities (Polls/Quizzes) 2-50

Chapter 3 Summarizing Data 3-1

3.1 Creating an Accumulating Total Variable 3-3

Exercises 3-14

3.2 Accumulating Totals for a Group of Data 3-18

Exercises......3-34

3.3 Solutions......3-38

Solutions to Exercises......3-38

Solutions to Student Activities (Polls/Quizzes)......3-42

Chapter 4 Reading Raw Data Files......4-1

4.1 Reading Raw Data Files with Formatted Input......4-3

Exercises......4-17

4.2 Controlling when a Record Loads......4-20

Exercises......4-41

4.3 Solutions......4-45

Solutions to Exercises......4-45

Solutions to Student Activities......4-47

Chapter 5 Data Transformations......5-1

5.1 Introduction......5-3

5.2 Manipulating Character Values (Part 1)......5-8

Exercises......5-19

5.3 Manipulating Character Values (Part 2)......5-23

Exercises......5-39

5.4 Manipulating Numeric Values......5-43

Exercises......5-51

5.5 Converting Variable Type......5-54

Exercises......5-76

5.6 Solutions......5-78

Solutions to Exercises......5-78

Solutions to Student Activities (Polls/Quizzes)......5-84

Chapter 6 Debugging Techniques ... 6-1

6.1 Using the PUTLOG Statement ... 6-3

Demonstration: Determining Logic Errors ... 6-8

Exercises ... 6-12

6.2 Solutions ... 6-12

Solutions to Exercises ... 6-12

Solutions to Student Activities (Polls/Quizzes) ... 6-13

Chapter 7 Processing Data Iteratively ... 7-1

7.1 DO Loop Processing ... 7-3

Exercises ... 7-16

7.2 Conditional DO Loop Processing ... 7-17

Exercises ... 7-28

7.3 SAS Array Processing ... 7-30

Exercises ... 7-40

7.4 Using SAS Arrays ... 7-44

Exercises ... 7-59

7.5 Solutions ... 7-61

Solutions to Exercises ... 7-61

Solutions to Student Activities (Polls/Quizzes) ... 7-66

Chapter 8 Restructuring a Data Set ... 8-1

8.1 Rotating with the DATA Step ... 8-3

Exercises ... 8-22

8.2 Solutions ... 8-24

Solutions to Exercises ... 8-24

Solutions to Student Activities (Polls/Quizzes) ... 8-26

Chapter 9 Combining SAS® Data Sets 9-1

9.1 Using Data Manipulation Techniques with Match-Merging 9-3

Demonstration: Performing a Match-Merge on Data Sets That Lack a Common Variable 9-13

Exercises 9-20

9.2 Solutions 9-24

Solutions to Exercises 9-24

Solutions to Student Activities (Polls/Quizzes) 9-25

Chapter 10 Creating and Maintaining Permanent Formats 10-1

10.1 Creating Permanent Formats 10-3

Demonstration: Using a Control Data Set to Create a Format 10-11

Demonstration: Maintaining Permanent Formats 10-17

Exercises 10-18

10.2 Solutions 10-20

Solutions to Exercises 10-20

Solutions to Student Activities (Polls/Quizzes) 10-24

Chapter 11 Other SAS® Languages 11-1

11.1 An Overview of Other Languages 11-3

11.2 Using the SQL Procedure 11-5

Exercises 11-19

11.3 The SAS Macro Language 11-23

Exercises 11-33

11.4 Solutions 11-35

Solutions to Exercises 11-35

Solutions to Student Activities (Polls/Quizzes) 11-37

Chapter 12 Learning More 12-1

12.1 Introduction 12-3

Course Description

This course is for those who need to learn data manipulation techniques using SAS DATA and procedure steps to access, transform, and summarize SAS data sets. The course builds on the concepts that are presented in the SAS® Programming 1: Essentials course and is not recommended for beginning SAS software users.

To learn more…

For information about other courses in the curriculum, contact the SAS Education Division at 1-800-333-7660, or send e-mail to training@sas.com. You can also find this information on the Web at support.sas.com/training/ as well as in the Training Course Catalog.

For a list of other SAS books that relate to the topics covered in this Course Notes, USA customers can contact our SAS Publishing Department at 1-800-727-3228 or send e-mail to sasbook@sas.com. Customers outside the USA, please contact your local SAS office.

Also, see the Publications Catalog on the Web at support.sas.com/pubs for a complete list of books and a convenient order form.

Prerequisites

Before attending this course, you should have at least six months of experience writing SAS programs or have completed the SAS® Programming 1: Essentials course and used SAS for at least one month. Specifically, you should be able to

- submit a SAS program
- diagnose and correct syntax errors
- examine descriptor and data portions of a SAS data set
- access SAS data libraries
- read and create SAS data sets
- read Excel spreadsheets
- read delimited raw data files
- examine data errors when reading raw data files
- use SAS procedures to validate data
- clean invalid data
- create variables
- combine SAS data sets
- use global statements
- use labels and formats, including user-defined formats
- subset observations
- produce summary reports using the FREQ and MEANS procedures

Chapter 1 Introduction

1.1 An Overview of SAS Foundation 1-3

1.2 Course Logistics 1-6

1.3 Course Data Files 1-12

Demonstration: Creating Course Data Flies 1-13

Exercises 1-14

1.1 An Overview of SAS Foundation

Objectives

- Characterize SAS software.
- Describe the functionality of Base SAS and SAS Foundation tools.

3

What Is SAS?

SAS is a suite of business solutions and technologies to help organizations solve business problems.

sas

4

What Can You Do with SAS?

SAS software enables you to do the following:

- access data across multiple sources
- manage data
- perform sophisticated analyses
- deliver information across your organization

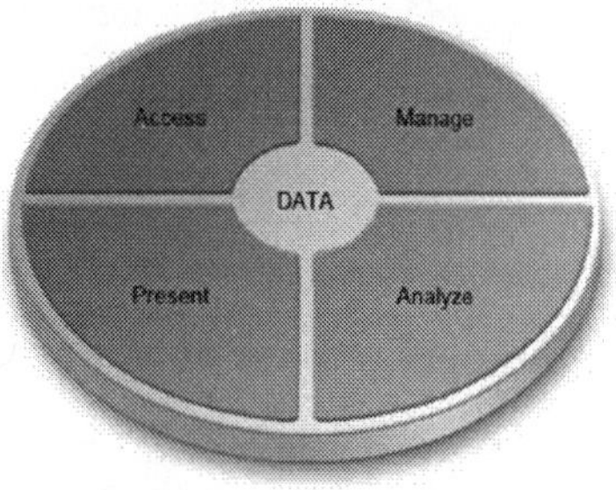

5

What Is Base SAS?

Base SAS is the centerpiece of all SAS software.

Base SAS is a product within the SAS Foundation set of products that provides

- a highly flexible, highly extensible fourth-generation programming language
- a rich library of encapsulated programming procedures
- a graphic user interface for administering SAS tasks.

6

About This Class

This class focuses on manipulating data with the DATA step, including

- creating multiple SAS data sets
- accumulating totals and summarizing data
- reading fixed column raw data files
- manipulating variable values with functions
- performing DO loop and SAS array processing
- rotating data sets
- merging data sets.

7

1.01 Poll

Have you worked with the DATA step?

a. yes, just maintaining programs
b. no, not at all

8

1.2 Course Logistics

Objectives

- Describe the data used in the course.
- Designate the editors and processing mode available for workshops.
- Specify the naming convention used for course files.
- Define the three levels of exercises.
- Discuss accessing the Help facility.

11

Orion Star Sports & Outdoors

This course focuses on a fictitious global sports and outdoors retailer that has traditional stores, an online store, and a large catalog business.

12

Orion Star Data

Large amounts of data are stored in transactional systems in various formats.

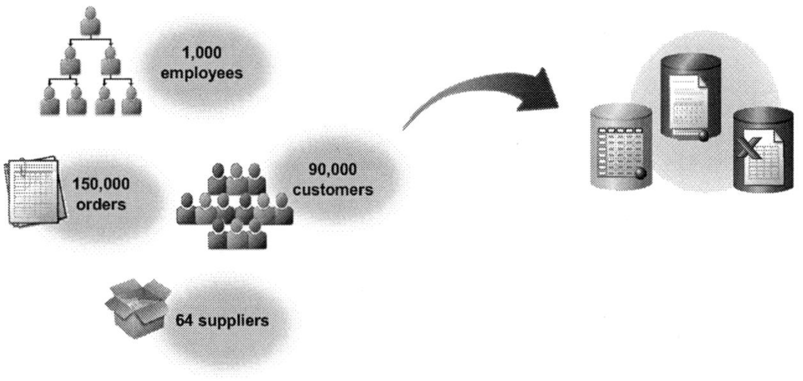

13

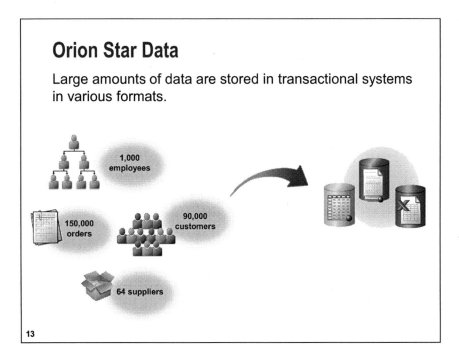

Writing and Running SAS Programs

In this course, you ***write*** and ***process*** SAS programs that access Orion Star data and create reports using an editor.

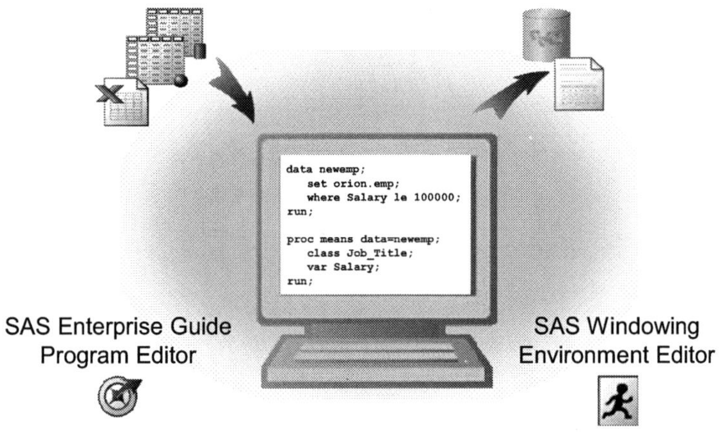

14

	SAS Enterprise Guide	SAS Windowing Environment
Editor	Program Editor	Enhanced Editor or Program Editor
Formatting	Automatic	Manual
Syntax Help	Context-sensitive	Menu- or function key-based
Output	SAS Report	HTML
Projects	Yes	No
Autocomplete	Yes	No
Program Flow Analysis	Yes	No

What Is SAS Enterprise Guide?

SAS Enterprise Guide is a powerful Windows client application that provides a GUI for transparently accessing the power of SAS.

It provides the following:

- a point-and-click interface with menus and wizards that enable the user to define tasks
- SAS code generation and execution based on user selections
- a full programming interface that can be used to write, edit, and submit SAS code

This class uses the programming interface.

15

What Is the SAS Windowing Environment?

The *SAS windowing environment* consists of a series of windows that you can use to edit and submit programs, and view the results.

The SAS windowing environment editor contains the following windows:

- the Enhanced Editor and Program Editor windows for preparing and submitting a program
- the Log window for viewing notes, warning messages, and error messages
- the Output window, which contains the output generated by most SAS procedures

16

1.02 Multiple Choice Poll

Which editor will you use to write SAS programs?

a. SAS Enterprise Guide Program Editor
b. Program Editor in the SAS windowing environment
c. a different editor
d. I do not know.

17

Program Naming Conventions

In this course, you retrieve and save SAS programs using the structure below.

- ❶ course ID
- ❷ chapter #
- ❸ type
  - a=activity
  - d=demo
  - e=exercise
  - s=solution
- ❹ item #
- ❺ placeholder

```
p204d01x
```

❶ ❷ ❸ ❹ ❺

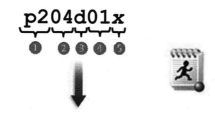

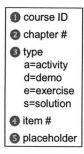

Programming 2, Chapter 4, Demo 1

18

Filename and Library Name References

In this course, macro variable references are used to give a more flexible approach for locating files.

Examples

```
%let path=s:\workshop;
libname orion "s:\workshop";
```

```
filename sales "&path\sales.dat";
```

```
infile "&path\payroll.dat";
```

19

Three Levels of Exercises

The course is designed to have you complete only ***one*** set of exercises. Select the level most appropriate for your skill set.

Level 1	Provides step-by-step instructions.
Level 2	Provides less information and guidance.
Challenge	Provides minimal information and guidance. Students might need to use the Help facility.

20

Getting Help

In class, you can get product help in several ways, depending on the editor being used.

- Getting Started tutorials
- Help facilities included in the software
- web-based help, if web access is available

21

Extending Your Learning

After class, you will have access to an extended learning page that was created for this course. The page includes

- course data and program files
- a PDF file of the course notes
- other course-specific resources.

✎ This page might also be available during class.

22

1.3 Course Data Files

Objectives

- Execute a SAS program to create the course data files.
- Execute a SAS program to define the data location.

25

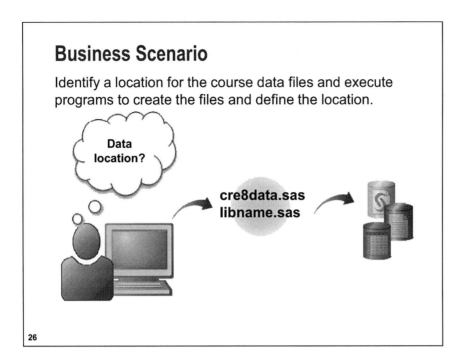

Business Scenario

Identify a location for the course data files and execute programs to create the files and define the location.

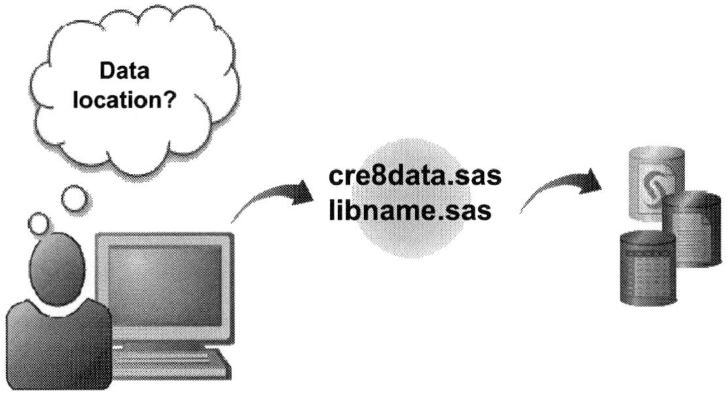

26

Creating Course Data Flies

cre8data

The **cre8data** program creates data files for this course. The program must be executed once, at the start of the ***course***.

1. Define target locations for your course data files. The default location for all course data is **s:\workshop**. If your data files are to be created in a location other than **s:\workshop**, you must identify a location for the course data files.

   Create the SAS data files here: ________________________________

2. Select **File** ⇨ **Open** ⇨ **Program**.

3. Navigate to the data folder, select **cre8data**, and click **Open**. The program is displayed in an editor.

   Notice the default value for the %LET statement.

4. If your files are to be created at a location other than **s:\workshop**, change the %LET statements as follows:

   Change the value assigned to PATH= to reflect the location of the SAS data files.

   ✎ If your files are to be created in **s:\workshop**, then no change is needed.

5. Press F3 to submit the program.

6. View the Results window and verify that the output contains a list of data files.

Defining the Data Location

libname

The **libname** program tells SAS where to find the course data files. This program must be executed each time you start a new ***session***.

1. Open the **libname** program. The LIBNAME statement starts with an asterisk. This means it is commented out and SAS does not execute this statement. At this point, you only want SAS to execute the %LET statement to tell SAS where the data files are located. You learn about the LIBNAME statement and the use of comments later in this course.

```
%let path=s:\workshop;
*libname orion "s:\workshop";
```

   The data location might be different in your **libname** program. It is defined based on the data location specified in **cre8data**.

2. Submit the program. View the log and verify that there are no errors or warnings.

Exercises

You ***must*** complete the exercises to create the course data files. If you do not create the data files, all programs in this course will fail.

Required Exercise

1. Creating Course Data

   a. The default location for all course data is **s:\workshop**. If your data files are to be created in a location other than **s:\workshop**, you must identify a location for your course data files.

   Create the SAS data files here: ____________________________________

   b. Select **File** ⇨ **Open** ⇨ **Program**.

   c. Navigate to the data folder, select **cre8data**, and click **Open**. The program is displayed in an editor.

   Observe the default values for the %LET statements.

```
/* Windows/UNIX */

/* STEP 1: Notice the default values for the %LET statements. */

/* STEP 2: If your files are not to be located in S:\workshop */
/* change the value of PATH= %LET statement to */
/* reflect your data location. */

/* STEP 3: Submit the program to create the course data files. */
```

```
/* STEP 4: Go to the Results-SAS Report tab in Enterprise Guide*/
/* or the Results Viewer in SAS and verify the CONTENTS    */
/*procedure report lists the names of the SAS data sets that */
/*were created.*/

%let path=s:\workshop;

/*++++++++++++++++++++++++++++++++++++++++++++++++*/
/* WARNING: DO NOT ALTER CODE BELOW THIS LINE */
/*++++++++++++++++++++++++++++++++++++++++++++++++*/
```

d. If your files are to be created at a location other than **s:\workshop**, change the %LET statements as follows:

Change the value assigned to PATH= to reflect the location of the SAS data files.

If your files are to be created in **s:\workshop**, then no change is needed.

e. Press F3 to submit the program.

f. View the Results window and verify that the output contains a list of data files, similar to the list below.

The SAS System

The CONTENTS Procedure

Directory	
Libref	ORION
Engine	V9
Physical Name	s:\workshop
Filename	s:\workshop

#	Name	Member Type	File Size	Last Modified
1	APRSALES	DATA	5120	27Sep12:13:17:59
2	APRSALES2	DATA	5120	27Sep12:13:17:59
3	AU_SALESFORCE	DATA	9216	27Sep12:13:17:59

2. **Defining the Data Location**

a. Open the **libname** program. Do not change anything in this program.

b. Submit the program.

c. View the log and verify that there are no errors or warnings.

Chapter 2 Controlling Input and Output

2.1 Writing Observations Explicitly 2-3

Exercises 2-14

2.2 Writing to Multiple SAS Data Sets 2-17

Demonstration: Creating Multiple Data Sets 2-21

Exercises 2-26

2.3 Selecting Variables and Observations 2-29

Exercises 2-43

2.4 Solutions 2-46

Solutions to Exercises 2-46

Solutions to Student Activities (Polls/Quizzes) 2-50

2.1 Writing Observations Explicitly

Objectives

- Explicitly control the output of multiple observations to a SAS data set.

3

Business Scenario

You have been asked to forecast the growth rate of six departments at Orion Star for a two-year period.

Current Employee Count

Department	Total_ Employees	Increase
Administration	34	0.25
Engineering	9	0.30
IS	25	0.10
Marketing	20	0.20
Sales	201	0.30
Sales Management	11	0.10

Predicted Two-Year Growth Rate

Department	Total_ Employees	Increase	Year
Administration	42.500	0.25	1
Administration	53.125	0.25	2
Engineering	11.700	0.30	1
Engineering	15.210	0.30	2
IS	27.500	0.10	1
IS	30.250	0.10	2

4

2.01 Quiz

Which of the following occurs at the end of a DATA step iteration?

```
data forecast;
   set orion.growth;
   total_employees=
      total_employees * (1+increase);
run;
```

a. reinitialize the PDV
b. implicit OUTPUT and implicit RETURN
c. read the next observation

5

Explicit Output

The explicit OUTPUT statement writes the contents of the program data vector (PDV) to the data set or data sets being created. The presence of an explicit OUTPUT statement overrides implicit output.

```
data forecast;
   set orion.growth;
   Year=1;
   Total_Employees=Total_Employees*(1+Increase);
   output;
   Year=2;
   Total_Employees=Total_Employees*(1+Increase);
   output;
run;
```

OUTPUT *<SAS-data-set-1 ... SAS-data-set-n>*;

No implicit OUTPUT;
Implicit RETURN;

7 **p202d01**

Using an explicit OUTPUT statement without arguments causes the current observation to be written to all data sets that are named in the DATA statement.

> The explicit OUTPUT statement causes immediate output but not an immediate return to the top of the DATA step. The implicit RETURN statement still occurs at the bottom of the step.

Compilation

```
data forecast;
   set orion.growth;
   Year=1;
   Total_Employees=Total_Employees*(1+Increase);
   output;
   Year=2;
   Total_Employees=Total_Employees*(1+Increase);
   output;
run;
```

PDV – Program Data Vector

Department $ 20	Total_ Employees N 8	Increase N 8

8 ...

Compilation

```
data forecast;
   set orion.growth;
   Year=1;
   Total_Employees=Total_Employees*(1+Increase);
   output;
   Year=2;
   Total_Employees=Total_Employees*(1+Increase);
   output;
run;
```

PDV

Department $ 20	Total_ Employees N 8	Increase N 8	Year N 8

9 ...

Compilation

```
data forecast;
   set orion.growth;
   Year=1;
   Total_Employees=Total_Employees*(1+Increase);
   output;
   Year=2;
   Total_Employees=Total_Employees*(1+Increase);
   output;
run;
```

Write descriptor portion of output data set.

PDV

Department $ 20	Total_ Employees N 8	Increase N 8	Year N 8

work.forecast

Department $ 20	Total_ Employees N 8	Increase N 8	Year N 8

10

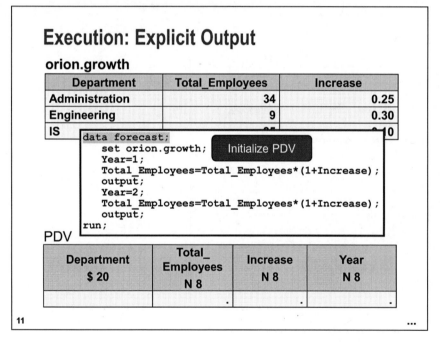

Execution: Explicit Output

orion.growth

Department	Total_Employees	Increase
Administration	34	0.25
Engineering	9	0.30
IS	[illegible]	0.10

```
data forecast;
   set orion.growth;
   Year=1;
   Total_Employees=Total_Employees*(1+Increase);
   output;
   Year=2;
   Total_Employees=Total_Employees*(1+Increase);
   output;
run;
```

Initialize PDV

PDV

Department $ 20	Total_ Employees N 8	Increase N 8	Year N 8
	.	.	.

11 ...

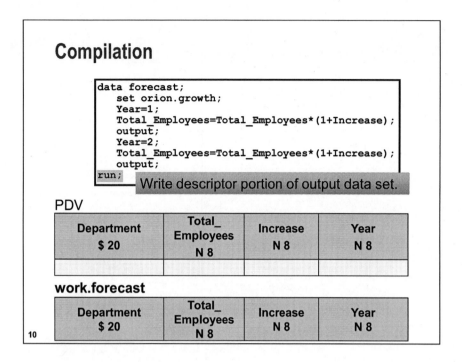

Execution: Explicit Output

orion.growth

Department	Total_Employees	Increase
Administration	34	0.25
Engineering	9	0.30
IS		

```
data forecast;
   set orion.growth;
   Year=1;
   Total_Employees=Total_Employees*(1+Increase);
   output;
   Year=2;
   Total_Employees=Total_Employees*(1+Increase);
   output;
run;
```

PDV

Department $ 20	Total_ Employees N 8	Increase N 8	Year N 8
Administration	34	0.25	.

12 ...

Execution: Explicit Output

orion.growth

Department	Total_Employees	Increase
Administration	34	0.25
Engineering	9	0.30
IS		

```
data forecast;
   set orion.growth;
   Year=1;
   Total_Employees=Total_Employees*(1+Increase);
   output;
   Year=2;
   Total_Employees=Total_Employees*(1+Increase);
   output;
run;
```

PDV

Department $ 20	Total_ Employees N 8	Increase N 8	Year N 8
Administration	34	0.25	1

13 ...

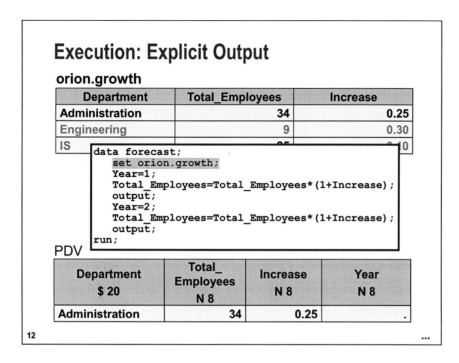

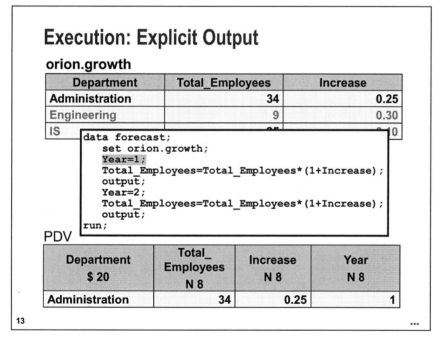

Execution: Explicit Output

orion.growth

Department	Total_Employees	Increase
Administration	34	0.25
Engineering	9	0.30
IS		

```
data forecast;
   set orion.growth;
   Year=1;
   Total_Employees=Total_Employees*(1+Increase);
   output;
   Year=2;
   Total_Employees=Total_Employees*(1+Increase);
   output;
run;
```

34 * (1 + 0.25)

PDV

Department $ 20	Total_ Employees N 8	Increase N 8	Year N 8
Administration	42.5	0.25	1

14 ...

Execution: Explicit Output

orion.growth

Department	Total_Employees	Increase
Administration	34	0.25
Engineering	9	0.30
IS		

```
data forecast;
   set orion.growth;
   Year=1;
   Total_Employees=Total_Employees*(1+Increase);
   output;
   Year=2;
   Total_Employees=Total_Employees*(1+Increase);
   output;
run;
```

Output current observation

PDV

Department $ 20	Total_ Employees N 8	Increase N 8	Year N 8
Administration	42.5	0.25	1

15 ...

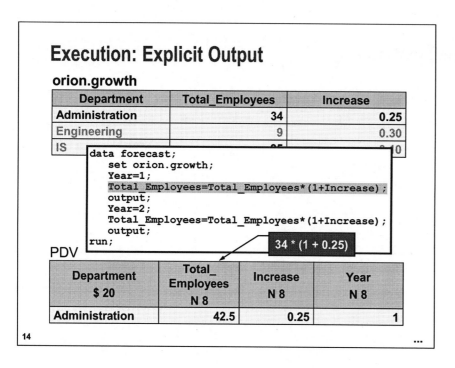

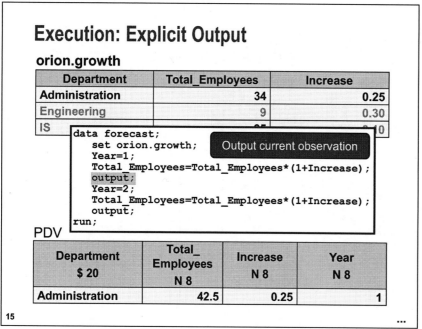

Execution: Explicit Output

orion.growth

Department	Total_Employees	Increase
Administration	34	0.25
Engineering	9	0.30
IS		

```
data forecast;
   set orion.growth;
   Year=1;
   Total_Employees=Total_Employees*(1+Increase);
   output;
   Year=2;
   Total_Employees=Total_Employees*(1+Increase);
   output;
run;
```

PDV

Department $ 20	Total_ Employees N 8	Increase N 8	Year N 8
Administration	42.5	0.25	2

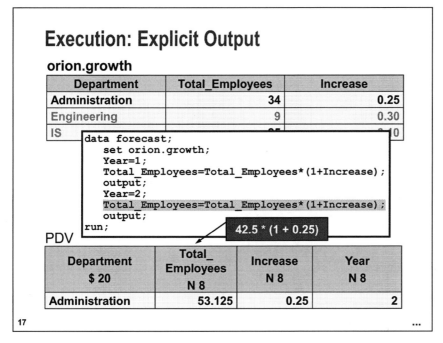

16 ...

Execution: Explicit Output

orion.growth

Department	Total_Employees	Increase
Administration	34	0.25
Engineering	9	0.30
IS		

```
data forecast;
   set orion.growth;
   Year=1;
   Total_Employees=Total_Employees*(1+Increase);
   output;
   Year=2;
   Total_Employees=Total_Employees*(1+Increase);
   output;
run;
```

42.5 * (1 + 0.25)

PDV

Department $ 20	Total_ Employees N 8	Increase N 8	Year N 8
Administration	53.125	0.25	2

17 ...

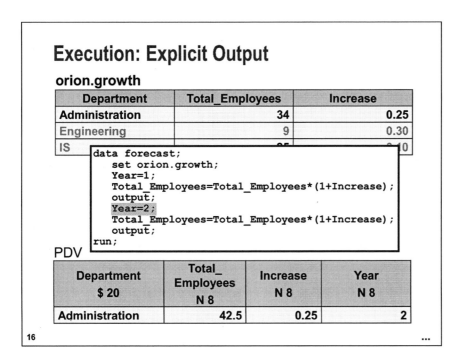

Execution: Explicit Output

orion.growth

Department	Total_Employees	Increase
Administration	34	0.25
Engineering	9	0.30
IS		

```
data forecast;
   set orion.growth;
   Year=1;
   Total_Employees=Total_Employees*(1+Increase);
   output;
   Year=2;
   Total_Employees=Total_Employees*(1+Increase);
   output;
run;
```

Output current observation

PDV

Department $ 20	Total_ Employees N 8	Increase N 8	Year N 8
Administration	53.125	0.25	2

18

...

Execution: Explicit Output

orion.growth

Department	Total_Employees	Increase
Administration	34	0.25
Engineering	9	0.30
IS		

```
data forecast;
   set orion.growth;
   Year=1;
   Total_Employees=Total_Employees*(1+Increase);
   output;
   Year=2;
   Total_Employees=Total_Employees*(1+Increase);
   output;
run;
```

No implicit OUTPUT;
Implicit RETURN;

PDV

Department $ 20	Total_ Employees N 8	Increase N 8	Year N 8
Administration	53.125	0.25	2

19

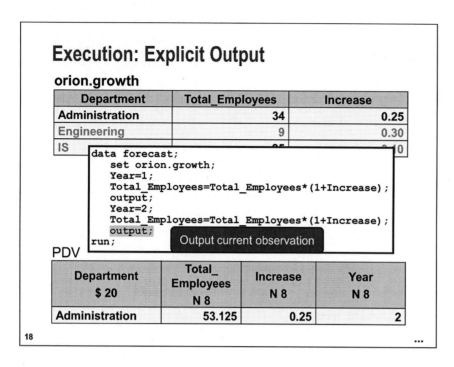

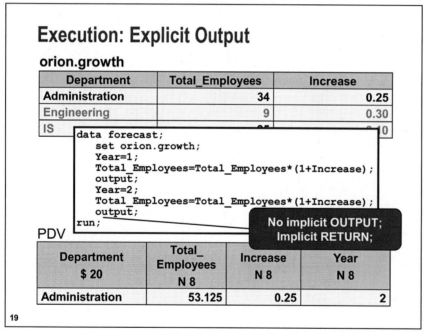

Output: A Forecasting Application

The **forecast** data set contains two observations after the first iteration of the DATA step.

work.forecast

Department	Total_ Employees	Increase	Year
Administration	42.500	0.25	1
Administration	53.125	0.25	2

20

Setup for the Poll

Prior to the second iteration of the DATA step, variables in the program data vector might be reinitialized.

```
data forecast;
   set orion.growth;
   Year=1;
   Total_Employees=Total_Employees*(1+Increase);
   output;
   Year=2;
   Total_Employees=Total_Employees*(1+Increase);
   output;
run;
```

PDV

Department $ 20	Total_ Employees N 8	Increase N 8	Year N 8
Administration	53.125	0.25	2

21

2.02 Multiple Answer Poll

Which variable or variables are reinitialized?

a. **Department**
b. **Total_Employees**
c. **Increase**
d. **Year**

22

Execution: Explicit Output

orion.growth

Department	Total_Employees	Increase
Administration	34	0.25
Engineering	9	0.30
IS		0.10

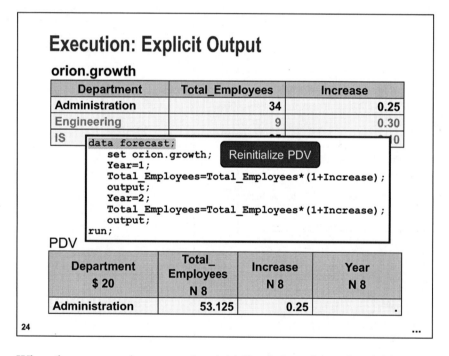

```
data forecast;
   set orion.growth;
   Year=1;
   Total_Employees=Total_Employees*(1+Increase);
   output;
   Year=2;
   Total_Employees=Total_Employees*(1+Increase);
   output;
run;
```

Reinitialize PDV

PDV

Department $ 20	Total_ Employees N 8	Increase N 8	Year N 8
Administration	53.125	0.25	.

24 ...

When the program data vector is reinitialized, the values of variables created by the assignment statements are set to missing. Variables that you read with a SET statement are not set to missing, because they are overwritten when the next observation is read.

Execution: Explicit Output

orion.growth

Department	Total_Employees	Increase
Administration	34	0.25
Engineering	9	0.30
IS		

```
data forecast;
   set orion.growth;
   Year=1;
   Total_Employees=Total_Employees*(1+Increase);
   output;
   Year=2;
   Total_Employees=Total_Employees*(1+Increase);
   output;
run;
```

PDV

Department $ 20	Total_ Employees N 8	Increase N 8	Year N 8
Engineering	9	0.30	.

25 ...

Execution: Explicit Output

orion.growth

Department	Total_Employees	Increase
Administration	34	0.25
Engineering	9	0.30
IS		

```
data forecast;
   set orion.growth;
   Year=1;
   Total_Employees=Total_Employees*(1+Increase);
   output;
   Year=2;
   Total_Employees=Total_Employees*(1+Increase);
   output;
run;
```

Continue until EOF

PDV

Department $ 20	Total_ Employees N 8	Increase N 8	Year N 8
Engineering	9	0.30	1

26

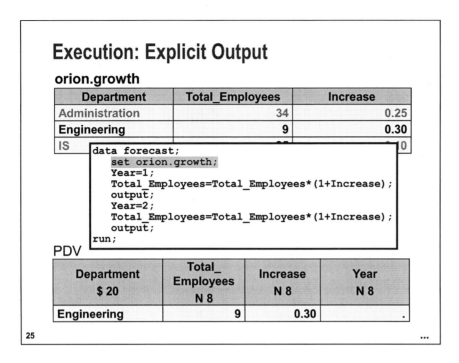

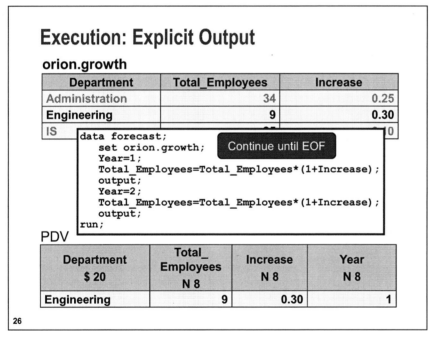

Check the Results

Partial SAS Log

```
NOTE: There were 6 observations read from the data set
      ORION.GROWTH.
NOTE: The data set WORK.FORECAST has 12 observations
      and 4 variables.
```

Partial PROC PRINT Output

Department	Total_ Employees	Year
Administration	42.500	1
Administration	53.125	2
Engineering	11.700	1
Engineering	15.210	2
IS	27.500	1
IS	30.250	2
Marketing	24.000	1
Marketing	28.800	2

27

2.03 Quiz

Open and submit **p202a01**. Modify the DATA step to write only one observation per department. Show the number of employees after two years.

How did you modify the DATA step?

Desired Results

Department	Total_ Employees	Year
Administration	53.125	2
Engineering	15.210	2
IS	30.250	2
Marketing	28.800	2
Sales	339.690	2
Sales Management	13.310	2

28 p202a01

Exercises

If you restarted your SAS session since the last exercise, open and submit the **libname.sas** program found in the data folder.

Level 1

1. Writing Observations Explicitly

The **orion.prices** data set contains price information for Orion Star products.

Partial **orion.prices** (50 Total Observations)

Product_ID	Unit_Price	Factor
210200100009	$34.70	1.01
210200100017	$40.00	1.01
210200200023	$19.80	1.01
210200600067	$67.00	1.01
210200600085	$39.40	1.01

a. Write a DATA step to create a new data set that forecasts unit prices for the next three years. This data set contains three observations for each input observation read from **orion.prices**.

- Open file **p202e01**. It reads **orion.prices** and creates a new data set named **work.price_increase**.
- Use explicit OUTPUT statements to forecast unit prices for the next three years, using **Factor** as the annual rate of increase.

b. Print the new data set.

- Include only **Product_ID**, **Unit_Price**, and **Year** in the report.
- Verify your results.

Partial PROC PRINT Output (150 Total Observations)

Obs	Product_ID	Unit_Price	Year
1	210200100009	$35.05	1
2	210200100009	$35.40	2
3	210200100009	$35.75	3
4	210200100017	$40.40	1
5	210200100017	$40.80	2

Level 2

2. Writing Observations Explicitly

The data set **orion.discount** contains information about various discounts that Orion Star runs on its products.

Partial **orion.discount**

Product_ID	Start_ Date	End_Date	Unit_Sales_ Price	Discount
210100100027	01MAY2011	31MAY2011	$17.99	70%
210100100030	01AUG2011	31AUG2011	$32.99	70%
210100100033	01AUG2011	31AUG2011	$161.99	70%
210100100034	01AUG2011	31AUG2011	$187.99	70%
210100100035	01MAY2011	31MAY2011	$172.99	70%

a. Due to excellent sales, all discounts from December 2011 are repeated in July 2012. Both the December 2011 and the July 2012 discounts are called the Happy Holidays promotion.

- Create a new data set named **work.extended** that contains all discounts for the Happy Holidays promotion.
- Use a WHERE statement to read only observations with a start date of 01Dec2011.
- Create a new variable, **Promotion**, which has the value *Happy Holidays* for each observation.
- Create another new variable, **Season**, that has a value of *Winter* for the December observations and *Summer* for the July observations.
- July 2012 discounts should have a start date of 01Jul2012 and an end date of 31Jul2012.
- Drop the **Unit_Sales_Price** variable.
- Use explicit OUTPUT to write two observations for each observation read.

b. Print the new data set.

- Add an appropriate title
- Verify the results.

Partial PROC PRINT (332 Total Observations)

Obs	Product_ID	Start_ Date	End_Date	Discount	Promotion	Season
1	210200100007	01DEC2011	31DEC2011	50%	Happy Holidays	Winter
2	210200100007	01JUL2012	31JUL2012	50%	Happy Holidays	Summer
3	210200300013	01DEC2011	31DEC2011	50%	Happy Holidays	Winter
4	210200300013	01JUL2012	31JUL2012	50%	Happy Holidays	Summer
5	210200300025	01DEC2011	31DEC2011	50%	Happy Holidays	Winter

Challenge

3. Using Conditional Logic to Output Multiple Observations

The data set **orion.country** contains information about country names as well as various lookup codes.

orion.country

Country	Country_Name	Population	Country_ ID	Continent_ ID	Country_Former Name
AU	Australia	20,000,000	160	96	
CA	Canada	.	260	91	
DE	Germany	80,000,000	394	93	East/West Germany
IL	Israel	5,000,000	475	95	
TR	Turkey	70,000,000	905	95	
US	United States	280,000,000	926	91	
ZA	South Africa	43,000,000	801	94	

a. Create a new data set that contains one observation for each current country name as well as one observation for each former country name.

- Use conditional logic and explicit OUTPUT statements to create a data set named **work.lookup**.
- If a country has a former country name, write two observations: one with the current name in the **Country_Name** variable and another with the former country name in the **Country_Name** variable.

- Drop the variables **Country_FormerName** and **Population**.
- Create a new variable named **Outdated** with values of either *Y* or *N* to indicate whether the observation represents the current country name.

b. Print the new data set with an appropriate title.

PROC PRINT Output

Current and Outdated Country Name Data

Obs	Country	Country_Name	Country_ ID	Continent_ ID	Outdated
1	AU	Australia	160	96	N
2	CA	Canada	260	91	N
3	DE	Germany	394	93	N
4	DE	East/West Germany	394	93	Y
5	IL	Israel	475	95	N
6	TR	Turkey	905	95	N
7	US	United States	926	91	N
8	ZA	South Africa	801	94	N

2.2 Writing to Multiple SAS Data Sets

Objectives

- Create multiple SAS data sets in a single DATA step.
- Use conditional processing to control the data set (or data sets) to which an observation is written.

33

Business Scenario

Use the input data set as to create three new data sets.

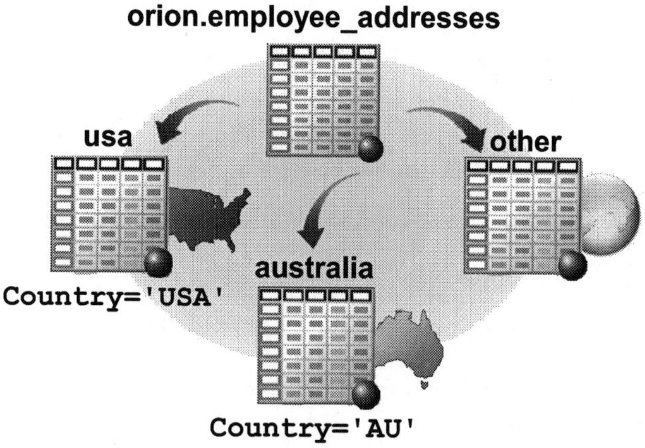

34

Browse the Input Data Set

```
proc print data=orion.employee_addresses;
   var Employee_Name City Country;
run;
```

Partial PROC PRINT Output (424 Total Observations)

Obs	Employee_Name	City	Country
1	Abbott, Ray	Miami-Dade	US
2	Aisbitt, Sandy	Melbourne	AU
3	Akinfolarin, Tameaka	Philadelphia	US
4	Amos, Salley	San Diego	US
5	Anger, Rose	Philadelphia	US
6	Anstey, David	Miami-Dade	US
7	Antonini, Doris	Miami-Dade	US
8	Apr, Nishan	San Diego	US
9	Ardskin, Elizabeth	Miami-Dade	US
10	Areu, Jeryl	Miami-Dade	US
11	Arizmendi, Gilbert	San Diego	US
12	Armant, Debra	San Diego	US

35 p202d02

Creating Multiple SAS Data Sets

Multiple data sets can be created in a DATA step by listing the names of the output data sets in the DATA statement.

Create three new data sets: **usa**, **australia**, and **other**.

DATA *<SAS-data-set-1 ... SAS-data-set-n>*;

```
data usa australia other;
   set orion.employee_addresses;
   if Country='AU' then output australia;
   else if Country='US' then output usa;
   else output other;
run;
```

You can direct output to a specific data set or data sets by listing the data set names in the OUTPUT statement.

36

p202d03

If you do not specify a SAS data set name or the reserved name _NULL_ in a DATA statement, then SAS creates data sets automatically with the names **data1**, **data2**, and so on in the Work library by default.

Data sets named in the OUTPUT statement ***must*** appear in the DATA statement.

To specify multiple data sets in a single OUTPUT statement, separate the data set names with a space.

```
output data1 data2;
```

Check the SAS Log

Three data sets were created. The log shows that *US* was the most frequently occurring value.

Partial SAS Log

```
NOTE: There were 424 observations read from the data set
      ORION.EMPLOYEE_ADDRESSES.
NOTE: The data set WORK.USA has 311 observations and 9
      variables.
NOTE: The data set WORK.AUSTRALIA has 105 observations and
      9  variables.
NOTE: The data set WORK.OTHER has 8 observations and 9
      variables.
```

37

Efficient Conditional Processing

It is more efficient to check values in order of decreasing frequency.

```
data usa australia other;
   set orion.employee_addresses;
   if Country='US' then output usa;
   else if Country='AU' then output australia;
   else output other;
run;
```

```
NOTE: There were 424 observations read from the data set
      ORION.EMPLOYEE_ADDRESSES.
NOTE: The data set WORK.USA has 311 observations and 9
      variables.
NOTE: The data set WORK.AUSTRALIA has 105 observations and
      9 variables.
NOTE: The data set WORK.OTHER has 8 observations and 9
      variables.
```

38

2.04 Quiz

Consider the results of the previous DATA step.

Can all three data sets be printed with a single PRINT procedure?

Partial SAS Log

```
NOTE: There were 424 observations read from the data set
      ORION.EMPLOYEE_ADDRESSES.
NOTE: The data set WORK.USA has 311 observations and 9
      variables.
NOTE: The data set WORK.AUSTRALIA has 105 observations and
      9 variables.
NOTE: The data set WORK.OTHER has 8 observations and 9
      variables.
```

39

Displaying Multiple SAS Data Sets

The PRINT procedure can print only one data set. A separate PROC PRINT step is required for each data set.

```
title 'Employees in the United States';
proc print data=usa;
run;

title 'Employees in Australia';
proc print data=australia;
run;

title 'Non US and AU Employees';
proc print data=other;
run;

title;
```

41

p202a02s

Creating Multiple Data Sets

p202d03a

This demonstration illustrates the creation of multiple data sets.

1. Open **p202d03a** and submit only the DATA step to create three data sets: **usa**, **australia**, and **other**. Examine the log. Most observations were written to **usa** and **australia**, whereas only eight observations were written to **other**.

   Partial SAS Log

   ```
   NOTE: There were 424 observations read from the data set ORION.EMPLOYEE_ADDRESSES.
   NOTE: The data set WORK.USA has 311 observations and 9 variables.
   NOTE: The data set WORK.AUSTRALIA has 105 observations and 9 variables.
   NOTE: The data set WORK.OTHER has 8 observations and 9 variables.
   ```

2. Submit the three PROC PRINT steps to display the data sets. Examine the values of the **Country** variable in the output. The observations in **other** have lowercase **Country** values: *au* and *us*. The UPCASE function can be used to cause case to be ignored.

3. Submit the modified DATA step to use the UPCASE function to handle case-insensitive comparisons as shown below.

   ```
   data usa australia other;
      set orion.employee_addresses;
      if upcase(Country)='AU' then output australia;
      else if upcase(Country)='US' then output usa;
      else output other;
   run;
   ```

   The following is an alternate approach that converts the **Country** values to be stored as uppercase:

```
data usa australia other;
   set orion.employee_addresses;
   Country=upcase(Country);
   if Country='AU' then output australia;
   else if Country='US' then output usa;
   else output other;
run;
```

4. Examine the log. No observations were written to **other**.

```
NOTE: There were 424 observations read from the data set ORION.EMPLOYEE_ADDRESSES.
NOTE: The data set WORK.USA has 316 observations and 9 variables.
NOTE: The data set WORK.AUSTRALIA has 108 observations and 9 variables.
NOTE: The data set WORK.OTHER has 0 observations and 9 variables.
```

Using a SELECT Group

The previous task can be rewritten using a SELECT group:

```
data usa australia other;
   set orion.employee_addresses;
   select (Country);
      when ('US') output usa;
      when ('AU') output australia;
      otherwise output other;
   end;
run;
```

SELECT <(*select-expression*)>;
WHEN-1 (*value-1* <*...,value-n*>)
statement;
<...**WHEN-*n*** (*value-1* <*...,value-n*>)
statement;>
<**OTHERWISE** *statement*;>
END;

44

p202d04

Check the SAS Log

Results using SELECT are the same as IF-THEN/ELSE results.

Partial SAS Log

```
NOTE: There were 424 observations read from the data set
      ORION.EMPLOYEE_ADDRESSES.
NOTE: The data set WORK.USA has 311 observations and 9
      variables.
NOTE: The data set WORK.AUSTRALIA has 105 observations and 9
      variables.
NOTE: The data set WORK.OTHER has 8 observations and 9
      variables.
```

45

2.05 Quiz

Open the file **p202a03** and submit it. View the log, identify and correct the problem, and resubmit the program.

```
data usa australia;
   set orion.employee_addresses;
   select (Country);
      when ('US') output usa;
      when ('AU') output australia;
   end;
run;
```

46

p202a03

OTHERWISE Statement

The OTHERWISE statement is optional, but omitting it results in an error when all WHEN conditions are false.

```
data usa australia;
   set orion.employee_addresses;
   select (Country);
      when ('US') output usa;
      when ('AU') output australia;
      otherwise;
   end;
run;
```

48 p202a03s

Test for Multiple Values in a WHEN Statement

Multiple values can be listed in the WHEN expression.

```
data usa australia other;
   set orion.employee_addresses;
   select (Country);
      when ('US','us') output usa;
      when ('AU','au') output australia;
      otherwise output other;
   end;
run;
```

Partial SAS Log

```
NOTE: There were 424 observations read from the data set
      ORION.EMPLOYEE_ADDRESSES.
NOTE: The data set WORK.USA has 316 observations and 9 variables.
NOTE: The data set WORK.AUSTRALIA has 108 observations and 9
      variables.
NOTE: The data set WORK.OTHER has 0 observations and 9 variables.
```

49 p202d04

Using Functions in a SELECT Expression

An alternate solution uses the UPCASE function.

```
data usa australia other;
   set orion.employee_addresses;
   select (upcase(Country));
      when ('US') output usa;
      when ('AU') output australia;
      otherwise output other;
   end;
run;
```

Partial SAS Log

```
NOTE: There were 424 observations read from the data set
      ORION.EMPLOYEE_ADDRESSES.
NOTE: The data set WORK.USA has 316 observations and 9 variables.
NOTE: The data set WORK.AUSTRALIA has 108 observations and 9
      variables.
NOTE: The data set WORK.OTHER has 0 observations and 9 variables.
```

50 p202d04

Using DO-END in a SELECT Group

Use DO and END statements to execute multiple statements when an expression is true.

```
data usa australia other;
   set orion.employee_addresses;
   select (upcase(country));
      when ('US') do;
         Benefits=1;
         output usa;
      end;
      when ('AU') do;
         Benefits=2;
         output australia;
      end;
      otherwise do;
         Benefits=0;
         output other;
      end;
   end;
run;
```

51 p202d04

Omitting the Select Expression

This version of the current example omits the SELECT expression.

```
data usa australia other;
   set orion.employee_addresses;
   select;
      when (country='US') output usa;
      when (country='AU') output australia;
      otherwise output other;
   end;
run;
```

```
SELECT;
   WHEN (expression-1)
      statement;
   <...WHEN (expression-n)
      statement;>
   <OTHERWISE statement;>
END;
```

52 p202d04

See SAS documentation for more information about using SELECT groups.

Exercises

If you restarted your SAS session since the last exercise, open and submit the **libname.sas** program found in the data folder.

Level 1

4. Creating Multiple SAS Data Sets

The data set **orion.employee_organization** contains information about employee job titles, departments, and managers.

Partial **orion.employee_organization** (424 Total Observations)

Employee_ ID	Job_Title	Department	Manager_ ID
120101	Director	Sales Management	120261
120102	Sales Manager	Sales Management	120101
120103	Sales Manager	Sales Management	120101
120104	Administration Manager	Administration	120101
120105	Secretary I	Administration	120101

a. Create a separate data set for each department.

Name the data sets **work.admin**, **work.stock**, and **work.purchasing**.

Use conditional logic and explicit OUTPUT statements to write to these data sets depending on whether the value of **Department** is *Administration*, *Stock & Shipping*, or *Purchasing*, respectively. Ignore all other **Department** values.

Hint: Be careful with capitalization and the spelling of the **Department** values.

b. Print **work.admin** and verify your results. Add an appropriate title.

Partial **work.admin** (34 Total Observations)

Administration Employees

Obs	Employee_ ID	Job_Title	Department	Manager_ ID
1	120104	Administration Manager	Administration	120101
2	120105	Secretary I	Administration	120101
3	120106	Office Assistant II	Administration	120104
4	120107	Office Assistant III	Administration	120104
5	120108	Warehouse Assistant II	Administration	120104

c. Print **work.stock** and verify your results. Add an appropriate title.

Partial **work.stock** (26 Total Observations)

Stock and Shipping Employees

Obs	Employee_ ID	Job_Title	Department	Manager_ ID
1	120670	Shipping Manager	Stock & Shipping	120659
2	120671	Shipping Agent III	Stock & Shipping	120670
3	120672	Shipping Manager	Stock & Shipping	120659
4	120673	Shipping Agent II	Stock & Shipping	120672
5	120677	Shipping Manager	Stock & Shipping	120659

d. Print **work.purchasing** and verify your results. Add an appropriate title.

Partial **work.purchasing** (18 Total Observations)

Purchasing Employees

Obs	Employee_ ID	Job_Title	Department	Manager_ ID
1	120728	Purchasing Agent II	Purchasing	120735
2	120729	Purchasing Agent I	Purchasing	120735
3	120730	Purchasing Agent I	Purchasing	120735
4	120731	Purchasing Agent II	Purchasing	120735
5	120732	Purchasing Agent III	Purchasing	120736

Level 2

5. Creating Multiple SAS Data Sets with Derived Values

The data set **orion.orders** contains information about in-store, catalog, and Internet orders as well as delivery dates.

Partial **orion.orders** (490 Total Observations)

Order_ID	Order_ Type	Employee_ID	Customer_ID	Order_ Date	Delivery_ Date
1230058123	1	121039	63	11JAN2007	11JAN2007
1230080101	2	99999999	5	15JAN2007	19JAN2007
1230106883	2	99999999	45	20JAN2007	22JAN2007
1230147441	1	120174	41	28JAN2007	28JAN2007
1230315085	1	120134	183	27FEB2007	27FEB2007

a. Orion Star wants to study catalog and Internet orders that were delivered quickly, as well as those that went slowly.

- Create three data sets named **work.fast**, **work.slow**, and **work.veryslow**.
- Write a WHERE statement to read only the observations with **Order_Type** equal to *2* (catalog) or *3* (Internet).
- Create a variable named **ShipDays** that is the number of days between when the order is placed and when the order is delivered.
- Handle the output as follows:
  - Output to **work.fast** when the value of **ShipDays** is less than *3*.
  - Output to **work.slow** when the value of **ShipDays** is *5* to *7*.
  - Output to **work.veryslow** when the value of **ShipDays** is greater than *7*.
  - Do not output an observation when the value of **ShipDays** is *3* or *4*.
- Drop the variable **Employee_ID**.
- There should be 80 observations in **work.fast**, 69 observations in **work.slow**, and 5 observations in **work.veryslow**.

Of the 490 observations in **orion.orders**, only 230 are read due to the WHERE statement.

b. Print your results from **work.veryslow** with an appropriate title.

work.veryslow

Orders taking more than 7 days to deliver

Obs	Order_ID	Order_ Type	Customer_ID	Order_ Date	Delivery_ Date	Ship Days
1	1231305521	2	16	27AUG2007	04SEP2007	8
2	1236483576	2	70108	22JUL2009	02AUG2009	11
3	1236965430	3	70165	08SEP2009	18SEP2009	10
4	1237165927	3	79	27SEP2009	08OCT2009	11
5	1241298131	2	2806	29JAN2011	08FEB2011	10

Challenge

6. Using a SELECT Group

Write a solution to the previous exercise using SELECT logic instead of IF-THEN/ELSE logic. Refer to SAS documentation to explore the use of a compound expression in a SELECT statement. Print the data set **work.veryslow**.

2.3 Selecting Variables and Observations

Objectives

- Control which variables are written to an output data set during a DATA step.
- Control which variables are read from an input data set during a DATA step.
- Control how many observations are processed from an input data set during a DATA or PROC step.

56

Business Scenario

You have controlled the observations written to the three new data sets, and now you want to control the variables that are written to each.

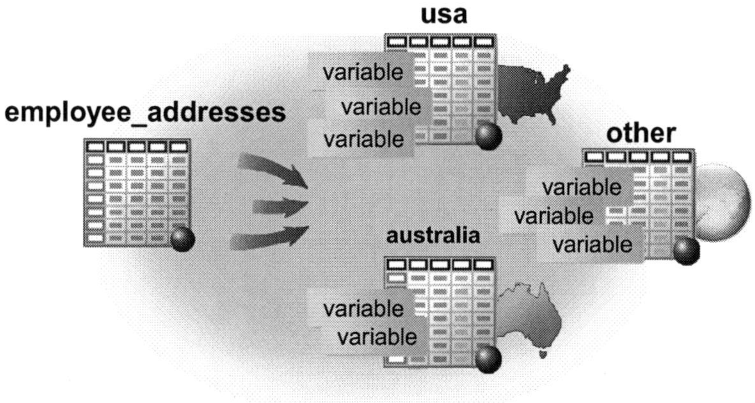

57

Controlling Variable Output (Review)

By default, SAS writes all variables from the input data set to every output data set.

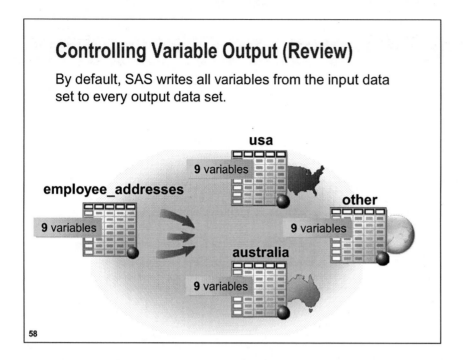

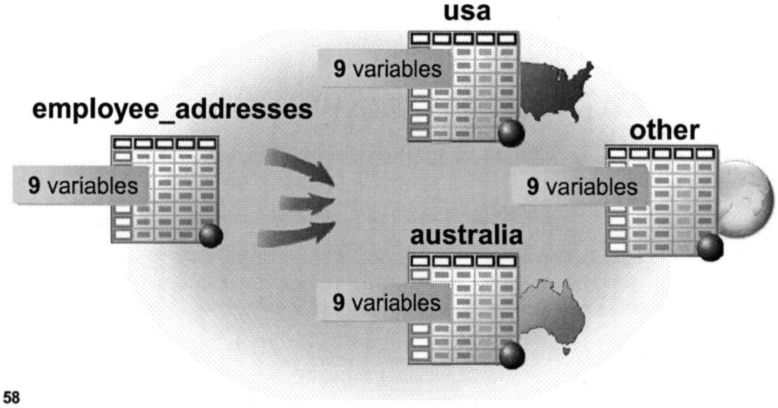

58

Controlling Variable Output (Review)

In the DATA step, the DROP and KEEP statements can be used to control which variables are written to output data sets.

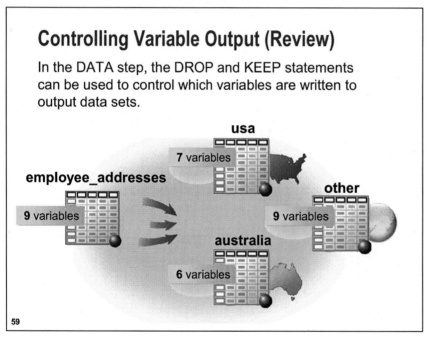

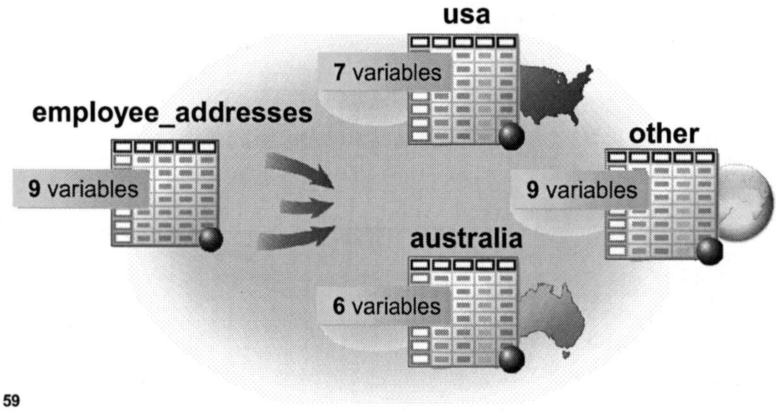

59

Controlling Variable Output (Review)

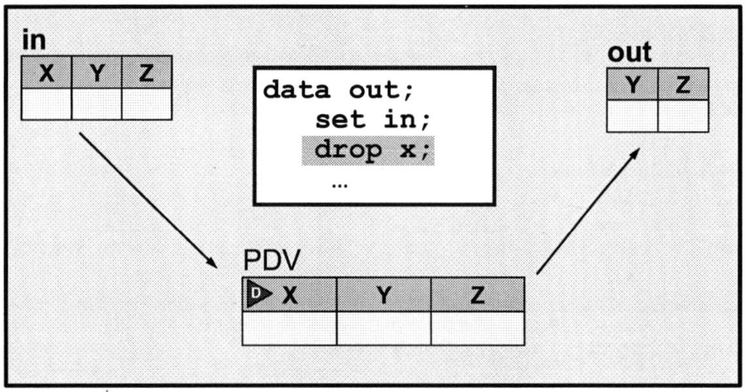

The DROP and KEEP statements affect output data sets. The statements can be used when reading from a SAS data set or from a raw data file.

60

Displaying Information about the Variables

The **orion.employee_addresses** data set contains nine variables.

```
proc contents data=orion.employee_addresses;
run;
```

Partial PROC CONTENTS Output

```
---Alphabetic List of Variables and Attributes---

     #    Variable          Type    Len

     6    City              Char     30
     9    Country           Char      2
     1    Employee_ID       Num       8
     2    Employee_Name     Char     40
     8    Postal_Code       Char     10
     7    State             Char      2
     3    Street_ID         Num       8
     5    Street_Name       Char     40
     4    Street_Number     Num       8
```

61 p202d05

Use the VARNUM option in the PROC CONTENTS statement to print a list of the variables by their position in the data set.

DROP Statement

The *DROP statement* drops variables from every output data set.

```
data usa australia other;
   drop Street_ID;
   set orion.employee_addresses;
   if Country='US' then output usa;
   else if Country='AU' then output australia;
   else output other;
run;
```

Partial SAS Log

```
NOTE: There were 424 observations read from the data set
      ORION.EMPLOYEE_ADDRESSES.
NOTE: The data set WORK.USA has 311 observations and 8 variables.
NOTE: The data set WORK.AUSTRALIA has 105 observations and 8
      variables.
NOTE: The data set WORK.OTHER has 8 observations and 8 variables.
```

62 p202d05

Controlling Variable Output

The task is to drop **Street_ID** and **Country** from **usa**, drop **Street_ID**, **Country**, and **State** from **australia**, and keep all variables in **other**.

USA

Employee_ ID	Employee_Name	Street_ Number	Street_Name	City	State	Postal_ Code
121044	Abbott, Ray	2267	Edwards Mill Rd	Miami-Dade	FL	33135
120761	Akinfolarin, Tameaka	5	Donnybrook Rd	Philadelphia	PA	19145
120656	Amos, Salley	3524	Calico Ct	San Diego	CA	92116

Australia

Employee_ ID	Employee_Name	Street_ Number	Street_Name	City	Postal_ Code
120145	Aisbitt, Sandy	30	Bingera Street	Melbourne	2001
120185	Bahlman, Sharon	24	LaTrobe Street	Sydney	2165
120109	Baker, Gabriele	166	Toorak Road	Sydney	2119

Other

Employee_ ID	Employee_Name	Street_ID	Street_ Number	Street_Name	City	State	Postal_ Code	Country
121019	Desanctis, Scott	9260121087	765	Greenhaven Ln	Philadelphia	PA	19102	us
120997	Donathan, Mary	9260121069	4923	Gateridge Dr	Philadelphia	PA	19152	us
120747	Farthing, Zashia	9260123756	763	Chatterson Dr	San Diego	CA	92116	us

63

DROP= Option in an Output Data Set

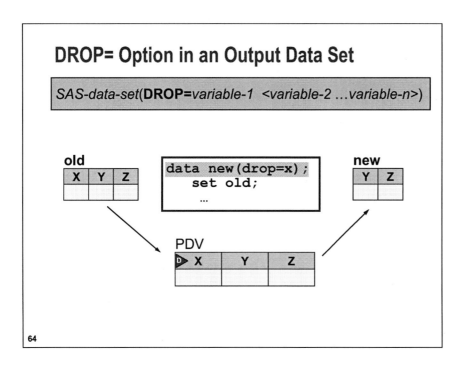

SAS-data-set(**DROP=***variable-1 <variable-2 ...variable-n>*)

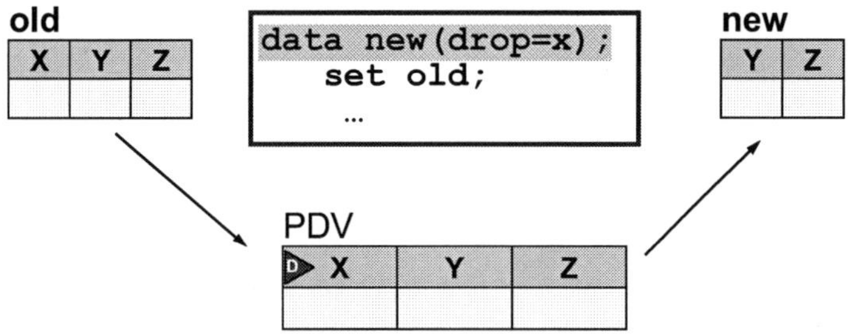

64

Using the DROP= Data Set Option

```
data usa(drop=Street_ID Country)
     australia(drop=Street_ID State Country)
     other;
   set orion.employee_addresses;
   if Country='US' then output usa;
   else if Country='AU' then
        output australia;
   else output other;
run;
```

```
NOTE: There were 424 observations read from the data set
      ORION.EMPLOYEE_ADDRESSES.
NOTE: The data set WORK.USA has 311 observations
      and 7 variables.
NOTE: The data set WORK.AUSTRALIA has 105 observations
      and 6 variables.
NOTE: The data set WORK.OTHER has 8 observations
      and 9 variables.
```

65 p202d06

KEEP= Option in an Output Data Set

SAS-data-set(**KEEP=***variable-1 <variable-2 ...variable-n>*)

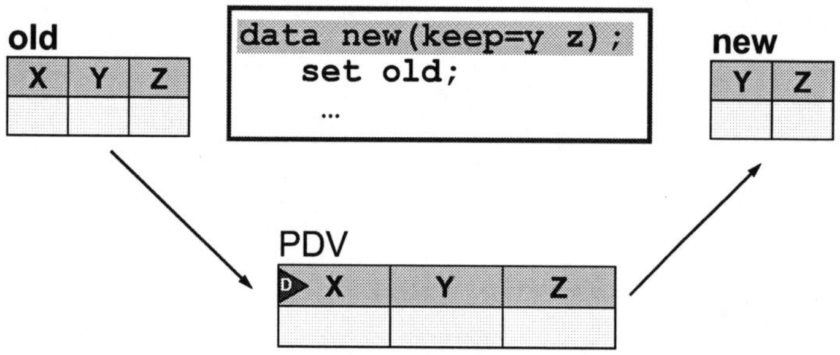

66

Using the DROP= and KEEP= Options

The DROP= and KEEP= options can both be used in a SAS program.

```
data usa(keep=Employee_Name City State)
     australia(drop=Street_ID State)
     other;
   set orion.employee_addresses;
   if Country='US' then output usa;
   else if Country='AU' then output australia;
   else output other;
run;
```

67 p202d07

In many cases, you have a choice between using a DROP= or KEEP= data set option (or DROP or KEEP statements). Often the data set option or statement that minimizes the amount of typing is selected.

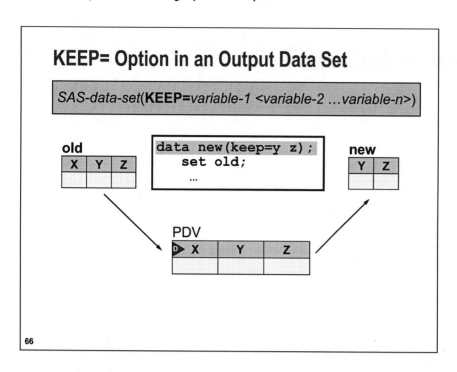

2.06 Quiz

The data set **orion.employee_addresses** contains nine variables. How many variables are in the **usa**, **australia**, and **other** data sets?

```
data usa(keep=Employee_Name City State Country)
     australia(drop=Street_ID State Country)
     other;
   set orion.employee_addresses;
   if Country='US' then output usa;
   else if Country='AU' then output australia;
   else output other;
run;
```

68 p202a04

Using DROP= in an Input Data Set

When a **DROP=** data set option is used in an input data set, the specified variables are not read into the PDV and therefore are ***not*** available for processing.

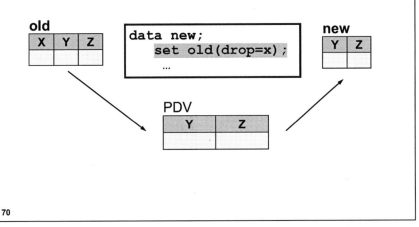

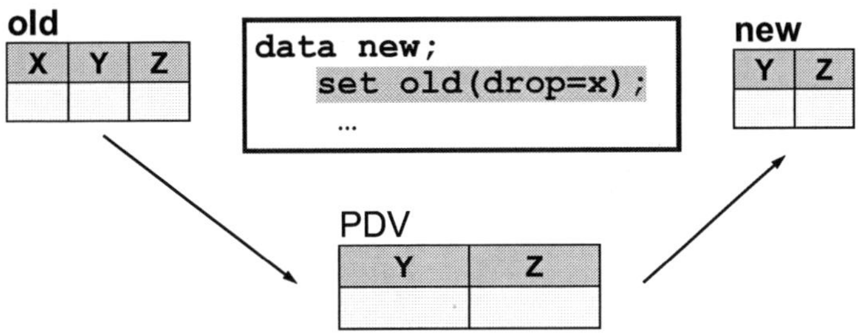

70

Using KEEP= in an Input Data Set

When a **KEEP=** data set option is used in an input data set, only the specified variables are read into the PDV and therefore are available for processing.

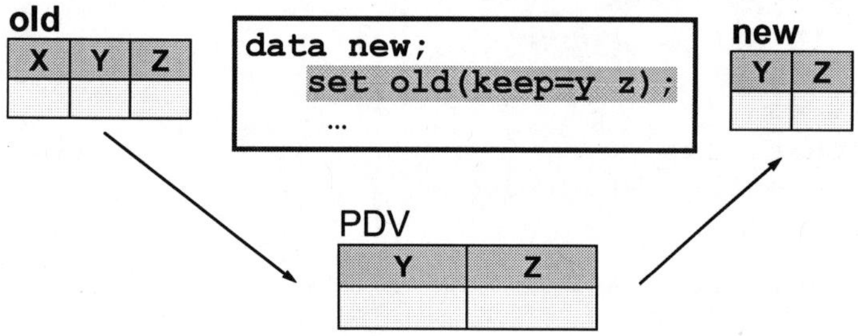

71

2.07 Quiz

Open file **p202a05** and submit it. The intent is to drop **Country**, **Street_ID**, and **Employee_ID** from every data set, and to drop **State** from **australia**. What is wrong with the program?

```
data usa australia(drop=State) other;
   set orion.employee_addresses
       (drop=Country Street_ID Employee_ID);
   if Country='US' then output usa;
   else if Country='AU' then output australia;
   else output other;
run;
```

72 p202a05

Improved Solution

Use a combination of the DROP= option and the DROP statement to achieve the desired results.

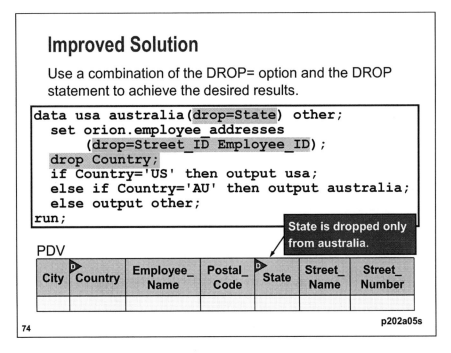

```
data usa australia(drop=State) other;
  set orion.employee_addresses
      (drop=Street_ID Employee_ID);
  drop Country;
  if Country='US' then output usa;
  else if Country='AU' then output australia;
  else output other;
run;
```

State is dropped only from australia.

PDV

City	Country (D)	Employee_ Name	Postal_ Code	State (D)	Street_ Name	Street_ Number

74 p202a05s

If a DROP or KEEP statement is used in the same step as a data set option, the statement is applied first.

Attempting to drop and keep the same variable in a data set results in a warning.

Check the SAS Log

```
NOTE: There were 424 observations read from the data set
      ORION.EMPLOYEE_ADDRESSES.
NOTE: The data set WORK.USA has 311 observations
      and 6 variables.
NOTE: The data set WORK.AUSTRALIA has 105 observations
      and 5 variables.
NOTE: The data set WORK.OTHER has 8 observations
      and 6 variables.
```

75

Controlling Variable Input

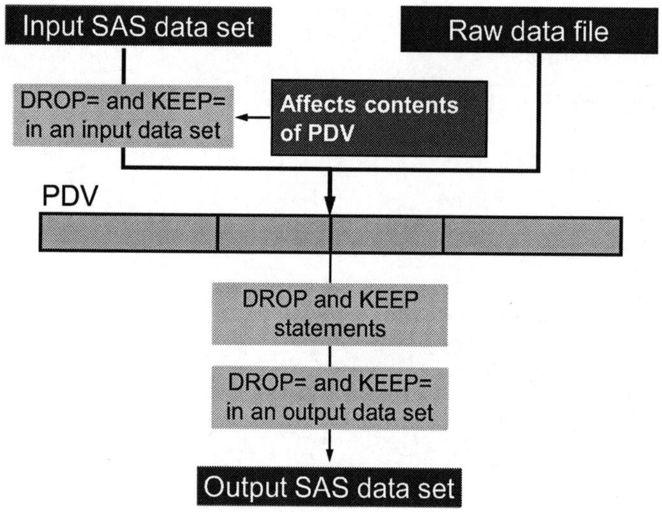

76

The DROP= and KEEP= data set options can be used to exclude variables from processing during a PROC step.

```
proc print data=orion.employee_addresses
               (keep=Employee_Name City State Country);
run;
```

However, the DROP= and KEEP= data set options do ***not*** affect the order in which the variables are processed.

Controlling Which Observations Are Read

By default, SAS processes every observation in a SAS data set, from the first observation to the last. The FIRSTOBS= and OBS= data set options can be used to control which observations are processed.

The FIRSTOBS= and OBS= options are used with input data sets. You cannot use either option with output data sets.

78

Using the OBS= Data Set Option

This OBS= data set option causes the DATA step to stop processing after observation 100.

SAS-data-set(**OBS=***n*)

```
data australia;
   set orion.employee_addresses (obs=100);
   if Country='AU' then output;
run;
```

Partial SAS Log

```
NOTE: There were 100 observations read from the data set
      ORION.EMPLOYEE_ADDRESSES.
NOTE: The data set WORK.AUSTRALIA has 24 observations and
      9 variables.
```

79 p202d08

n specifies a positive integer that is less than or equal to the number of observations in the data set, or zero.

Using OBS= and FIRSTOBS= Data Set Options

The FIRSTOBS= and OBS= data set options cause the SET statement below to read 51 observations from **orion.employee_addresses**. Processing begins with observation 50 and ends after observation 100.

```
data australia;
   set orion.employee_addresses
       (firstobs=50 obs=100);
   if Country='AU' then output;
run;
```

80 p202d09

Check the SAS Log

Partial SAS Log

```
640  data australia;
641       set orion.employee_addresses(firstobs=50 obs=100);
642       if Country='AU' then output;
643  run;

NOTE: There were 51 observations read from the data set
      ORION.EMPLOYEE_ADDRESSES.
NOTE: The data set WORK.AUSTRALIA has 13 observations and
      9 variables.
```

81

Controlling Which Records Are Read

The FIRSTOBS= and OBS= options can be used in an INFILE statement when SAS reads from raw data files.

```
data employees;
   infile "&path\emps.dat" firstobs=11 obs=15;
   input @1 EmpID 8. @9 EmpName $40.
         @153 Country $2.;
run;
proc print data=employees;
run;
```

✎ The syntax is different. In an INFILE statement, the options are not enclosed in parentheses.

82 p202d10

Check the Output

Partial SAS Log

```
45   data employees;
46     infile "&path\emps.dat" firstobs=11 obs=15;
47     input @1 EmpID 8. @9 EmpName $40. @153 Country $2.;
48   run;

NOTE: 5 records were read from the infile 'emps.dat'.
NOTE: The data set WORK.EMPLOYEES has 5 observations and
      3 variables.
```

PROC PRINT Output

Obs	EmpID	EmpName	Country
1	121017	Arizmendi, Gilbert	US
2	121062	Armant, Debra	US
3	121119	Armogida, Bruce	US
4	120812	Arruza, Fauver	US
5	120756	Asta, Wendy	US

83

Using OBS= and FIRSTOBS= in a PROC Step

The FIRSTOBS= and OBS= data set options can also be used in SAS procedures. The PROC PRINT step below begins processing at observation 10 and ends after observation 15.

```
proc print data=orion.employee_addresses
           (firstobs=10 obs=15);
   var Employee_Name City State Country;
run;
```

84

p202d11

Check the Output

Partial SAS Log

```
417  proc print data=orion.employee_addresses
418            (firstobs=10 obs=15);
419     var Employee_Name City State Country;
420  run;

NOTE: There were 6 observations read from the data set
      ORION.EMPLOYEE_ADDRESSES.
```

PROC PRINT Output

PROC PRINT output shows the original observation numbers.

```
Obs   Employee_Name         City           State    Country

 10   Areu, Jeryl           Miami-Dade      Fl        US
 11   Arizmendi, Gilbert    San Diego       CA        US
 12   Armant, Debra         San Diego       CA        US
 13   Armogida, Bruce       Philadelphia    PA        US
 14   Arruza, Fauver        Miami-Dade      FL        US
 15   Asta, Wendy           Philadelphia    PA        US
```

85

Adding a WHERE Statement

When the FIRSTOBS= or OBS= option and the WHERE statement are used together, the following occurs:

- The subsetting WHERE is applied first.
- The FIRSTOBS= and OBS= options are applied to the resulting observations.

The following step includes a WHERE statement and an OBS= option:

```
proc print data=orion.employee_addresses
           (obs=10);
   where Country='AU';
   var Employee_Name City Country;
run;
```

86 p202d12

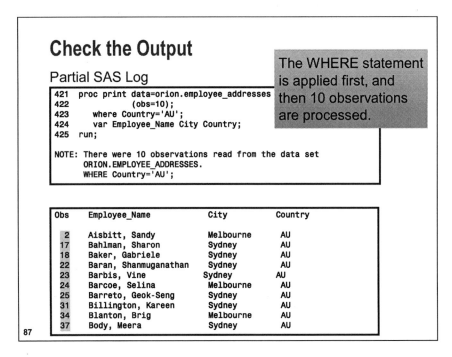

Check the Output

Partial SAS Log

```
421  proc print data=orion.employee_addresses
422             (obs=10);
423     where Country='AU';
424     var Employee_Name City Country;
425  run;

NOTE: There were 10 observations read from the data set
      ORION.EMPLOYEE_ADDRESSES.
      WHERE Country='AU';
```

The WHERE statement is applied first, and then 10 observations are processed.

```
Obs    Employee_Name             City         Country

  2    Aisbitt, Sandy            Melbourne      AU
 17    Bahlman, Sharon           Sydney         AU
 18    Baker, Gabriele           Sydney         AU
 22    Baran, Shanmuganathan     Sydney         AU
 23    Barbis, Vine              Sydney         AU
 24    Barcoe, Selina            Melbourne      AU
 25    Barreto, Geok-Seng        Sydney         AU
 31    Billington, Kareen        Sydney         AU
 34    Blanton, Brig             Melbourne      AU
 37    Body, Meera               Sydney         AU
```

87

The procedure processes observations 1 through 10 after the subsetting WHERE is applied. The value in the OBS column reflects the observation number from the original data set.

Exercises

If you restarted your SAS session since the last exercise, open and submit the **libname.sas** program found in the data folder.

Level 1

7. Specifying Variables and Observations

The data set **orion.employee_organization** contains information about employee job titles, departments, and managers.

Partial **orion.employee_organization** (424 Total Observations)

Employee_ ID	Job_Title	Department	Manager_ ID
120101	Director	Sales Management	120261
120102	Sales Manager	Sales Management	120101
120103	Sales Manager	Sales Management	120101
120104	Administration Manager	Administration	120101
120105	Secretary I	Administration	120101

a. Create two data sets: one for the Sales Department and another for the Executive Department.

- Name the data sets **work.sales** and **work.exec**.
- Output to these data sets depending on whether the value of **Department** is *Sales* or *Executives*, respectively. Ignore all other **Department** values.
- The **work.sales** data set should contain three variables (**Employee_ID, Job_Title**, and **Manager_ID)** and have 201 observations.
- The **work.exec** data set should contain two variables (**Employee_ID** and **Job_Title)** and have four observations.

b. Print only the first six observations from **work.sales**.

- Use a data set option to display only the first six observations.
- Add an appropriate title.

PROC PRINT Output

```
                 Sales Employees

          Employee_                          Manager_
  Obs        ID            Job_Title            ID

    1      120121       Sales Rep. II        120102
    2      120122       Sales Rep. II        120102
    3      120123       Sales Rep. I         120102
    4      120124       Sales Rep. I         120102
    5      120125       Sales Rep. IV        120102
    6      120126       Sales Rep. II        120102
```

c. Print selected observations from **work.exec**.

- Use data set options to process only observations 2 and 3.
- Add an appropriate title.

PROC PRINT Output

```
                                    Executives

                             Employee_
                      Obs       ID             Job_Title

                        2     120260     Chief Marketing Officer
                        3     120261     Chief Sales Officer
```

Level 2

8. Specifying Variables and Observations

The data set **orion.orders** contains information about in-store, catalog, and Internet orders as well as delivery dates.

Partial **orion.orders** (490 Total Observations)

Order_ID	Order_ Type	Employee_ID	Customer_ID	Order_ Date	Delivery_ Date
1243992813	2	99999999	70187	23NOV2011	28NOV2011
1244066194	2	99999999	2806	30NOV2011	04DEC2011
1244086685	3	99999999	14104	03DEC2011	06DEC2011
1244107612	1	121107	45	05DEC2011	05DEC2011
1244117101	1	121109	45	06DEC2011	06DEC2011
1244296274	1	121040	5	26DEC2011	26DEC2011

a. Create two data sets, **work.instore** and **work.delivery**, to analyze in-store sales.

- Use a WHERE statement to read only observations with **Order_Type** equal to 1.
- Create a variable **ShipDays** that is the number of days between when the order was placed and when the order was delivered.
- Output to **work.instore** when **ShipDays** is equal to 0.
- Output to **work.delivery** when **ShipDays** is greater than 0.
- The **work.instore** data set should contain three variables (**Order_ID**, **Customer_ID**, and **Order_Date**).

  The **work.delivery** data set should contain four variables (**Order_ID**, **Customer_ID**, **Order_Date**, and **ShipDays**).
- Test this program by reading the first 30 observations that satisfy the WHERE statement. Check the SAS log to verify that no warnings or errors were reported.

b. Modify the program to read the full **orion.orders** data set. Of the 490 observations in **orion.orders**, only 260 are read due to the WHERE statement.

c. Print your results from **work.delivery** with an appropriate title.

Partial **work.delivery** (10 Total Observations)

Deliveries from In-store Purchases

Obs	Order_ID	Customer_ID	Order_ Date	Ship Days
1	1231468750	52	25SEP2007	5
2	1231657078	63	29OCT2007	4
3	1232648239	49	07APR2008	8
4	1241063739	89	03JAN2011	1
5	1241235281	171	23JAN2011	7

d. Use PROC FREQ to display the number of orders per year in **work.instore**. Add an appropriate title.

Hint: Format the variable **Order_Date** with a YEAR. format. Restrict the analysis to the variable **Order_Date** with a TABLES statement.

PROC FREQ Output

```
                    In-stock Store Purchases, By Year

                           The FREQ Procedure

                    Date Order was placed by Customer

                                                  Cumulative    Cumulative
      Order_Date    Frequency     Percent         Frequency       Percent
      ---------------------------------------------------------------------
            2007           43       17.20                43         17.20
            2008           50       20.00                93         37.20
            2009           27       10.80               120         48.00
            2010           67       26.80               187         74.80
            2011           63       25.20               250        100.00
```

2.4 Solutions

Solutions to Exercises

1. Writing Observations Explicitly

```
data work.price_increase;
   set orion.prices;
   Year=1;
   Unit_Price=Unit_Price * Factor;
   output;
   Year=2;
   Unit_Price=Unit_Price * Factor;
   output;
   Year=3;
   Unit_Price=Unit_Price * Factor;
   output;
run;

proc print data=work.price_increase;
   var Product_ID Unit_Price Year;
run;
```

2. Writing Observations Explicitly

```
data work.extended;
   set orion.discount;
   drop unit_sales_price;
   where Start_Date='01dec2011'd;
   Promotion='Happy Holidays';
   Season='Winter';
   output;
   Start_Date='01jul2012'd;
   End_Date='31jul2012'd;
   Season='Summer';
   output;
```

```
run;

title 'All discount ranges with the Happy Holidays promotion';
proc print data=work.extended;
run;
title;
```

3. **Using Conditional Logic to Output Multiple Observations**

```
data work.lookup;
   set orion.country;
   Outdated='N';
   output;
   if Country_FormerName ne ' ' then do;
      Country_Name=Country_FormerName;
         Outdated='Y';
         output;
   end;
   drop Country_FormerName Population;
run;

title 'Current and Outdated Country Name Data';
proc print data=work.lookup;
run;
title;
```

4. **Creating Multiple SAS Data Sets**

```
data work.admin work.stock work.purchasing;
   set orion.employee_organization;
   if Department='Administration' then output work.admin;
   else if Department='Stock & Shipping' then output work.stock;
   else if Department='Purchasing' then output work.purchasing;
run;

title 'Administration Employees';
proc print data=work.admin;
run;
title;

title 'Stock and Shipping Employees';
proc print data=work.stock;
run;
title;

title 'Purchasing Employees';
proc print data=work.purchasing;
run;
title;
```

Alternate Solution

```
data work.admin work.stock work.purchasing;
   set orion.employee_organization;
   select (Department);
      when ('Administration') output work.admin;
      when ('Stock & Shipping') output work.stock;
      when ('Purchasing') output work.purchasing;
      otherwise;
   end;
run;

title 'Administration Employees';
proc print data=work.admin;
run;
title;

title 'Stock and Shipping Employees';
proc print data=work.stock;
run;
title;

title 'Purchasing Employees';
proc print data=work.purchasing;
run;
title;
```

5. Creating Multiple SAS Data Sets with Derived Values

```
data work.fast work.slow work.veryslow;
   set orion.orders;
   where Order_Type in (2,3);
    /* There are several correct ways to write this WHERE statement */
   ShipDays=Delivery_Date-Order_Date;
   if ShipDays<3 then output work.fast;
   else if 5<=ShipDays<=7 then output work.slow;
   else if ShipDays>7 then output work.veryslow;
   drop Employee_ID;
run;

title 'Orders taking more than 7 days to deliver';
proc print data=work.veryslow;
run;
title;
```

6. Using a SELECT Group

```
data work.fast work.slow work.veryslow;
   set orion.orders;
   where Order_Type in (2,3);
    /* There are several correct ways to write this WHERE statement */
   ShipDays=Delivery_Date-Order_Date;
   select;
```

```
      when (ShipDays<3) output work.fast;
      when (5<=ShipDays<=7)  output work.slow;
      when (ShipDays>7) output work.veryslow;
     otherwise;
   end;
   drop Employee_ID;
run;

title 'Orders taking more than 7 days to deliver';
proc print data=work.veryslow;
run;
```

7. Specifying Variables and Observations

```
data work.sales (keep=Employee_ID Job_Title Manager_ID)
     work.exec (keep=Employee_ID Job_Title);
   set orion.employee_organization;
   if Department='Sales' then output work.sales;
   else if Department='Executives' then output work.exec;
run;

title 'Sales Employees';
proc print data=work.sales (obs=6);
run;
title;

title 'Executives';
proc print data=work.exec (firstobs=2 obs=3);
run;
title;
```

8. Specifying Variables and Observations

```
data work.instore (keep=Order_ID Customer_ID Order_Date)
     work.delivery (keep=Order_ID Customer_ID Order_Date ShipDays);
   set orion.orders (obs=30);
   where Order_Type=1;
   ShipDays=Delivery_Date-Order_Date;
   if ShipDays=0 then output work.instore;
   else if ShipDays>0 then output work.delivery;
run;

data work.instore (keep=Order_ID Customer_ID Order_Date)
     work.delivery (keep=Order_ID Customer_ID Order_Date ShipDays);
   set orion.orders;
   where Order_Type=1;
   ShipDays=Delivery_Date-Order_Date;
   if ShipDays=0 then output work.instore;
   else if ShipDays>0 then output work.delivery;
run;

title 'Deliveries from In-store Purchases';
proc print data=work.delivery;
```

```
run;
title;

title 'In-stock Store Purchases, By Year';
proc freq data=work.instore;
   tables Order_Date;
   format Order_Date year.;
run;
title;
```

Solutions to Student Activities (Polls/Quizzes)

2.01 Quiz – Correct Answer

Which of the following occurs at the end of a DATA step iteration?

```
data forecast;
   set orion.growth;
   total_employees=
      total_employees * (1+increase);
run;
```

Implicit OUTPUT;
Implicit RETURN;

By default, every DATA step performs an implicit OUTPUT and implicit RETURN at the end of each iteration.

6

2.02 Multiple Answer Poll – Correct Answers

Which variable or variables are reinitialized?

a. **Department**
b. **Total_Employees**
c. **Increase**
(d.) **Year**

Variables created by INPUT and assignment statements are reinitialized. Variables read with a SET statement are not.

23

2.03 Quiz – Correct Answer

There are several ways to modify the DATA step.

Here is one solution:

```
data forecast;
   set orion.growth;
   Year=1;
   Total_Employees=Total_Employees*(1+Increase);
   Year=2;
   Total_Employees=Total_Employees*(1+Increase);
   output;
run;
```

29

p202a01s

2.04 Quiz – Correct Answer

Consider the results of the previous DATA step.

Can all three data sets be printed with a single PRINT procedure?

Partial SAS Log

```
NOTE: There were 424 observations read from the data set
      ORION.EMPLOYEE_ADDRESSES.
NOTE: The data set WORK.USA has 311 observations and 9
      variables.
NOTE: The data set WORK.AUSTRALIA has 105 observations and
      9 variables.
NOTE: The data set WORK.OTHER has 8 observations and 9
      variables.
```

No, a separate PRINT procedure is needed for each data set.

40

2.05 Quiz – Correct Answer

Open the file **p202a03** and submit it. View the log, identify and correct the problem, and resubmit the program.

```
150  data usa australia;
151     set orion.employee_addresses;
152     select (Country);
153        when ('US') output usa;
154        when ('AU') output australia;
155     end;
156  run;
ERROR: Unsatisfied WHEN clause and no OTHERWISE clause at
line 155 column 4.
```

```
data usa australia;
   set orion.employee_addresses;
   select (Country);
      when ('US') output usa;
      when ('AU') output australia;
      otherwise;
   end;
run;
```

An OTHERWISE statement is needed.

47

p202a03s

2.06 Quiz – Correct Answer

The data set **orion.employee_addresses** contains nine variables. How many variables will be in the **usa**, **australia**, and **other** data sets? **4, 6, 9**

```
data usa(keep=Employee_Name City State Country)
     australia(drop=Street_ID State Country)
     other;
   set orion.employee_addresses;
   if Country='US' then output usa;
   else if Country='AU' then output australia;
   else output other;
run;
```

Four variables are kept in usa, three are dropped from australia, and there is no DROP or KEEP for other.

69

2.07 Quiz – Correct Answer

Country is dropped on input, and therefore it is not available for processing. Every observation is written to other.

```
data usa australia(drop=State) other;
   set orion.employee_addresses
       (drop=Country Street_ID Employee_ID);
   if Country='US' then output usa;
   else if Country='AU' then output australia;
   else output other;
run;
```

Country is not included in the PDV.

PDV

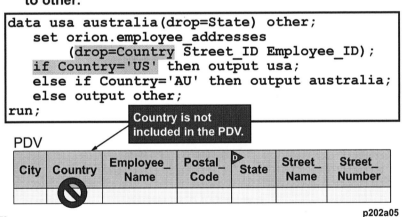

City	Country	Employee_ Name	Postal_ Code	D State	Street_ Name	Street_ Number

73

p202a05

Chapter 3 Summarizing Data

3.1 Creating an Accumulating Total Variable 3-3

Exercises 3-14

3.2 Accumulating Totals for a Group of Data 3-18

Exercises 3-34

3.3 Solutions 3-38

Solutions to Exercises 3-38

Solutions to Student Activities (Polls/Quizzes) 3-42

3.1 Creating an Accumulating Total Variable

Objectives

- Explain how SAS initializes the value of a variable in the PDV.
- Prevent reinitialization of a variable in the PDV.
- Create an accumulating variable.

3

Business Scenario

A manager has asked to see daily sales for April, as well as a month-to-date total for each day for her department.

Partial **orion.aprsales**

SaleDate	SaleAmt
01APR2011	498.49
02APR2011	946.50
03APR2011	994.97
04APR2011	564.59
05APR2011	783.01
06APR2011	228.82
07APR2011	930.57

Partial **mnthtot**

SaleDate	Sale Amt	Mth2Dte
01APR2011	498.49	498.49
02APR2011	+ 946.50	= 1444.99
03APR2011	994.97	2439.96
04APR2011	564.59	3004.55
05APR2011	783.01	3787.56

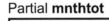

4

3.01 Quiz

Open and submit the program in **p203a01**. Does this program create the correct values for **Mth2Dte**?

```
data mnthtot;
   set orion.aprsales;
   Mth2Dte=Mth2Dte+SaleAmt;
run;
```

Partial **orion.aprsales**

SaleDate	SaleAmt
01APR2011	498.49
02APR2011	946.50
03APR2011	994.97
04APR2011	564.59
05APR2011	783.01

5

p203a01

Creating an Accumulating Variable

By default, variables created with an assignment statement are initialized to missing at the top of each iteration of the DATA step.

Initialized to missing at the top of the DATA step

```
data mnthtot;
   set orion.aprsales;
   Mth2Dte=Mth2Dte+SaleAmt;
run;
```

Mth2Dte is an example of an accumulating variable that needs to keep its value from one observation to the next.

7

Creating an Accumulating Variable

Retain the values of **Mth2Dte** and set an initial value.

```
data mnthtot;
   set orion.aprsales;
   retain Mth2Dte 0;
   Mth2Dte=Mth2Dte+SaleAmt;
run;
```

RETAIN *variable-name <initial-value> ...*;

If you do not supply an initial value, all the values of **Mth2Dte** will be missing.

8

p203d02

RETAIN Statement: Details

The RETAIN statement

- retains the value of the variable in the PDV across iterations of the DATA step
- initializes the retained variable to missing or a specified initial value before the first iteration of the DATA step
- is a compile-time-only statement.

The RETAIN statement has no effect on variables read with SET, MERGE, or UPDATE statements. Variables read from SAS data sets are retained automatically.

9

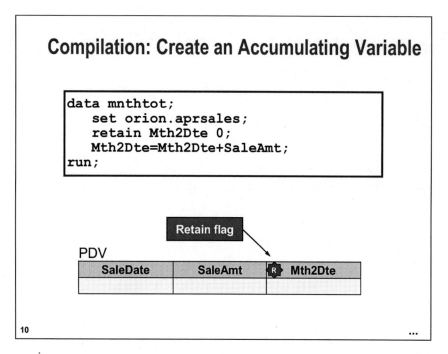

Compilation: Create an Accumulating Variable

```
data mnthtot;
   set orion.aprsales;
   retain Mth2Dte 0;
   Mth2Dte=Mth2Dte+SaleAmt;
run;
```

Retain flag

PDV

SaleDate	SaleAmt	(R) Mth2Dte

10 ...

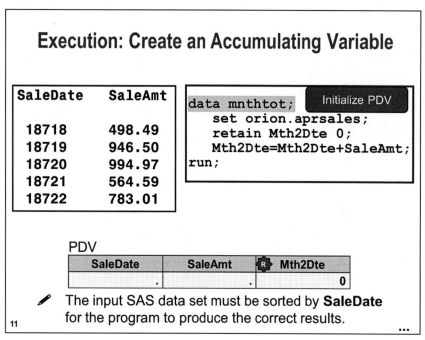

Execution: Create an Accumulating Variable

SaleDate	SaleAmt
18718	498.49
18719	946.50
18720	994.97
18721	564.59
18722	783.01

```
data mnthtot;
   set orion.aprsales;
   retain Mth2Dte 0;
   Mth2Dte=Mth2Dte+SaleAmt;
run;
```

Initialize PDV

PDV

SaleDate	SaleAmt	(R) Mth2Dte
.	.	0

✎ The input SAS data set must be sorted by **SaleDate** for the program to produce the correct results.

11 ...

Execution: Create an Accumulating Variable

SaleDate	SaleAmt
18718	498.49
18719	946.50
18720	994.97
18721	564.59
18722	783.01

```
data mnthtot;
   set orion.aprsales;
   retain Mth2Dte 0;
   Mth2Dte=Mth2Dte+SaleAmt;
run;
```

PDV

SaleDate	SaleAmt	R Mth2Dte
18718	498.49	0

12 ...

Execution: Create an Accumulating Variable

SaleDate	SaleAmt
18718	498.49
18719	946.50
18720	994.97
18721	564.59
18722	783.01

```
data mnthtot;
   set orion.aprsales;
   retain Mth2Dte 0;
   Mth2Dte=Mth2Dte+SaleAmt;
run;
```

0 + 498.49

PDV

SaleDate	SaleAmt	R Mth2Dte
18718	498.49	498.49

13 ...

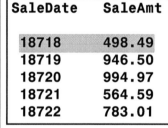

Execution: Create an Accumulating Variable

SaleDate	SaleAmt
18718	498.49
18719	946.50
18720	994.97
18721	564.59
18722	783.01

```
data mnthtot;
   set orion.aprsales;
   retain Mth2Dte 0;
   Mth2Dte=Mth2Dte+SaleAmt;
run;
```

Implicit OUTPUT;
Implicit RETURN;

PDV

SaleDate	SaleAmt	R Mth2Dte
18718	498.49	498.49

Write observation to **mnthtot**

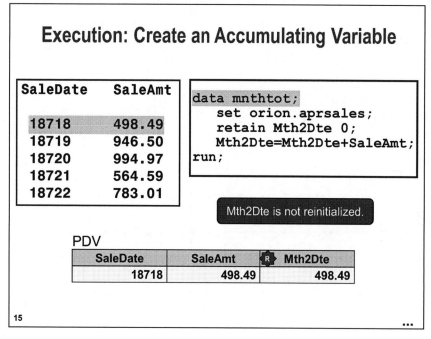

14 ...

Execution: Create an Accumulating Variable

SaleDate	SaleAmt
18718	498.49
18719	946.50
18720	994.97
18721	564.59
18722	783.01

```
data mnthtot;
   set orion.aprsales;
   retain Mth2Dte 0;
   Mth2Dte=Mth2Dte+SaleAmt;
run;
```

Mth2Dte is not reinitialized.

PDV

SaleDate	SaleAmt	R Mth2Dte
18718	498.49	498.49

15 ...

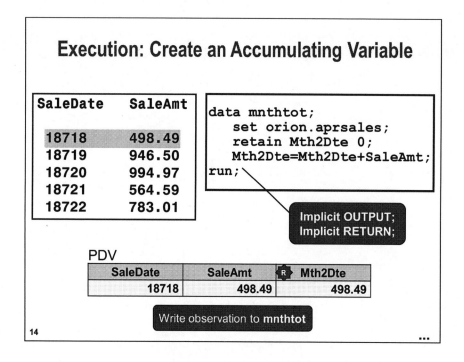

Execution: Create an Accumulating Variable

SaleDate	SaleAmt
18718	498.49
18719	946.50
18720	994.97
18721	564.59
18722	783.01

```
data mnthtot;
   set orion.aprsales;
   retain Mth2Dte 0;
   Mth2Dte=Mth2Dte+SaleAmt;
run;
```

PDV

SaleDate	SaleAmt	R Mth2Dte
18718	946.50	498.49

16 ...

Execution: Create an Accumulating Variable

SaleDate	SaleAmt
18718	498.49
18719	946.50
18720	994.97
18721	564.59
18722	783.01

```
data mnthtot;
   set orion.aprsales;
   retain Mth2Dte 0;
   Mth2Dte=Mth2Dte+SaleAmt;
run;
```

498.49 + 946.50

PDV

SaleDate	SaleAmt	R Mth2Dte
18719	946.50	1444.99

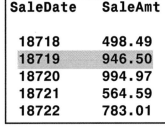

17 ...

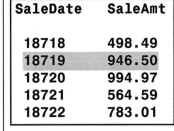

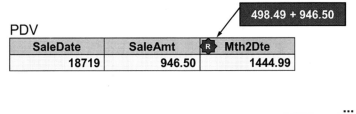

Execution: Create an Accumulating Variable

SaleDate	SaleAmt
18718	498.49
18719	946.50
18720	994.97
18721	564.59
18722	783.01

```
data mnthtot;
   set orion.aprsales;
   retain Mth2Dte 0;
   Mth2Dte=Mth2Dte+SaleAmt;
run;
```

Implicit OUTPUT;
Implicit RETURN;

PDV

SaleDate	SaleAmt	R Mth2Dte
18719	946.50	1444.99

Write observation to **mnthtot**

18 ...

Execution: Create an Accumulating Variable

SaleDate	SaleAmt
18718	498.49
18719	946.50
18720	994.97
18721	564.59
18722	783.01

```
data mnthtot;
   set orion.aprsales;
   retain Mth2Dte 0;
   Mth2Dte=Mth2Dte+SaleAmt;
run;
```

Mth2Dte is not reinitialized.

PDV

SaleDate	SaleAmt	R Mth2Dte
18719	946.50	1444.99

19 ...

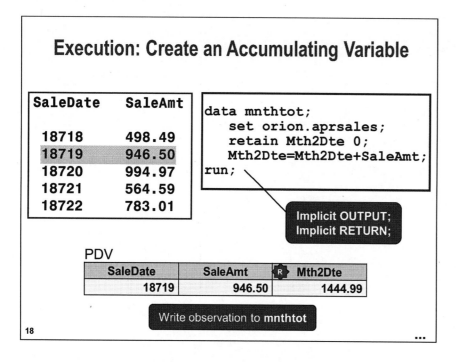

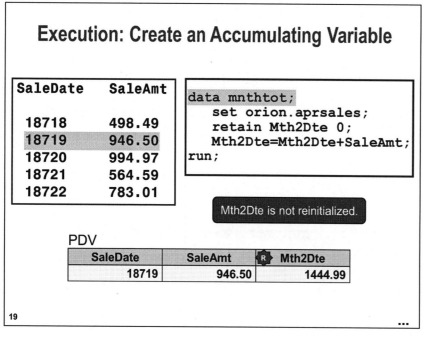

Execution: Create an Accumulating Variable

SaleDate	SaleAmt
18718	498.49
18719	946.50
18720	994.97
18721	564.59
18722	783.01

```
data mnthtot;
   set orion.aprsales;
   retain Mth2Dte 0;
   Mth2Dte=Mth2Dte+SaleAmt;
run;
```

Continue until EOF

PDV

SaleDate	SaleAmt	R Mth2Dte
18719	946.50	1444.99

20

Creating an Accumulating Variable

```
proc print data=mnthtot noobs;
   format SaleDate date9.;
run;
```

Partial PROC PRINT Output

```
              Sale
 SaleDate      Amt      Mth2Dte

01APR2011    498.49      498.49
02APR2011    946.50     1444.99
03APR2011    994.97     2439.96
04APR2011    564.59     3004.55
05APR2011    783.01     3787.56
```

21 p203d02

Setup for the Poll

What happens if there are missing values for **SaleAmt**?

Open and submit **p203a02** and examine the output.

Partial **orion.Aprsales2**

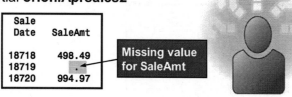

Sale Date	SaleAmt
18718	498.49
18719	.
18720	994.97

Missing value for SaleAmt

22

3.02 Multiple Choice Poll

What effect did the missing value for **SaleAmt** have on **Mth2Dte**?

a. The missing value is ignored; **Mth2Dte** values are not affected.

b. The missing value causes the DATA step to stop processing.

c. The missing value causes the subsequent values for **Mth2Dte** to be set to missing.

23

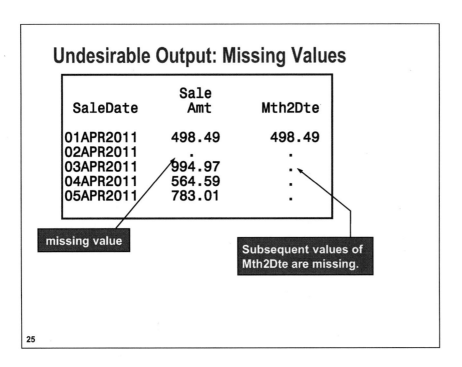

Undesirable Output: Missing Values

SaleDate	Sale Amt	Mth2Dte
01APR2011	498.49	498.49
02APR2011	.	.
03APR2011	994.97	.
04APR2011	564.59	.
05APR2011	783.01	.

missing value

Subsequent values of Mth2Dte are missing.

25

SUM Function

A RETAIN statement along with a SUM function in an assignment statement can be used to create **Mth2Dte**.

```
data mnthtot;
   set orion.aprsales;
   retain Mth2Dte 0;
   Mth2Dte=sum(Mth2Dte,SaleAmt);
run;
```

The SUM function ignores missing values.

26

Sum Statement

Use the sum statement to create **Mth2Dte**.

```
data mnthtot2;
   set work.aprsales2;
   Mth2Dte+SaleAmt;
run;
```

variable **+** *expression*;

Specifics about **Mth2Dte**:

- initialized to zero
- automatically retained
- increased by the value of **SaleAmt** for each observation
- ignored missing values of **SaleAmt**

27

p203d03

Sum Statement

```
proc print data=mnthtot2 noobs;
   format SaleDate date9.;
run;
```

Partial PROC PRINT Output (30 Total Observations)

SaleDate	SaleAmt	Mth2Dte
01APR2011	498.49	498.49
02APR2011	.	498.49
03APR2011	994.97	1493.46
04APR2011	564.59	2058.05
05APR2011	783.01	2841.06

28

Exercises

If you restarted your SAS session since the last exercise, open and submit the **libname.sas** program found in the data folder.

Level 1

1. Creating Accumulating Totals

The data set **orion.order_fact** contains information about orders for several years, sorted by **Order_Date**. Each observation represents one order, and **Total_Retail_Price** contains the sales value for the order.

Partial Listing of **orion.order_fact** (617 Total Observations, 12 Total Variables)

Order_ID	Order_ Date	Total_Retail_ Price
1230058123	11JAN2007	$16.50
1230080101	15JAN2007	$247.50
1230106883	20JAN2007	$28.30
1230147441	28JAN2007	$32.00
1230315085	27FEB2007	$63.60

a. Orion Star would like to examine growth in sales during the date range of 01Nov2008 to 14Dec2008.

- Open file **p203e01**. It creates and prints a data set named **work.mid_q4** from **orion.order_fact**. The DATA step uses the following WHERE statement to read only the observations in the specified date range:

```
where '01nov2008'd <= Order_Date <= '14dec2008'd;
```

- Modify the program to create an accumulating total, **Sales2Dte**, to display the sales-to-date total.
- Also create an accumulating variable, **Num_Orders**, indicating how many orders-to-date that total represents. Each observation counts as one order.

b. Modify the PROC PRINT step to show your results.

- Display **Sales2Dte** with a DOLLAR10.2 format.
- Show only the columns **Order_ID**, **Order_Date**, **Total_Retail_Price**, **Sales2Dte**, and **Num_Orders**.

Partial PROC PRINT Output

Orders from 01Nov2008 through 14Dec2008

Obs	Order_ID	Order_ Date	Total_Retail_ Price	Sales2Dte	Num_ Orders
1	1234033037	01NOV2008	$53.70	$53.70	1
2	1234092222	10NOV2008	$7.20	$60.90	2
3	1234133789	17NOV2008	$328.30	$389.20	3
4	1234186330	25NOV2008	$200.10	$589.30	4
	...				
10	1234301319	11DEC2008	$105.60	$1,664.20	10

Level 2

2. Creating Accumulating Totals with Conditional Logic

The data set **orion.order_fact** contains a group of orders across several years, sorted by **Order_Date**.

Partial Listing of **orion.order_fact** (617 Total Observations, 12 Total Variables)

Order_ID	Order_ Type	Order_ Date	Quantity
1230058123	1	11JAN2007	1
1230080101	2	15JAN2007	1
1230106883	2	20JAN2007	1
1230147441	1	28JAN2007	2
1230315085	1	27FEB2007	3

a. Orion Star would like to analyze 2009 data by creating accumulating totals for the number of items sold from retail, catalog, and Internet channels.

- The value of **Order_Type** indicates whether the sale was retail (=*1*), catalog (=*2*), or Internet (=*3*).
- Create a data set named **work.typetotals** with accumulating totals for **TotalRetail**, **TotalCatalog**, and **TotalInternet**, as described above.

  The variable **Quantity** contains the number of items sold for each order.

- For testing your program in this step, read only the first 10 observations that satisfy the WHERE statement.

  Remember to process only those rows where **Order_Date** occurs in 2009.

b. Continue testing your program by printing the results from part **a**. Print all the variables and verify that the program is correctly calculating values for the accumulating totals.

PROC PRINT Output

Obs	Customer_ID	Employee_ID	Street_ID	Order_ Date	Delivery_ Date	Order_ID	Order_ Type	Product_ID
1	195	120150	1600101663	02JAN2009	02JAN2009	1234437760	1	230100600028
2	36	99999999	9260128237	11JAN2009	14JAN2009	1234534069	3	240800100026
3	183	120121	1600100760	12JAN2009	12JAN2009	1234537441	1	240100200001
4	16	99999999	3940105865	12JAN2009	14JAN2009	1234538390	2	220200300015
	...							
10	183	120179	1600100760	31JAN2009	31JAN2009	1234727966	1	240700400004

Obs	Quantity	Total_Retail_ Price	CostPrice_ Per_Unit	Discount	Total Retail	Total Catalog	Total Internet
1	2	$193.40	$48.45	.	2	0	0
2	4	$525.20	$58.55	.	2	0	4
3	1	$16.00	$6.35	.	3	0	4
4	1	$115.00	$52.40	.	3	1	4
	...						
10	1	$13.20	$5.95	.	4	6	6

c. When the results from parts **a** and **b** are correct, do the following:

- Modify the program to read all observations satisfying the WHERE statement. The resulting report contains 90 observations.
- Keep only the variables **Order_Date**, **Order_ID**, **TotalRetail**, **TotalCatalog**, and **TotalInternet**.
- Print your results with an appropriate title.

Challenge

3. Creating Accumulating Totals by Month

The data set **orion.order_fact** contains a group of orders across several years, sorted by **Order_Date**.

Partial **orion.order_fact** (617 Total Observations, 12 Total Variables)

Order_ID	Order_ Date	Total_Retail_ Price
1230058123	11JAN2007	$16.50
1230080101	15JAN2007	$247.50
1230106883	20JAN2007	$28.30
1230147441	28JAN2007	$32.00
1230315085	27FEB2007	$63.60

Orion Star would like to generate the following report showing all orders in 2011 along with an accumulating total:

- The accumulating total should reset to zero at the start of each new month.
- Remember to process only those rows where **Order_Date** occurs in 2011.

Partial PROC PRINT Output (148 Total Observations)

Accumulating Totals by Month in 2011

Obs	Order_ Date	Order_ID	Total_ Retail_ Price	MonthSales
1	02JAN2011	1241054779	$195.60	$195.60
2	03JAN2011	1241063739	$160.80	$356.40
3	04JAN2011	1241066216	$306.20	$662.60
4	06JAN2011	1241086052	$37.80	$700.40
5	13JAN2011	1241147641	$362.60	$1,063.00

3.2 Accumulating Totals for a Group of Data

Objectives

- Define First. and Last. processing.
- Calculate an accumulating total for groups of data.
- Use a subsetting IF statement to output selected observations.

32

Business Scenario

The **Salary** variable represents the portion of the employee's salary allocated to a project. An analyst would like to create a new data set and listing report that has the salary totals for each department.

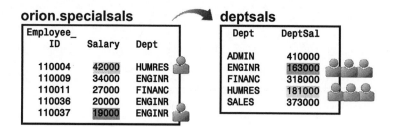

orion.specialsals

Employee_ ID	Salary	Dept
110004	42000	HUMRES
110009	34000	ENGINR
110011	27000	FINANC
110036	20000	ENGINR
110037	19000	ENGINR

deptsals

Dept	DeptSal
ADMIN	410000
ENGINR	163000
FINANC	318000
HUMRES	181000
SALES	373000

33

Processing Needed

Dept	Salary
ADMIN	20000
ADMIN	100000
ADMIN	50000
ENGINR	25000
ENGINR	20000
ENGINR	23000
ENGINR	27000
FINANC	10000
FINANC	12000

DeptSal

Step 1 Sort the data by **Dept**.

34

Processing Needed

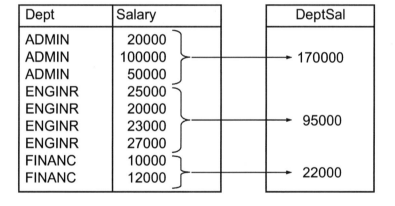

Dept	Salary	DeptSal
ADMIN	20000	
ADMIN	100000	170000
ADMIN	50000	
ENGINR	25000	
ENGINR	20000	
ENGINR	23000	95000
ENGINR	27000	
FINANC	10000	
FINANC	12000	22000

Step 2 Summarize the observations by department groups.

35

BY-Group Processing

The BY statement in the DATA step enables SAS to process data in groups.

```
proc sort data=orion.specialsals
          out=salsort;
   by Dept;
run;

data deptsals(keep=Dept DeptSal);
   set salsort;
   by Dept;
   <additional SAS statements>
run;
```

Step 1: Sort by Dept.

Step 2: Process by Dept groups.

First.*BY-variable*
Last.*BY-variable*

A BY statement in a DATA step creates two temporary variables for each variable listed in the BY statement.

36

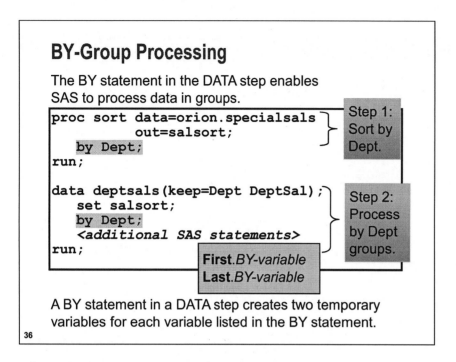

When a BY statement is used with a SET statement, the data must be sorted by the BY variable(s) or have an index based on the BY variable(s).

The SORT procedure

- orders SAS data set observations by the values of one or more character or numeric variables
- either replaces the original data set or creates a new data set
- produces only an output data set.

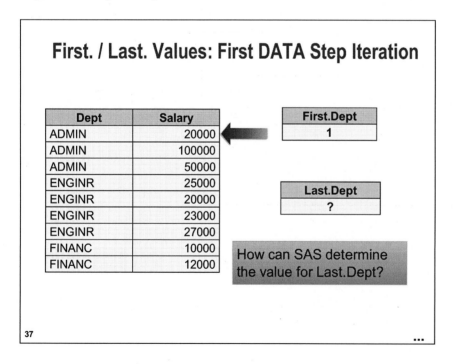

First. / Last. Values: First DATA Step Iteration

Dept	Salary
ADMIN	20000
ADMIN	100000
ADMIN	50000
ENGINR	25000
ENGINR	20000
ENGINR	23000
ENGINR	27000
FINANC	10000
FINANC	12000

First.Dept
1

Last.Dept
?

How can SAS determine the value for Last.Dept?

37 ...

First. / Last. Values: First DATA Step Iteration

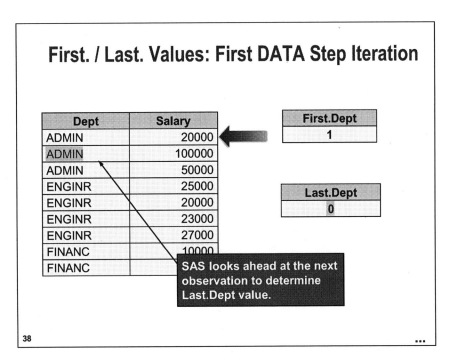

Dept	Salary
ADMIN	20000
ADMIN	100000
ADMIN	50000
ENGINR	25000
ENGINR	20000
ENGINR	23000
ENGINR	27000
FINANC	10000
FINANC	

First.Dept
1

Last.Dept
0

SAS looks ahead at the next observation to determine Last.Dept value.

38 ...

First. / Last. Values: Second DATA Step Iteration

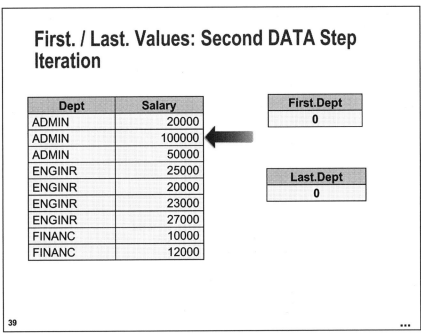

Dept	Salary
ADMIN	20000
ADMIN	100000
ADMIN	50000
ENGINR	25000
ENGINR	20000
ENGINR	23000
ENGINR	27000
FINANC	10000
FINANC	12000

First.Dept
0

Last.Dept
0

39 ...

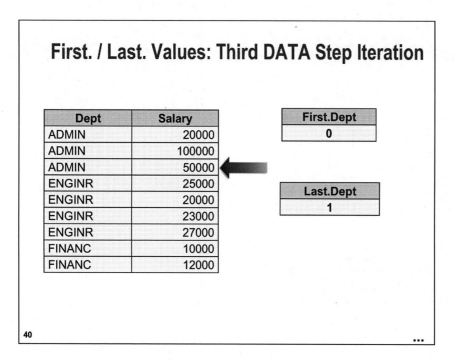

First. / Last. Values: Third DATA Step Iteration

Dept	Salary
ADMIN	20000
ADMIN	100000
ADMIN	50000
ENGINR	25000
ENGINR	20000
ENGINR	23000
ENGINR	27000
FINANC	10000
FINANC	12000

First.Dept
0

Last.Dept
1

40

...

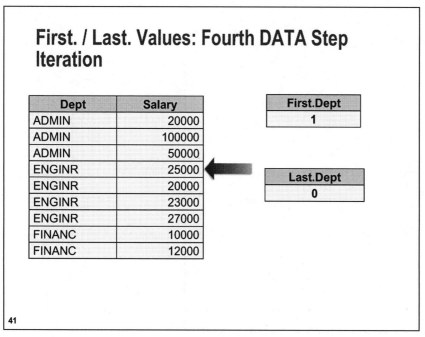

First. / Last. Values: Fourth DATA Step Iteration

Dept	Salary
ADMIN	20000
ADMIN	100000
ADMIN	50000
ENGINR	25000
ENGINR	20000
ENGINR	23000
ENGINR	27000
FINANC	10000
FINANC	12000

First.Dept
1

Last.Dept
0

41

3.03 Quiz

What are the values for **First.Dept** and **Last.Dept** when the DATA step is processing the observation indicated by the arrow?

Dept	Salary
ADMIN	20000
ADMIN	100000
ADMIN	50000
ENGINR	25000 ←
FINANC	10000
FINANC	12000

First.Dept
?

Last.Dept
?

42

What Must Happen When?

There is a three-step process for using the DATA step to summarize grouped data.

Step 1	Initialize: Set the accumulating variable to zero at the start of each BY group.
Step 2	Accumulate: Increment the accumulating variable with a sum statement (automatically retains).
Step 3	Output: Write only the last observation of each BY group.

44

Summarizing Data by Groups

Step 1 Initialize

```
data deptsals(keep=Dept DeptSal);
   set SalSort;
   by Dept;
   if First.Dept then DeptSal=0;
   <additional SAS statements>
run;
```

The condition is considered true when **First.Dept** has a value of *1*.

45

Summarizing Data by Groups

Step 2 Accumulate

```
data deptsals(keep=Dept DeptSal);
   set SalSort;
   by Dept;
   if First.Dept then DeptSal=0;
   DeptSal+Salary;
   <additional SAS statements>
run;
```

46

Summarizing Data by Groups

Step 3 Output

Dept	Salary	DeptSal
ADMIN	20000	20000
ADMIN	100000	120000
ADMIN	50000	170000
ENGINR	25000	25000
ENGINR	20000	45000
ENGINR	23000	68000
ENGINR	27000	95000
FINANC	10000	10000
FINANC	12000	22000

47

Summarizing Data by Groups

Step 3 Output

```
data deptsals(keep=Dept DeptSal);
   set SalSort;
   by Dept;
   if First.Dept then DeptSal=0;
   DeptSal+Salary;
   if Last.Dept;
run;
```

✎ The subsetting IF defines a condition that the observation must meet to be further processed by the DATA step.

48

p203d04

Summarizing Data by Groups

```
proc print data=deptsals noobs;
run;
```

PROC PRINT Output

Dept	DeptSal
ADMIN	410000
ENGINR	163000
FINANC	318000
HUMRES	181000
SALES	373000

Partial SAS Log

```
NOTE: There were 39 observations read
      from the data set WORK.SALSORT.
NOTE: The data set WORK.DEPTSALS has 5
      observations and 2 variables.
```

49

3.04 Multiple Answer Poll

What must happen in the DATA step to summarize data by groups? (Circle all that apply.)

a. Sort the input data.
b. Set the accumulating variable to zero at the start of each BY group.
c. Increment the accumulating variable.
d. Output only the last observation of each BY group.

50

Business Scenario

Each employee listed in **orion.projsals** is assigned to a special project. A business analyst would like to see the salary totals from each department for each special project.

Partial **orion.projsals**

Employee_ ID	Salary	Proj	Dept
110004	42000	EZ	HUMRES
110009	34000	WIN	ENGINR
110011	27000	WIN	FINANC
110036	20000	WIN	ENGINR
110037	19000	EZ	ENGINR
110048	19000	EZ	FINANC
110077	27000	CAP1	ADMIN
110097	20000	EZ	ADMIN
110107	31000	EZ	ENGINR

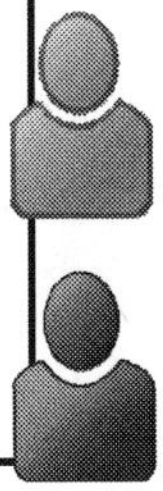

52

Business Scenario: Desired Output

Create a new data set, **pdsals**, that shows the number of employees and salary totals from each department for each special project.

Partial **pdsals**

Proj	Dept	Dept Sal	Num Emps
CAP1	ADMIN	70000	2
EZ	ADMIN	83000	3
EZ	ENGINR	109000	4
EZ	FINANC	122000	3
EZ	HUMRES	178000	5
NGEN	ADMIN	37000	2

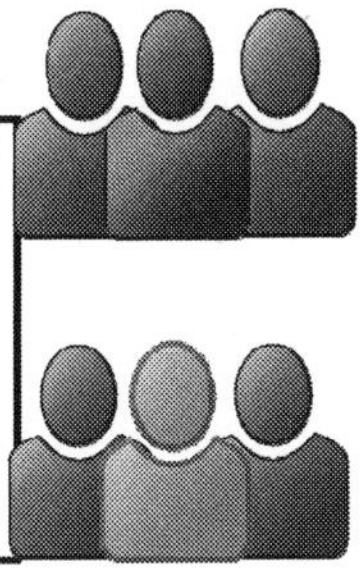

53

Sorting by Project and Department

This is similar to the previous business scenario except that now the data must be sorted by multiple BY variables: **Proj** and **Dept**.

```
proc sort data=orion.projsals
          out=projsort;
   by Proj Dept;
run;
```

primary sort variable (Proj)

secondary sort variable (Dept)

54 p203d05

Sorting by Project and Department

```
proc print data=projsort noobs;
   var Pro Dept Salary;
run;
```

Partial PROC PRINT Output (14 Total Observations)

Proj	Dept	Salary
CAP1	ADMIN	27000
CAP1	ADMIN	43000
EZ	ADMIN	20000
EZ	ADMIN	31000
EZ	ADMIN	32000
EZ	ENGINR	19000

55 p203d05

Idea Exchange

The DATA step must include both **Proj** and **Dept** in the BY statement.

```
data pdsals;
   set projsort;
   by Proj Dept;
   <additional SAS statements>
run;
```

How does the DATA step set First. and Last. values for multiple BY variables?

56

First. / Last. Values: First DATA Step Iteration

Proj	Dept
A	ADMIN
A	ADMIN
A	ADMIN
B	ADMIN
B	ENGINR
B	ENGINR
C	ENGINR
C	SALES
C	SALES
C	SALES
C	SALES

First.Proj
1

First.Dept
1

Last.Proj
?

Last.Dept
?

57 ...

First. / Last. Values: First DATA Step Iteration

Proj	Dept
A	ADMIN
A	ADMIN
A	ADMIN
B	ADMIN
B	ENGINR
B	ENGINR
C	ENGINR
C	SALES
C	SALES
C	
C	

SAS looks ahead at the next observation to determine the values for Last.Proj and Last.Dept.

First.Proj
1

First.Dept
1

Last.Proj
0

Last.Dept
0

58

...

First. / Last. Values: Second DATA Step Iteration

Proj	Dept
A	ADMIN
A	ADMIN
A	ADMIN
B	ADMIN
B	ENGINR
B	ENGINR
C	ENGINR
C	SALES
C	SALES
C	SALES
C	SALES

First.Proj
0

First.Dept
0

Last.Proj
0

Last.Dept
0

59

...

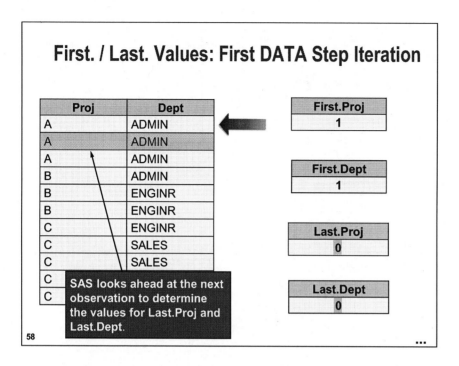

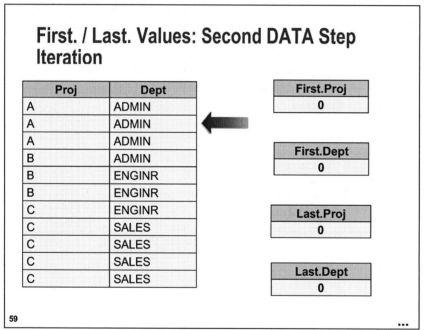

First. / Last. Values: Third DATA Step Iteration

Proj	Dept
A	ADMIN
A	ADMIN
A	ADMIN
B	ADMIN
B	ENGINR
B	ENGINR
C	ENGINR
C	SALES
C	SALES
C	SALES
C	SALES

First.Proj
0

First.Dept
0

Last.Proj
1

Last.Dept
1

60

...

First. / Last. Values: Fourth DATA Step Iteration

Proj	Dept
A	ADMIN
A	ADMIN
A	ADMIN
B	ADMIN
B	ENGINR
B	ENGINR
C	ENGINR
C	SALES
C	SALES
C	SALES
C	SALES

First.Proj
1

First.Dept
1

Last.Proj
0

Last.Dept
1

61

...

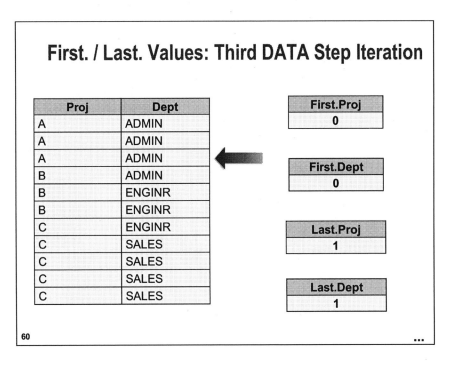

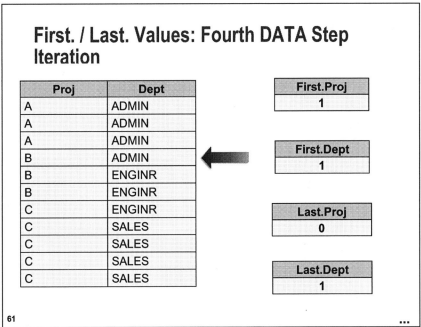

First. / Last. Values: Fifth DATA Step Iteration

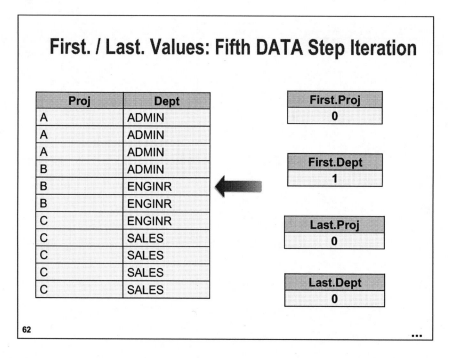

Proj	Dept
A	ADMIN
A	ADMIN
A	ADMIN
B	ADMIN
B	ENGINR
B	ENGINR
C	ENGINR
C	SALES
C	SALES
C	SALES
C	SALES

First.Proj
0

First.Dept
1

Last.Proj
0

Last.Dept
0

62

...

3.05 Quiz

What are the values for First. and Last. variables when the DATA step is processing the observation indicated by the arrow?

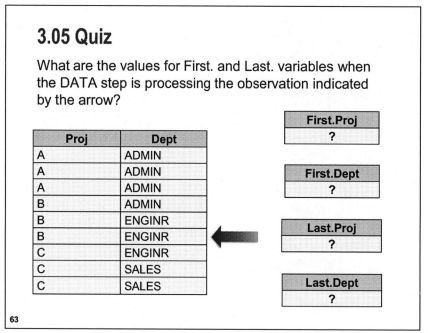

Proj	Dept
A	ADMIN
A	ADMIN
A	ADMIN
B	ADMIN
B	ENGINR
B	ENGINR
C	ENGINR
C	SALES
C	SALES

First.Proj
?

First.Dept
?

Last.Proj
?

Last.Dept
?

63

First. and Last. for Multiple BY Variables

When you use more than one variable in the BY statement, **Last.***BY-variable*=1 for the ***primary variable*** forces **Last.***BY-variable*=1 for the ***secondary variable(s)***.

Proj	Dept	First.Proj	Last.Proj	First.Dept	Last.Dept
A	ADMIN	1	0	1	0
A	ADMIN	0	0	0	0
A	ADMIN	0	1	0	1
B	ADMIN	1	0	1	1
B	ENGINR	0	0	1	0

change in Primary

change in Secondary

65

Multiple BY Variables

Here is the complete DATA step.

```
data pdsals(keep=Proj Dept
                 DeptSal NumEmps);
   set projsort;
   by Proj Dept;
   if First.Dept then do;
      DeptSal=0;
      NumEmps=0;
   end;
   DeptSal+Salary;
   NumEmps+1;
   if Last.Dept;
run;
```

66 p203d05

Multiple BY Variables

Partial SAS Log

```
NOTE: There were 39 observations read
      from the data set WORK.PROJSORT.
NOTE: The data set WORK.PDSALS has 14
      observations and 4 variables.
```

67

Multiple BY Variables

```
proc print data=pdsals noobs;
run;
```

Partial PROC PRINT Output (14 Total Observations)

Proj	Dept	Dept Sal	Num Emps
CAP1	ADMIN	70000	2
EZ	ADMIN	83000	3
EZ	ENGINR	109000	4
EZ	FINANC	122000	3

68 p203d05

Exercises

If you restarted your SAS session since the last exercise, open and submit the **libname.sas** program found in the data folder.

Level 1

4. Summarizing Data Using the DATA Step

The data set **orion.order_summary** contains information about sales in a particular year for each customer, separated by month. For a given customer, there might be some months that he did not place an order.

Partial Listing of **orion.order_summary** (101 Total Observations)

Customer_ID	Order_ Month	Sale_Amt
5	5	478.00
5	6	126.80
5	9	52.50
5	12	33.80
10	3	32.60

a. Sort the input data set, **orion.order_summary**, by **Customer_ID**. Use the OUT= option to avoid overwriting the original data set. Name the output data set **work.sumsort**.

b. Create a new data set showing a total sales value for each customer.

- Name the new data set **work.customers**.
- Name the new variable **Total_Sales**. This variable contains the total of sales across all months for each customer.

c. Print your result.

- Display **Total_Sales** with a DOLLAR11.2 format.
- Add an appropriate title.

Partial PROC PRINT Output (37 Total Observations)

Total Sales to each Customer

Obs	Customer_ID	Total_Sales
1	5	$691.10
2	10	$3,479.09
3	11	$78.20
4	12	$253.20
5	18	$29.40

Level 2

5. Summarizing and Grouping Data Using the DATA Step

The data set **orion.order_qtrsum** contains information about sales in a particular year for each customer, separated by month.

- For a given customer, there might be some months (and quarters) that the customer did not place an order.
- The variable **Order_Qtr** contains the appropriate quarter.

Partial **orion.order_qtrsum** (101 Total Observations)

Customer_ID	Order_ Qtr	Order_ Month	Sale_Amt
69	4	10	3.2
70187	4	11	8.2
10	2	6	12.2
70079	4	10	14.6
70165	3	7	16.6

The data set is not sorted by **Customer_ID** and **Order_Qtr**.

a. Create a data set named **work.qtrcustomers** that summarizes sales based on customer and quarter.

- The variable **Total_Sales** should contain the total sales for each quarter within each **Customer_ID** value.
- Create a variable named **Num_Months** that counts the total months within each quarter that the customer had an order.

b. Print your results.

- Display **Total_Sales** with a DOLLAR11.2 format.
- Add an appropriate title.

Partial PROC PRINT Output (74 Total Observations)

Total Sales to each Customer for each Quarter

Obs	Customer_ID	Order_ Qtr	Total_Sales	Num_ Months
1	5	2	$604.80	2
2	5	3	$52.50	1
3	5	4	$33.80	1
4	10	1	$32.60	1
5	10	2	$342.80	3

6. (Optional) Summarizing Data and Conditional Output

The data set **orion.usorders04** contains a group of orders from U.S. customers.

Partial **orion.usorders04** (83 Total Observations, 9 Total Variables)

Order_ID	Customer_ID	Customer_Name	Order_ Type	Total_Retail_ Price
1241054779	24	Robyn Klem	3	$195.60
1241063739	89	Wynella Lewis	1	$160.80
1241286432	27	Cynthia Mccluney	3	$174.40
1241359997	12	David Black	1	$117.60
1241461856	18	Tonie Asmussen	1	$29.40
1241623505	24	Robyn Klem	3	$46.90

a. Orion Star wants to reward customers who spent $100 or more through any particular sales channel (retail, catalog, or Internet).

- Create three data sets: **work.discount1**, **work.discount2**, and **work.discount3**.

- The value of **Order_Type** indicates whether the sale was retail (=*1*), catalog (=*2*), or Internet (=*3*).
- The variable **Total_Retail_Price** contains the amount that the customer spent on each individual order.
- Create a variable named **TotSales** to hold the total sales to each customer by order type.
- Output to each of the three data sets based on the following table:

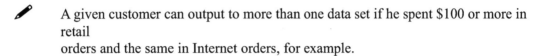

Customer spent $100 or more in…	Output to…
Retail orders	**work.discount1**
Catalog orders	**work.discount2**
Internet orders	**work.discount3**

A given customer can output to more than one data set if he spent $100 or more in retail
orders and the same in Internet orders, for example.

- Keep the variables **Customer_ID**, **Customer_Name**, and **TotSales**.
- Verify that the data sets **work.discount1**, **work.discount2**, and **work.discount3** have 8, 2, and 5 observations, respectively.

b. Print your results from **work.discount1**.

- Format **TotSales** with a DOLLAR11.2 format.
- Add an appropriate title.

Partial **work.discount1**

```
                 Customers Spending $100 or more in Retail Orders

                    Customer_ID    Customer_Name            TotSales

                              5    Sandrina Stephano         $213.10
                             10    Karen Ballinger         $3,479.09
                             12    David Black               $253.20
                             31    Cynthia Martinez        $1,322.30
                             45    Dianne Patchin            $700.28
```

Challenge

7. Identifying Extreme Values in Each Group of Data

The data set **orion.customer_dim** contains information about Orion Star customers.

Partial **orion.customer_dim** (77 Total Observations, 11 Total Variables)

```
                                                                          Customer_
   Customer_ID    Customer_Name          Customer_Type                    BirthDate

             4    James Kvarniq          Orion Club members low activity          27JUN1978
             5    Sandrina Stephano      Orion Club Gold members medium activity  09JUL1983
             9    Cornelia Krahl         Orion Club Gold members medium activity  27FEB1978
            10    Karen Ballinger        Orion  Club members high activity        18OCT1988
            11    Elke Wallstab          Orion  Club members high activity        16AUG1978
```

Use First./Last. processing to create the report below. Show data on the oldest and youngest customers for each **Customer_Type**.

- The variable **o_ID** is the **Customer_ID** value of the oldest customer and **y_ID** is the **Customer_ID** value of the youngest customer for each group.
- Create a variable named **agerange** to indicate the spread between these oldest and youngest customers.
- Use **Customer_BirthDate**, rather than **Customer_Age**, for all age determinations because this is more accurate.

Partial PROC PRINT Output (7 Total Observations)

```
                    Oldest and Youngest Customers of each Customer Type

Customer_Type                                oldest      youngest      o_ID     y_ID    agerange

Internet/Catalog Customers                  08JUL1938    18AUG1973       29    54655      35.1
Orion  Club members high activity           28SEP1938    24OCT1990       89    46966      52.1
Orion  Club members medium activity         20JAN1938    16SEP1992    70059     2806      54.7
Orion Club Gold members high activity       16JAN1938    25JUL1988       50       39      50.5
Orion Club Gold members low activity        19DEC1973    21JUL1992    70201       13      18.6
```

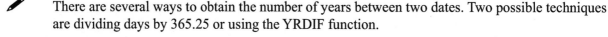

There are several ways to obtain the number of years between two dates. Two possible techniques are dividing days by 365.25 or using the YRDIF function.

3.3 Solutions

Solutions to Exercises

1. **Creating Accumulating Totals**

```
data work.mid_q4;
   set orion.order_fact;
   where '01nov2008'd <= Order_Date <= '14dec2008'd;
   Sales2Dte+Total_Retail_Price;
   Num_Orders+1;
run;

title 'Orders from 01Nov2008 through 14Dec2008';
proc print data=work.mid_q4;
   format Sales2Dte dollar10.2;
   var Order_ID Order_Date Total_Retail_Price Sales2Dte Num_Orders;
run;
title;
```

2. **Creating Accumulating Totals with Conditional Logic**

```
data work.typetotals;
   set orion.order_fact (obs=10);
   where year(Order_Date)=2009;
   /* There are equivalent WHERE statements that would work */
   if Order_Type=1 then TotalRetail+Quantity;
   else if Order_Type=2 then TotalCatalog+Quantity;
   else if Order_Type=3 then TotalInternet+Quantity;
```

```
run;

proc print data=work.typetotals;
run;

data work.typetotals;
   set orion.order_fact;
   where year(Order_Date)=2009;
   /* There are equivalent WHERE statements that would work */
   if Order_Type=1 then TotalRetail+Quantity;
   else if Order_Type=2 then TotalCatalog+Quantity;
   else if Order_Type=3 then TotalInternet+Quantity;
   keep Order_ID Order_Date TotalRetail
        TotalCatalog TotalInternet;
run;

title '2005 Accumulating Totals for Each Type of Order';
proc print data=work.typetotals;
run;
title;
```

3. **Creating Accumulating Totals by Month**

```
data work.monthtotals;
   set orion.order_fact;
   where year(Order_Date)=2011;
   retain rmonth;
   if month(Order_Date) ne rmonth then do;
      MonthSales=0;
      rmonth=month(Order_Date);
   end;
   monthsales+Total_Retail_Price;
   keep Order_ID Order_Date MonthSales Total_Retail_Price;
run;


title 'Accumulating Totals by Month in 2011';
proc print data=work.monthtotals;
   format Total_Retail_Price MonthSales dollar10.2;
run;
title;
```

4. **Summarizing Data Using the DATA Step**

```
proc sort data=orion.order_summary out=work.sumsort;
   by Customer_ID;
run;

data work.customers;
   set work.sumsort;
   by Customer_ID;
   if first.Customer_ID then Total_Sales=0;
   Total_Sales+Sale_Amt;
```

```
   if last.Customer_ID;
   keep Customer_ID Total_Sales;
run;

title 'Total Sales to each Customer';
proc print data=work.customers;
   format Total_Sales dollar11.2;
run;
title;
```

5. **Summarizing and Grouping Data Using the DATA Step**

```
proc sort data=orion.order_qtrsum out=work.custsort;
   by Customer_ID Order_Qtr;
run;

data work.qtrcustomers;
   set work.custsort;
   by Customer_ID Order_Qtr;
   if first.Order_Qtr=1 then do;
      Total_Sales=0;
    Num_Months=0;
   end;
   Total_Sales+Sale_Amt;
   Num_Months+1;
   if last.Order_Qtr=1;
   keep Customer_ID Order_Qtr Total_Sales Num_Months;
run;

title 'Total Sales to each Customer for each Quarter';
proc print data=work.qtrcustomers;
   format Total_Sales dollar11.2;
run;
title;
```

6. **(Optional) Summarizing Data and Conditional Output**

```
proc sort data=orion.usorders04 out=work.usorders04;
   by Customer_ID Order_Type;
run;

data work.discount1 work.discount2 work.discount3;
   set work.usorders04;
   by Customer_ID Order_Type;
   if first.Order_Type=1 then TotSales=0;
   TotSales+Total_Retail_Price;
   if last.Order_Type=1 and TotSales >= 100 then do;
      if Order_Type=1 then output discount1;
  else if Order_Type=2 then output discount2;
  else if Order_Type=3 then output discount3;
   end;
   keep Customer_ID Customer_Name TotSales;
run;
```

```
title 'Customers Spending $100 or more in Retail Sales';
proc print data=work.discount1 noobs;
   format TotSales dollar11.2;
run;
title;
```

7. **Identifying Extreme Values in Each Group of Data**

```
proc sort data=orion.customer_dim out=work.customers;
   by Customer_Type;
run;

data work.agecheck;
   set work.customers;
   by Customer_Type;
   retain oldest youngest o_ID y_ID;
   if first.Customer_Type=1 then do;
      oldest=Customer_BirthDate;
    youngest=Customer_BirthDate;
    o_ID=Customer_ID;
    y_ID=Customer_ID;
   end;
   if Customer_BirthDate < oldest then do;
      o_ID=Customer_ID;
      oldest=Customer_BirthDate;
   end;
   else if Customer_BirthDate > youngest then do;
      y_ID=Customer_ID;
      youngest=Customer_BirthDate;
   end;
   if last.Customer_Type=1 then do;
      agerange=(youngest-oldest)/365.25;
    output;
   end;
   keep Customer_Type oldest youngest o_ID y_ID agerange;
run;

title 'Oldest and Youngest Customers of each Customer Type';
proc print data=work.agecheck noobs;
   format oldest youngest date9. agerange 5.1;
run;
title;
```

Alternate Solution

```
proc sort data=orion.customer_dim out=work.customers;
   by Customer_Type Customer_BirthDate;
run;

data work.agecheck;
   set work.customers;
   by Customer_Type;
```

```
   /* Could instead use: by Customer_Type Customer_BirthDate;
      In this DATA step, either BY statement works. */
   retain oldest youngest o_ID y_ID;
   if first.Customer_Type=1 then do;
      o_ID=Customer_ID;
    oldest=Customer_BirthDate;
   end;
   /* Having sorted also on Customer_BirthDate, we know the first
   customer in each BY group will be the oldest (have the
   smallest SAS date value for a Birthday). */
   if last.Customer_Type=1 then do;
      y_ID=Customer_ID;
    youngest=Customer_BirthDate;
      agerange=(youngest-oldest)/365.25;
    output;
    end;
   /* Similar story: last in each BY group will be the youngest. */
   keep Customer_Type oldest youngest o_ID y_ID agerange;
run;

title 'Oldest and Youngest Customers of each Customer Type';
proc print data=work.agecheck noobs;
   format oldest youngest date9. agerange 5.1;
run;
title;
```

Solutions to Student Activities (Polls/Quizzes)

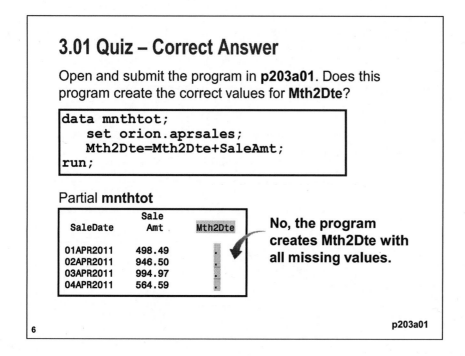

3.01 Quiz – Correct Answer

Open and submit the program in **p203a01**. Does this program create the correct values for **Mth2Dte**?

```
data mnthtot;
   set orion.aprsales;
   Mth2Dte=Mth2Dte+SaleAmt;
run;
```

Partial **mnthtot**

SaleDate	Sale Amt	Mth2Dte
01APR2011	498.49	.
02APR2011	946.50	.
03APR2011	994.97	.
04APR2011	564.59	.

No, the program creates Mth2Dte with all missing values.

6

p203a01

3.02 Multiple Choice Poll – Correct Answer

What effect did the missing value for **SaleAmt** have on **Mth2Dte**?

a. The missing value is ignored; **Mth2Dte** values are not affected.

b. The missing value causes the DATA step to stop processing.

(c.) The missing value causes the subsequent values for **Mth2Dte** to be set to missing.

24

3.03 Quiz – Correct Answer

What are the values for **First.Dept** and **Last.Dept** when the DATA step is processing the observation indicated by the arrow?

Dept	Salary
ADMIN	20000
ADMIN	100000
ADMIN	50000
ENGINR	25000 ⬅
FINANC	10000
FINANC	12000

First.Dept
1

Last.Dept
1

First.Dept and Last.Dept are both 1. This happens when a group consists of a single observation.

43

3.04 Multiple Answer Poll – Correct Answer

What must happen in the DATA step to summarize data by groups? (Circle all that apply.)

a. Sort the input data.
(b.) Set the accumulating variable to zero at the start of each BY group.
(c.) Increment the accumulating variable.
(d.) Output only the last observation of each BY group.

Choice a. does not apply because sorting is done with PROC SORT, not in the DATA step.

51

3.05 Quiz – Correct Answer

What are the values for First. and Last. variables when the DATA step is processing the observation indicated by the arrow?

Proj	Dept
A	ADMIN
A	ADMIN
A	ADMIN
B	ADMIN
B	ENGINR
B	ENGINR ←
C	ENGINR
C	SALES
C	SALES

First.Proj
0

First.Dept
0

Last.Proj
1

Last.Dept
1

64

Chapter 4 Reading Raw Data Files

4.1 Reading Raw Data Files with Formatted Input 4-3

Exercises 4-17

4.2 Controlling when a Record Loads 4-20

Exercises 4-41

4.3 Solutions 4-45

Solutions to Exercises 4-45

Solutions to Student Activities 4-47

4.1 Reading Raw Data Files with Formatted Input

Objectives

- Read raw data in fixed columns using formatted input.

3

Business Scenario

Management wants to analyze discount offer data. The data currently resides in a raw data file and needs to be converted to a SAS data set.

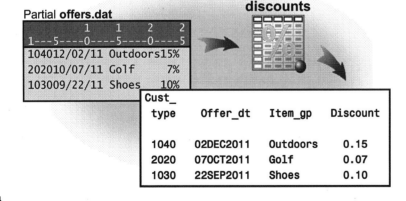

Partial **offers.dat**

```
         1    1    2    2
1---5----0----5----0----5
104012/02/11 Outdoors15%
202010/07/11 Golf     7%
103009/22/11 Shoes   10%
```

discounts

Cust_ type	Offer_dt	Item_gp	Discount
1040	02DEC2011	Outdoors	0.15
2020	07OCT2011	Golf	0.07
1030	22SEP2011	Shoes	0.10

4

4.01 Multiple Choice Poll

For your work, how often do you need to read raw data files?

a. all the time
b. occasionally
c. very rarely
d. never

5

Idea Exchange

The INPUT statement describes the arrangement of values in the input data record and assigns input values to the corresponding SAS variables.

What are the four styles of input?

6

Input Styles

Column input, formatted input, list input, and named input are all styles of writing INPUT statement specifications.

Style	Use for Reading
Column input	Standard data in fixed columns
Formatted input	Standard and nonstandard data in fixed columns
List input	Standard and nonstandard data separated by blanks or some other delimiter
Named input	Standard data that is preceded by the name of the variable and an equal sign (=)

7

Standard and Nonstandard Data (Review)

Standard data is data that SAS can read without any additional instruction.

- Character data is always standard.
- Some numeric values are standard and some are not.

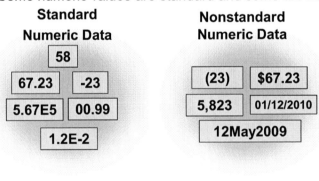

Standard Numeric Data	Nonstandard Numeric Data
58	(23)
67.23	$67.23
-23	5,823
5.67E5	01/12/2010
00.99	12May2009
1.2E-2	

8

The following are the only acceptable characters in a standard numeric field:

```
0 1 2 3 4 5 6 7 8 9 . E e D d - +
```

Leading or trailing blanks are also acceptable.

✎ **E**, **e**, **D**, and **d** represent exponential notation in a standard numeric field. An alternate way of writing **300000**, for example, is **3E5**.

Examples of nonstandard character data include preserving leading blanks in character values, hexadecimal characters, and values surrounded by matching quotation marks.

4.02 Quiz

Which style of INPUT statement specification should you choose to read the **offers.dat** raw data file?

Partial **offers.dat**

```
         1    1    2    2
1---5----0----5----0----5
104012/02/11 Outdoors15%
202010/07/11 Golf     7%
103009/22/11 Shoes   10%
103009/22/11 Clothes 10%
```

9

Reading Data Using Formatted Input

This SAS program uses formatted input to read the raw data file in **offers.dat**.

```
data work.discounts;
   infile "&path\offers.dat";
   input @1 Cust_type 4.
         @5 Offer_dt mmddyy8.
         @14 Item_gp $8.
         @22 Discount percent3.;
run;
```

INPUT *pointer-control variable informat . . .* ;

- starting position
- variable
- informat

11 p204d01

Statement	Description
DATA *output-SAS-data-set*;	The *DATA statement* begins a DATA step and provides the name of the SAS data set being created. *output-SAS-data-set* can refer to a temporary or permanent data set.

<table>
<tr><th>Statement</th><th>Description</th></tr>
<tr><td>INFILE 'raw-data-file-name';</td><td>The INFILE statement identifies the physical name of the raw data file to read with an INPUT statement.

'raw-data-file-name' is the physical name that the operating environment uses to access the file of raw data.

Examples:
<table>
<tr><td>Windows</td><td>infile 's:\workshop\offers.dat';</td></tr>
<tr><td>UNIX</td><td>infile '/users/userid/offers.dat';</td></tr>
<tr><td>z/OS (OS/390)</td><td>infile 'userid.workshop.rawdata(offers)';</td></tr>
</table>
The PAD and LRECL= options can be useful for reading variable-length records typically found in Windows and UNIX environments. See SAS Help and Documentation for more information about the PAD and LRECL= options.</td></tr>
<tr><td>INPUT specifications;</td><td>The INPUT statement describes the arrangement of values in the raw data file and assigns input values to the corresponding SAS variables.</td></tr>
</table>

Reading Data Using Formatted Input

Column pointer controls:

@n moves the pointer to column *n*.

+n moves the pointer *n* positions.

An informat specifies the following:

- the width of the input field
- how to read data values stored in the field

```
input @1 Cust_type 4.
      +1 Offer_dt mmddyy8.5
```

12

To move the pointer *n* positions backward, use +(-*n*).

SAS informats have the following form:

<$>*informat*<*w*>.<*d*>

where

$	indicates a character informat.
informat	names the SAS informat or user-defined informat.
w	specifies the number of columns to read in the input data.
.	is a required delimiter.

SAS Informat Examples

Examples of informats showing the raw data values and the converted SAS numeric values:

Informat	Raw Data Value	SAS Data Value
$8.	`Outdoors`	*Outdoors*
5.	`12345`	*12345*
COMMA7. DOLLAR7.	`$12,345`	*12345*
COMMAX7. DOLLARX7.	`$12.345`	*12345*
EUROX7.	`€12.345`	*12345*
PERCENT3.	`15%`	*.15*

13

The following table gives a brief definition for some of the informats. Complete information can be found in SAS OnlineDoc.

Informat	Definition
$*w*.	Reads standard character data.
w.d	Reads standard numeric data.
COMMA*w.d* DOLLAR*w.d*	Reads nonstandard numeric data and removes embedded commas, blanks, dollar signs, percent signs, and hyphens.
COMMAX*w.d* DOLLARX*w.d*	Operates like COMMA*w.d* and DOLLAR*w.d*, but reverses the role of the decimal point and comma. This convention is common in many European countries.
EUROX*w.d*	Reads nonstandard numeric data and removes embedded characters in European currency.

PERCENT*w.d*	Operates like COMMA*w.d* but divides the number by 100 if it is followed by a percent sign (%).

If the *d* is not specified, it defaults to 0. This means that COMMA7. and COMMA7.0 are equivalent.

If the data contains decimal points, SAS ignores the *d* value and reads the number of decimal places that are actually in the input data. If the data does not contain decimal places, *d* specifies the number of decimal places to imply.

DOLLAR*w.d* is an alias for COMMA*w.d*, and DOLLARX*w.d* is an alias for COMMAX*w.d*.

More information about EUROX*w.d* is available through SAS Help and Documentation.

SAS Date Informat Examples

Examples of date informats showing the nonstandard raw data values and the converted SAS numeric values:

Informat	Raw Data Value	SAS Date Value
MMDDYY6.	010160	*0*
MMDDYY8.	01/01/60	*0*
MMDDYY10.	01/01/1960	*0*
DDMMYY6.	311260	*365*
DDMMYY8.	31/12/60	*365*
DDMMYY10.	31/12/1960	*365*
DATE7.	31DEC59	*-1*
DATE9.	31DEC1959	*-1*

14

The ANYDTDTE*w.* informat can be used to read data that has a variety of date forms. More information about ANYDTDTE*w.* is available in SAS Help and Documentation.

Reading Data Using Formatted Input

Use formatted input to create a SAS data set named **discounts** from the raw data in **offers.dat**.

Layout: **offers.dat**

Description	Column
Customer Type	1-4
Offer Date	5-12
Item Group	14-21
Discount	22-24

Partial **offers.dat**

```
         1    1    2    2
1---5----0----5----0----5
104012/02/11 Outdoors15%
202010/07/11 Golf      7%
103009/22/11 Shoes    10%
103009/22/11 Clothes  10%
202007/08/11 Clothes  15%
203007/08/11 Clothes  25%
```

15

Writing INPUT Specifications

Identify the starting position, variable name, and informat for each input field.

```
input @1 Cust_type 4.
```

Layout: **offers.dat**

Description	Column
Customer Type	1-4
Offer Date	5-12
Item Group	14-21
Discount	22-24

Partial **offers.dat**

```
         1    1    2    2
1---5----0----5----0----5
104012/02/11 Outdoors15%
202010/07/11 Golf      7%
103009/22/11 Shoes    10%
103009/22/11 Clothes  10%
202007/08/11 Clothes  15%
203007/08/11 Clothes  25%
```

16

4.03 Quiz

Continue writing the INPUT statement to read Offer Date. (Hint: Use the MMDDYY8. informat.)

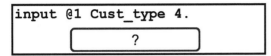

```
input @1 Cust_type 4.
          ?
```

Layout: **offers.dat**

Description	Column
Customer Type	1-4
Offer Date	5-12
Item Group	14-21
Discount	22-24

Partial **offers.dat**

```
         1    1    2    2
1---5----0----5----0----5
104012/02/11 Outdoors15%
202010/07/11 Golf      7%
103009/22/11 Shoes    10%
103009/22/11 Clothes  10%
202007/08/11 Clothes  15%
203007/08/11 Clothes  25%
```

17

Compilation: Formatted Input

```
data work.discounts;
   infile "&path\offers.dat";
   input @1 Cust_type 4.
         @5 Offer_dt mmddyy8.
         @14 Item_gp $8.
         @22 Discount percent3.;
run;
```

Input Buffer

```
                   1                   2
1 2 3 4 5 6 7 8 9 0 1 2 3 4 5 6 7 8 9 0 1 2 3 4 5
```


PDV

Cust_type N 8	Offer_dt N 8	Item_gp $ 8	Discount N 8

19 ...

Execution: Formatted Input

```
data work.discounts;
   infile "&path\offers.dat";
   input @1 Cust_type 4.
         @5 Offer_dt mmddyy8.
         @14 Item_gp $8.
         @22 Discount percent3.;
run;
```

Initialize PDV

Input Buffer

```
                  1                   2
1 2 3 4 5 6 7 8 9 0 1 2 3 4 5 6 7 8 9 0 1 2 3 4 5
```

PDV

Cust_type N 8	Offer_dt N 8	Item_gp $ 8	Discount N 8
.	.		.

20 ...

Execution: Formatted Input

Specify input data file

```
data work.discounts;
   infile "&path\offers.dat";
   input @1 Cust_type 4.
         @5 Offer_dt mmddyy8.
         @14 Item_gp $8.
         @22 Discount percent3.;
run;
```

Input Buffer

```
                  1                   2
1 2 3 4 5 6 7 8 9 0 1 2 3 4 5 6 7 8 9 0 1 2 3 4 5
```

PDV

Cust_type N 8	Offer_dt N 8	Item_gp $ 8	Discount N 8
.	.		.

21 ...

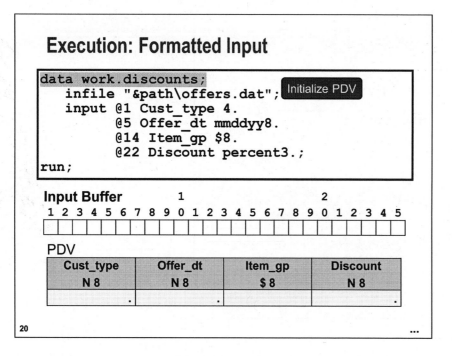

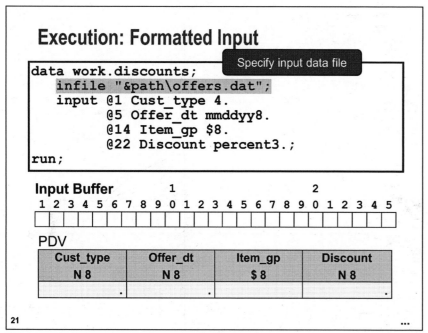

Execution: Formatted Input

Load input buffer

```
data work.discounts;
   infile "&path\offers.dat";
   input @1 Cust_type 4.
         @5 Offer_dt mmddyy8.
         @14 Item_gp $8.
         @22 Discount percent3.;
run;
```

Input Buffer

```
                    1                   2
1 2 3 4 5 6 7 8 9 0 1 2 3 4 5 6 7 8 9 0 1 2 3 4 5
1 0 4 0 1 2 / 0 2 / 1 1   O u t d o o r s 1 5 %
```

PDV

Cust_type N 8	Offer_dt N 8	Item_gp $ 8	Discount N 8
.	.		.

22 ...

Execution: Formatted Input

Load first value into PDV

```
data work.discounts;
   infile "&path\offers.dat";
   input @1 Cust_type 4.
         @5 Offer_dt mmddyy8.
         @14 Item_gp $8.
         @22 Discount percent3.;
run;
```

Input Buffer

```
                    1                   2
1 2 3 4 5 6 7 8 9 0 1 2 3 4 5 6 7 8 9 0 1 2 3 4 5
1 0 4 0 1 2 / 0 2 / 1 1   O u t d o o r s 1 5 %
```

PDV

Cust_type N 8	Offer_dt N 8	Item_gp $ 8	Discount N 8
1040	.		.

23 ...

Execution: Formatted Input

```
data work.discounts;
   infile "&path\offers.dat";
   input @1 Cust_type 4.
         @5 Offer_dt mmddyy8.
         @14 Item_gp $8.
         @22 Discount percent3.;
run;
```

Load second value into PDV

Input Buffer

1	2	3	4	5	6	7	8	9	10	11	12	13	14	15	16	17	18	19	20	21	22	23	24	25
1	0	4	0	1	2	/	0	2	/	1	1		O	u	t	d	o	o	r	s	1	5	%	

PDV

Cust_type N 8	Offer_dt N 8	Item_gp $ 8	Discount N 8
1040	18963		.

24 ...

Execution: Formatted Input

```
data work.discounts;
   infile "&path\offers.dat";
   input @1 Cust_type 4.
         @5 Offer_dt mmddyy8.
         @14 Item_gp $8.
         @22 Discount percent3.;
run;
```

Load third value into PDV

Input Buffer

1	2	3	4	5	6	7	8	9	10	11	12	13	14	15	16	17	18	19	20	21	22	23	24	25
1	0	4	0	1	2	/	0	2	/	1	1		O	u	t	d	o	o	r	s	1	5	%	

PDV

Cust_type N 8	Offer_dt N 8	Item_gp $ 8	Discount N 8
1040	18963	Outdoors	.

25 ...

Execution: Formatted Input

```
data work.discounts;
   infile "&path\offers.dat";
   input @1 Cust_type 4.
         @5 Offer_dt mmddyy8.
         @14 Item_gp $8.
         @22 Discount percent3.;
run;
```

Load fourth value into PDV

Input Buffer

1	2	3	4	5	6	7	8	9	10	1	2	3	4	5	6	7	8	9	20	1	2	3	4	5
1	0	4	0	1	2	/	0	2	/	1	1		O	u	t	d	o	o	r	s	1	5	%	

PDV

Cust_type N 8	Offer_dt N 8	Item_gp $ 8	Discount N 8
1040	18963	Outdoors	.15

26 ...

Execution: Formatted Input

```
data work.discounts;
   infile "&path\offers.dat";
   input @1 Cust_type 4.
         @5 Offer_dt mmddyy8.
         @14 Item_gp $8.
         @22 Discount percent3.;
run;
```

Implicit OUTPUT;
Implicit RETURN;

Input Buffer

1	2	3	4	5	6	7	8	9	10	1	2	3	4	5	6	7	8	9	20	1	2	3	4	5
1	0	4	0	1	2	/	0	2	/	1	1		O	u	t	d	o	o	r	s	1	5	%	

PDV

Cust_type N 8	Offer_dt N 8	Item_gp $ 8	Discount N 8
1040	18963	Outdoors	.15

27 ...

Execution: Formatted Input

Reinitialize PDV

```
data work.discounts;
   infile "&path\offers.dat";
   input @1 Cust_type 4.
         @5 Offer_dt mmddyy8.
         @14 Item_gp $8.
         @22 Discount percent3.;
run;
```

Continue until EOF

Input Buffer

1	2	3	4	5	6	7	8	9	10	1	2	3	4	5	6	7	8	9	20	1	2	3	4	5
3	0	1	0	0	5	/	1	7	/	1	1		C	l	o	t	h	e	s		1	5	%	

PDV

Cust_type N 8	Offer_dt N 8	Item_gp $ 8	Discount N 8
.	.		.

28

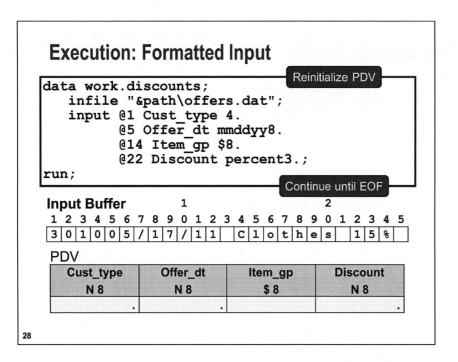

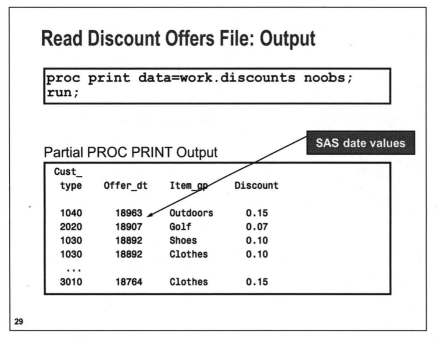

Read Discount Offers File: Output

```
proc print data=work.discounts noobs;
run;
```

Partial PROC PRINT Output

SAS date values

Cust_type	Offer_dt	Item_gp	Discount
1040	18963	Outdoors	0.15
2020	18907	Golf	0.07
1030	18892	Shoes	0.10
1030	18892	Clothes	0.10
...			
3010	18764	Clothes	0.15

29

Read Discount Offers File: Output

```
proc print data=work.discounts noobs;
   format Offer_dt date9.;
run;
```

Partial PROC PRINT Output

```
 Cust_
  type     Offer_dt    Item_gp     Discount

  1040    02DEC2011    Outdoors      0.15
  2020    07OCT2011    Golf          0.07
  1030    22SEP2011    Shoes         0.10
  1030    22SEP2011    Clothes       0.10
  ...
  3010    17MAY2011    Clothes       0.15
```

30

The FORMAT statement can also be used in the DATA step to permanently associate the DATE9. format with **Offer_dt**.

Exercises

If you restarted your SAS session since the last exercise, open and submit the **libname.sas** program found in the data folder.

Level 1

1. Using Formatted Input

The raw data file **sales1.dat** has employee information for the Australian and U.S. sales staff. The record layout is shown in the table below.

Layout for **sales1.dat**

	Field Description	Starting Column	Length of Field	Data Type
➡	Employee ID	1	6	Numeric
	First Name	8	12	Character
➡	Last Name	21	18	Character
	Gender	40	1	Character
➡	Job Title	43	20	Character

	Field Description	Starting Column	Length of Field	Data Type
➡	Salary	64	8	Numeric $100,000
	Country	73	2	Character 'AU' or 'US'
	Birth Date	76	10	Numeric mm/dd/yyyy
➡	Hire Date	87	10	Numeric mm/dd/yyyy

a. Create a new SAS data set named **sales_staff** that contains the fields indicated by arrows in the layout table.

b. Print **sales_staff** and add an appropriate title.

Partial PROC PRINT Output (165 Total Observations)

```
                         Australian and US Sales Staff

     Employee_                                                      Hire_
        ID        Last_Name         Job_Title          Salary       Date

      120102      Zhou            Sales Manager        108255      12205
      120103      Dawes           Sales Manager         87975       6575
      120121      Elvish          Sales Rep. II         26600       6575
      120122      Ngan            Sales Rep. II         27475       8217
      120123      Hotstone        Sales Rep. I          26190      18901
```

Level 2

2. Using Formatted Input and the Subsetting IF Statement

The raw data file **sales1.dat** has employee information for the Australian and U.S. sales staff. The record layout is shown in the table below.

Layout for **sales1.dat**

	Field Description	Starting Column	Length of Field	Data Type
➡	Employee ID	1	6	Numeric
	First Name	8	12	Character
➡	Last Name	21	18	Character
	Gender	40	1	Character
➡	Job Title	43	20	Character
➡	Salary	64	8	Numeric $100,000
➡	Country	73	2	Character 'AU' or 'US'

	Field Description	Starting Column	Length of Field	Data Type
	Birth Date	76	10	Numeric mm/dd/yyyy
➡	Hire Date	87	10	Numeric mm/dd/yyyy

a. Create two SAS data sets from the raw data file, and base them on the country of the trainee.

- Name the data sets **US_trainees** and **AU_trainees**. For this exercise, a trainee is anyone that has the job title of Sales Rep. I
- Each data set should contain the fields indicated by arrows in the layout table.
- Write only U.S. trainees to the **US_trainees** data set and only Australian trainees to the **AU_trainees** data set. Do ***not*** keep the **Country** variable in the output data sets.

b. Print both of the data sets with appropriate titles.

Partial **work.AU_trainees** (21 Total Observations)

```
                         Australian Trainees

     Employee_                                                Hire_
        ID        Last_Name         Job_Title        Salary    Date

      120123      Hotstone       Sales Rep. I        26190    18901
      120124      Daymond        Sales Rep. I        26480    18687
      120130      Lyon           Sales Rep. I        26955    18748
      120131      Surawski       Sales Rep. I        26910    18628
      120136      Leyden         Sales Rep. I        26605    18659
```

Partial **work.US_trainees** (42 Total Observations)

```
                             US Trainees

     Employee_                                                 Hire_
        ID        Last_Name          Job_Title        Salary    Date

      121023      Fuller          Sales Rep. I        26010    18748
      121028      Smades          Sales Rep. I        26585    18932
      121029      Mcelwee         Sales Rep. I        27225    18962
      121030      Areu            Sales Rep. I        26745    18659
      121036      Mesley          Sales Rep. I        25965    18901
```

Challenge

3. Using a Text String with Column Pointer Controls

- The raw data file **seminar.dat** contains comments and ratings from participants at a seminar given to Orion Star sales staff.
- The data file contains one line for each participant:
  - The first 15 characters are reserved for the name of the participant (if given).
  - There can be a comment of up to 60 characters.
  - The text **Rating:** is followed immediately by a numeric score from 1 to 5.

Listing of **seminar.dat**

```
J. Mitchell          Very Well done!  Rating:5
Amy Jung             Rating:4
Carl Heisman         Rating:4
Linda Deal           Not enough give aways  Rating:3
Gabrielle Heron      Nice! Rating:4
                     Not helpful at all Rating:2
Kyle Patterson       Very good. Need more like it  Rating:5
```

a. Create a new SAS data set named **seminar_ratings** that contains the names of the participants and the ratings that were given.

b. Print the data set and give it an appropriate title.

PROC PRINT Output

```
             Names and Ratings

      Obs    Name                  Rating

       1     J. Mitchell              5
       2     Amy Jung                 4
       3     Carl Heisman             4
       4     Linda Deal               3
       5     Gabrielle Heron          4
       6                              2
       7     Kyle Patterson           5
```

4.2 Controlling when a Record Loads

Objectives

- Read a raw data file with multiple records per observation.
- Read a raw data file with mixed record types.
- Subset from a raw data file with mixed record types.

34

Business Scenario

Create a SAS data set that contains the necessary information for a mailing label.

Partial **Address.dat**

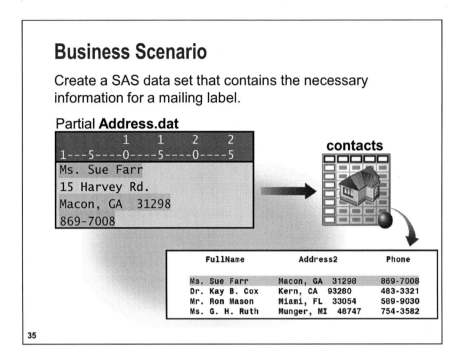

```
         1    1    2    2
1---5----0----5----0----5
Ms. Sue Farr
15 Harvey Rd.
Macon, GA  31298
869-7008
```

contacts

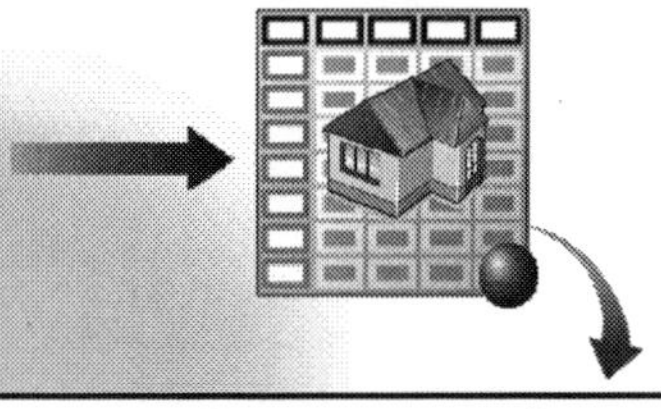

FullName	Address2	Phone
Ms. Sue Farr	Macon, GA 31298	869-7008
Dr. Kay B. Cox	Kern, CA 93280	483-3321
Mr. Ron Mason	Miami, FL 33054	589-9030
Ms. G. H. Ruth	Munger, MI 48747	754-3582

35

Multiple INPUT Statements

By default, SAS loads a new record into the input buffer when it encounters an INPUT statement.

You can have multiple INPUT statements in one DATA step.

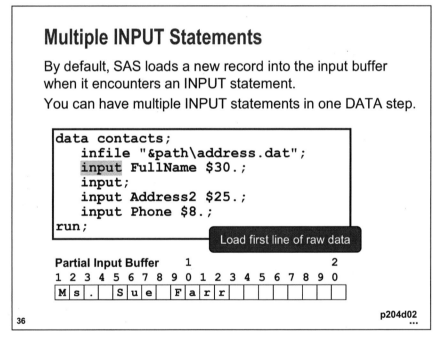

```
data contacts;
   infile "&path\address.dat";
   input FullName $30.;
   input;
   input Address2 $25.;
   input Phone $8.;
run;
```

Load first line of raw data

Partial Input Buffer

1	2	3	4	5	6	7	8	9	10	11	12	13	14	15	16	17	18	19	20
M	s	.		S	u	e		F	a	r	r								

36

p204d02

...

By default, SAS begins reading each new line of raw data at position 1 of the input buffer, so having @1 in the INPUT statement is not necessary.

Multiple INPUT Statements

```
data contacts;
   infile "&path\address.dat";
   input FullName $30.;
   input;
   input Address2 $25.;
   input Phone $8.;
run;
```

Load second line of raw data

Partial Input Buffer

1	2	3	4	5	6	7	8	9	10	11	12	13	14	15	16	17	18	19	20
1	5		H	a	r	v	e	y		R	d	.							

✎ Even though no variables are listed, the INPUT statement still loads the raw data line into the input buffer.

37 ...

Multiple INPUT Statements

```
data contacts;
   infile "&path\address.dat";
   input FullName $30.;
   input;
   input Address2 $25.;
   input Phone $8.;
run;
```

Load third line of raw data

Partial Input Buffer

1	2	3	4	5	6	7	8	9	10	11	12	13	14	15	16	17	18	19	20
M	a	c	o	n	,		G	A		3	1	2	9	8					

38 ...

Multiple INPUT Statements

```
data contacts;
   infile "&path\address.dat";
   input FullName $30.;
   input;
   input Address2 $25.;
   input Phone $8.;
run;
```

Load fourth line of raw data

Partial Input Buffer

1	2	3	4	5	6	7	8	9	10	1	2	3	4	5	6	7	8	9	20
8	6	9	-	7	0	0	8												

PDV

FullName $ 30	Address2 $ 25	Phone $ 8
Ms. Sue Farr	Macon, GA 31298	869-7008

39

Multiple INPUT Statements

Partial SAS Log

```
NOTE: 48 records were read from the infile 'address.dat'.
      The minimum record length was 18.
      The maximum record length was 30.
NOTE: The data set WORK.CONTACTS has 12 observations
      and 3 variables.
```

40

Multiple INPUT Statements

```
proc print data=contacts noobs;
run;
```

Partial PROC PRINT Output

```
        FullName              Address2              Phone

    Ms. Sue Farr        Macon, GA  31298          869-7008
    Dr. Kay B. Cox      Kern, CA  93280           483-3321
    Mr. Ron Mason       Miami, FL  33054          589-9030
    Ms. G. H. Ruth      Munger, MI  48747         754-3582
```

41

Line Pointer Controls

INPUT *specifications / specifications*;

```
data contacts;
   infile "&path\address.dat";
   input FullName $30. / /
         Address2 $25. /
         Phone $8. ;
run;
```

Load first line of raw data

Partial Input Buffer

1	2	3	4	5	6	7	8	9	10	1	2	3	4	5	6	7	8	9	20
M	s	.		S	u	e		F	a	r	r								

SAS loads the next record when it encounters a forward slash.

42

p204d03

...

Line Pointer Controls

```
data contacts;
   infile "&path\address.dat";
   input FullName $30. / /
         Address2 $25. /
         Phone $8. ;
run;
```

Load second line of raw data

Partial Input Buffer

1	2	3	4	5	6	7	8	9	10	1	2	3	4	5	6	7	8	9	20
1	5		H	a	r	v	e	y		R	d	.							

43 ...

Line Pointer Controls

```
data contacts;
   infile "&path\address.dat";
   input FullName $30. / /
         Address2 $25. /
         Phone $8. ;
run;
```

Load third line of raw data

Partial Input Buffer

1	2	3	4	5	6	7	8	9	10	1	2	3	4	5	6	7	8	9	20
M	a	c	o	n	,		G	A		3	1	2	9	8					

44 ...

Line Pointer Controls

```
data contacts;
   infile "&path\address.dat";
   input FullName $30. / /
         Address2 $25. /
         Phone $8. ;
run;
```

Load fourth line of raw data

Partial Input Buffer

1	2	3	4	5	6	7	8	9	10	11	12	13	14	15	16	17	18	19	20
8	6	9	-	7	0	0	8												

45

The forward slash is known as a *relative* line pointer control that moves the pointer relative to the line on which it currently positioned. There is also an *absolute* line pointer control that moves the pointer to a specific line in a group of lines. Here is an example.

```
data contacts;
   infile "&path\address.dat";
   input #1 FullName $30.
         #3 Address2 $25.
         #4 Phone $8.;
run;
```

✎ See SAS Help and Documentation for more information about absolute line pointer controls.

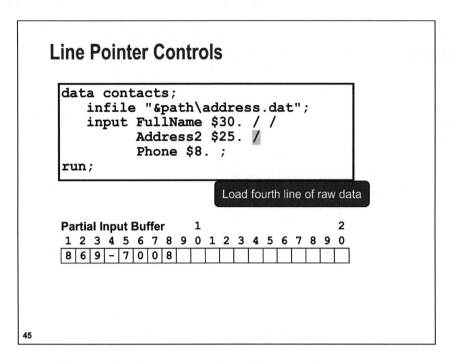

Line Pointer Controls

Partial SAS Log

```
NOTE: 48 records were read from the infile 'address.dat'.
      The minimum record length was 18.
      The maximum record length was 30.
NOTE: The data set WORK.CONTACTS has 12 observations
      and 3 variables.
```

46

Line Pointer Controls

```
proc print data=contacts noobs;
run;
```

Partial PROC PRINT Output

```
     FullName              Address2              Phone

 Ms. Sue Farr         Macon, GA  31298        869-7008
 Dr. Kay B. Cox       Kern, CA  93280         483-3321
 Mr. Ron Mason        Miami, FL  33054        589-9030
 Ms. G. H. Ruth       Munger, MI  48747       754-3582
```

47

4.04 Quiz

Using pen and paper, write an INPUT statement to read the data from the raw data file.

Raw Data

```
          1    1    2    2
1---5----0----5----0----5
10458Pine Mt. Sports
02/22/11 $2,405.50
00103RFG Textile Inc.
09/01/11 $1,095.30
24221Fifth Wheel Ltd.
06/04/11   $956.70
```

Line 1 Layout

Description	Column
Supplier Code	1-5
Supplier Name	6-25

Line 2 Layout

Description	Column
Shipment Date	1-8
Amount	10-18

✎ Supplier Code and Supplier Name contain character values.

48

Business Scenario: Read Top Sales Data

Create a SAS data set from the raw data that contains records that do not have the same format.

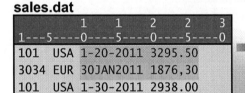

sales.dat

```
          1    1    2    2    3
1---5----0----5----0----5----0
101  USA 1-20-2011 3295.50
3034 EUR 30JAN2011 1876,30
101  USA 1-30-2011 2938.00
```

salesQ1

Sale ID	Location	Sale Date	Amount
101	USA	18647	3295.50
3034	EUR	18657	1876.30
101	USA	18657	2938.00
128	USA	18663	2908.74

51

Desired Output

work.salesQ1

Sale ID	Location	Sale Date	Amount
101	USA	18647	3295.50
3034	EUR	18657	1876.30
101	USA	18657	2938.00
128	USA	18663	2908.74
1345	EUR	18664	3145.60
109	USA	18703	2789.10

52

Mixed Record Types: First Attempt

This code is a good start to reading the mixed record types, but it gives unexpected results.

```
data salesQ1;
   infile "&path\sales.dat";
   input SaleID $4. @6 Location $3.;
   if Location='USA' then
      input @10 SaleDate mmddyy10.
            @20 Amount 7.;
   else if Location='EUR' then
      input @10 SaleDate date9.
            @20 Amount commax7.;
run;
```

53 p204d04

Execution: First Attempt

Initialize PDV

```
data salesQ1;
   infile "&path\sales.dat";
   input SaleID $4. @6 Location $3.;
   if Location='USA' then
      input @10 SaleDate mmddyy10.
            @20 Amount 7.;
   else if Location='EUR' then
      input @10 SaleDate date9.
            @20 Amount commax7.;
run;
```

Input Buffer

```
                  1                   2
1 2 3 4 5 6 7 8 9 0 1 2 3 4 5 6 7 8 9 0 1 2 3 4 5 6
```

PDV

SaleID $ 4	Location $ 3	SaleDate N 8	Amount N 8
		.	.

54 ...

Execution: First Attempt

Specify input data file

```
data salesQ1;
   infile "&path\sales.dat";
   input SaleID $4. @6 Location $3.;
   if Location='USA' then
      input @10 SaleDate mmddyy10.
            @20 Amount 7.;
   else if Location='EUR' then
      input @10 SaleDate date9.
            @20 Amount commax7.;
run;
```

Input Buffer

```
                  1                   2
1 2 3 4 5 6 7 8 9 0 1 2 3 4 5 6 7 8 9 0 1 2 3 4 5 6
```

PDV

SaleID $ 4	Location $ 3	SaleDate N 8	Amount N 8
		.	.

55 ...

Execution: First Attempt

Load input buffer

```
data salesQ1;
   infile "&path\sales.dat";
   input SaleID $4. @6 Location $3.;
   if Location='USA' then
      input @10 SaleDate mmddyy10.
            @20 Amount 7.;
   else if Location='EUR' then
      input @10 SaleDate date9.
            @20 Amount commax7.;
run;
```

Input Buffer

1	2	3	4	5	6	7	8	9	10	11	12	13	14	15	16	17	18	19	20	21	22	23	24	25	26
1	0	1			U	S	A		1	-	2	0	-	2	0	1	1		3	2	9	5	.	5	0

PDV

SaleID $ 4	Location $ 3	SaleDate N 8	Amount N 8
		.	.

56 ...

Execution: First Attempt

Load values into PDV

```
data salesQ1;
   infile "&path\sales.dat";
   input SaleID $4. @6 Location $3.;
   if Location='USA' then
      input @10 SaleDate mmddyy10.
            @20 Amount 7.;
   else if Location='EUR' then
      input @10 SaleDate date9.
            @20 Amount commax7.;
run;
```

Input Buffer

1	2	3	4	5	6	7	8	9	10	11	12	13	14	15	16	17	18	19	20	21	22	23	24	25	26
1	0	1			U	S	A		1	-	2	0	-	2	0	1	1		3	2	9	5	.	5	0

PDV

SaleID $ 4	Location $ 3	SaleDate N 8	Amount N 8
101	USA	.	.

57 ...

Execution: First Attempt

```
data salesQ1;
   infile "&path\sales.dat";
   input SaleID $4. @6 Location $3.;
   if Location='USA' then
      input @10 SaleDate mmddyy10.
            @20 Amount 7.;
   else if Location='EUR' then
      input @10 SaleDate date9.
            @20 Amount commax7.;
run;
```

True

Input Buffer

1	2	3	4	5	6	7	8	9	10	1	2	3	4	5	6	7	8	9	20	1	2	3	4	5	6
1	0	1			U	S	A		1	-	2	0	-	2	0	1	1		3	2	9	5	.	5	0

PDV

SaleID $ 4	Location $ 3	SaleDate N 8	Amount N 8
101	USA	.	.

58 ...

Execution: First Attempt

```
data salesQ1;
   infile "&path\sales.dat";
   input SaleID $4. @6 Location $3.;
   if Location='USA' then
      input @10 SaleDate mmddyy10.
            @20 Amount 7.;
   else if Location='EUR' then
      input @10 SaleDate date9.
            @20 Amount commax7.;
run;
```

Load input buffer

Input Buffer

1	2	3	4	5	6	7	8	9	10	1	2	3	4	5	6	7	8	9	20	1	2	3	4	5	6
3	0	3	4		E	U	R		3	0	J	A	N	2	0	1	1		1	8	7	6	,	3	0

PDV

SaleID $ 4	Location $ 3	SaleDate N 8	Amount N 8
101	USA	.	.

59 ...

Execution: First Attempt

```
data salesQ1;
   infile "&path\sales.dat";
   input SaleID $4. @6 Location $3.;
   if Location='USA' then
      input @10 SaleDate mmddyy10.
            @20 Amount 7.;
   else if Location='EUR' then
      input @10 SaleDate date9.
            @20 Amount commax7.;
run;
```

Invalid data message written to SAS log

Input Buffer

1	2	3	4	5	6	7	8	9	0	1	2	3	4	5	6	7	8	9	0	1	2	3	4	5	6
3	0	3	4		E	U	R		3	0	J	A	N	2	0	1	1		1	8	7	6	,	3	0

PDV

SaleID $ 4	Location $ 3	SaleDate N 8	Amount N 8
101	USA	.	.

60 ...

Execution: First Attempt

```
data salesQ1;
   infile "&path\sales.dat";
   input SaleID $4. @6 Location $3.;
   if Location='USA' then
      input @10 SaleDate mmddyy10.
            @20 Amount 7.;
   else if Location='EUR' then
      input @10 SaleDate date9.
            @20 Amount commax7.;
run;
```

Implicit OUTPUT;
Implicit RETURN;

Input Buffer

1	2	3	4	5	6	7	8	9	0 (1)	1	2	3	4	5	6	7	8	9	0 (2)	1	2	3	4	5	6
3	0	3	4		E	U	R		3	0	J	A	N	2	0	1	1		1	8	7	6	,	3	0

PDV

SaleID $ 4	Location $ 3	SaleDate N 8	Amount N 8
101	USA	.	.

61 ...

Execution: First Attempt

```
data salesQ1;
   infile "&path\sales.dat";
   input SaleID $4. @6 Location $3.;
   if Location='USA' then
      input @10 SaleDate mmddyy10.
            @20 Amount 7.;
   else if Location='EUR' then
      input @10 SaleDate date9.
            @20 Amount commax7.;
run;
```

Continue until EOF

Input Buffer

1	2	3	4	5	6	7	8	9	10	11	12	13	14	15	16	17	18	19	20	21	22	23	24	25	26
3	0	3	4		E	U	R		3	0	J	A	N	2	0	1	1		1	8	7	6	,	3	0

PDV

SaleID $ 4	Location $ 3	SaleDate N 8	Amount N 8
101	USA	.	.

62

First Attempt: Unexpected Output

Partial SAS Log

```
NOTE: Invalid data for SaleDate in line 2 10-19.
NOTE: Invalid data for Amount in line 2 20-26.
RULE:      ----+----1----+----2----+----3----+----4----+----5----+
           3034 EUR 30JAN2011 1876,30
SaleID=101 Location=USA SaleDate=. Amount=. _ERROR_=1 _N_=1
      .
      .
NOTE: 6 records were read from the infile 'sales.dat'.
      The minimum record length was 26.
      The maximum record length was 27.
NOTE: The data set WORK.SALESQ1 has 3 observations and 4 variables.
```

63

First Attempt: Unexpected Output

```
proc print data=salesQ1 noobs;
run;
```

PROC PRINT Output

Sale ID	Location	Sale Date	Amount
101	USA	.	.
101	USA	18663	2908.74
1345	EUR	.	278910.00

To get the correct results, SAS needs some way to keep the second INPUT statement from moving to the next line of raw data.

64

Mixed Record Types: Correct Program

The single trailing @ holds a raw data record in the input buffer until SAS does one of the following:

- executes an INPUT statement with no trailing @
- begins the next iteration of the DATA step

INPUT *specifications ...* @;

```
data salesQ1;
   infile "&path\sales.dat";
   input SaleID $4. @6 Location $3. @;
   if Location='USA' then
      input @10 SaleDate mmddyy10.
            @20 Amount 7.;
   else if Location='EUR' then
      input @10 SaleDate date9.
            @20 Amount commax7.;
run;
```

65 p204d05

Normally, each INPUT statement in a DATA step reads a new data record into the input buffer. When you use a trailing @, the following occur:

- The pointer position does not change.
- No new record is read into the input buffer.
- The next INPUT statement for the same iteration of the DATA step continues to read the same record rather than a new one.

SAS releases a record held by a trailing @ when

- a null INPUT statement executes (**input;**)
- an INPUT statement without a trailing @ executes
- the next iteration of the DATA step begins.

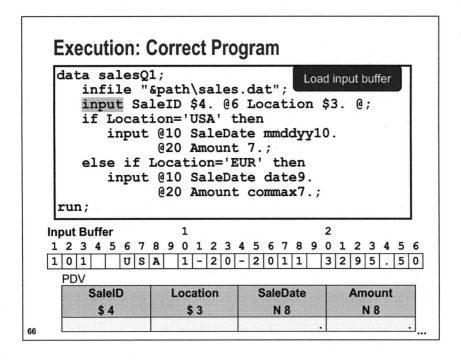

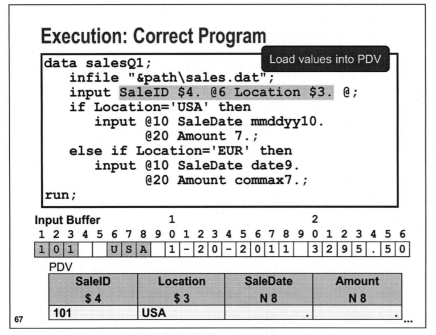

Execution: Correct Program

Load input buffer

```
data salesQ1;
   infile "&path\sales.dat";
   input SaleID $4. @6 Location $3. @;
   if Location='USA' then
      input @10 SaleDate mmddyy10.
            @20 Amount 7.;
   else if Location='EUR' then
      input @10 SaleDate date9.
            @20 Amount commax7.;
run;
```

Input Buffer

1	2	3	4	5	6	7	8	9	10	1	2	3	4	5	6	7	8	9	20	1	2	3	4	5	6
1	0	1			U	S	A		1	-	2	0	-	2	0	1	1		3	2	9	5	.	5	0

PDV

SaleID $ 4	Location $ 3	SaleDate N 8	Amount N 8
		.	.

66 ...

Execution: Correct Program

Load values into PDV

```
data salesQ1;
   infile "&path\sales.dat";
   input SaleID $4. @6 Location $3. @;
   if Location='USA' then
      input @10 SaleDate mmddyy10.
            @20 Amount 7.;
   else if Location='EUR' then
      input @10 SaleDate date9.
            @20 Amount commax7.;
run;
```

Input Buffer

1	2	3	4	5	6	7	8	9	10	1	2	3	4	5	6	7	8	9	20	1	2	3	4	5	6
1	0	1			U	S	A		1	-	2	0	-	2	0	1	1		3	2	9	5	.	5	0

PDV

SaleID $ 4	Location $ 3	SaleDate N 8	Amount N 8
101	USA	.	.

67 ...

Execution: Correct Program

```
data salesQ1;
   infile "&path\sales.dat";
   input SaleID $4. @6 Location $3. @;
   if Location='USA' then
      input @10 SaleDate mmddyy10.
            @20 Amount 7.;
   else if Location='EUR' then
      input @10 SaleDate date9.
            @20 Amount commax7.;
run;
```

Do not read new record at next INPUT statement

Hold

Input Buffer

1	2	3	4	5	6	7	8	9	10	11	12	13	14	15	16	17	18	19	20	21	22	23	24	25	26
1	0	1			U	S	A		1	-	2	0	-	2	0	1	1		3	2	9	5	.	5	0

PDV

SaleID $ 4	Location $ 3	SaleDate N 8	Amount N 8
101	USA	.	.

68 ...

Execution: Correct Program

```
data salesQ1;
   infile "&path\sales.dat";
   input SaleID $4. @6 Location $3. @;
   if Location='USA' then
      input @10 SaleDate mmddyy10.
            @20 Amount 7.;
   else if Location='EUR' then
      input @10 SaleDate date9.
            @20 Amount commax7.;
run;
```

True

Hold

Input Buffer

1	2	3	4	5	6	7	8	9	10	11	12	13	14	15	16	17	18	19	20	21	22	23	24	25	26
1	0	1			U	S	A		1	-	2	0	-	2	0	1	1		3	2	9	5	.	5	0

PDV

SaleID $ 4	Location $ 3	SaleDate N 8	Amount N 8
101	USA	.	.

69 ...

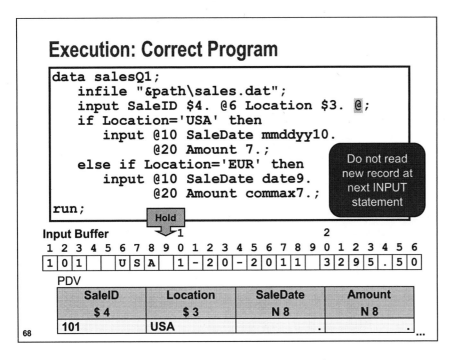

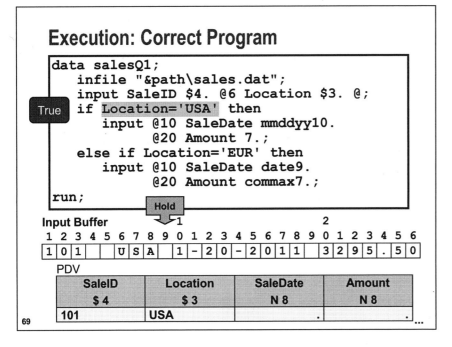

Execution: Correct Program

```
data salesQ1;
   infile "&path\sales.dat";
   input SaleID $4. @6 Location $3. @;
   if Location='USA' then
      input @10 SaleDate mmddyy10.
            @20 Amount 7.;
   else if Location='EUR' then
      input @10 SaleDate date9.
            @20 Amount commax7.;
run;
```

Do ***not*** load input buffer

Hold

Input Buffer

1	2	3	4	5	6	7	8	9	10	1	2	3	4	5	6	7	8	9	20	1	2	3	4	5	6
1	0	1			U	S	A		1	-	2	0	-	2	0	1	1		3	2	9	5	.	5	0

PDV

SaleID $ 4	Location $ 3	SaleDate N 8	Amount N 8
101	USA	.	.

70 ...

Execution: Correct Program

```
data salesQ1;
   infile "&path\sales.dat";
   input SaleID $4. @6 Location $3. @;
   if Location='USA' then
      input @10 SaleDate mmddyy10.
            @20 Amount 7.;
   else if Location='EUR' then
      input @10 SaleDate date9.
            @20 Amount commax7.;
run;
```

Input Buffer

1	2	3	4	5	6	7	8	9	10	1	2	3	4	5	6	7	8	9	20	1	2	3	4	5	6
1	0	1			U	S	A		1	-	2	0	-	2	0	1	1		3	2	9	5	.	5	0

PDV

SaleID $ 4	Location $ 3	SaleDate N 8	Amount N 8
101	USA	18647	3295.50

71 ...

Execution: Correct Program

```
data salesQ1;
   infile "&path\sales.dat";
   input SaleID $4. @6 Location $3. @;
   if Location='USA' then
      input @10 SaleDate mmddyy10.
            @20 Amount 7.;
   else if Location='EUR' then
      input @10 SaleDate date9.
            @20 Amount commax7.;
run;
```

Continue until EOF

Input Buffer

```
                  1                   2
1 2 3 4 5 6 7 8 9 0 1 2 3 4 5 6 7 8 9 0 1 2 3 4 5 6
1 0 1     U S A   1 - 2 0 - 2 0 1 1   3 2 9 5 . 5 0
```

PDV

SaleID $ 4	Location $ 3	SaleDate N 8	Amount N 8
101	USA	18647	3295.50

72

Correct Program: Output

Partial SAS Log

```
NOTE: 6 records were read from the infile 'sales.dat'.
      The minimum record length was 26.
      The maximum record length was 27.
NOTE: The data set WORK.SALESQ1 has 6 observations and 4 variables.
```

PROC PRINT Output

Sale ID	Location	Sale Date	Amount
101	USA	18647	3295.50
3034	EUR	18657	1876.30
101	USA	18657	2938.00
128	USA	18663	2908.74
1345	EUR	18664	3145.60
109	USA	18703	2789.10

73

Business Scenario

Create a SAS data set that contains only the European observations.

sales.dat

```
        1    1    2    2    3
1---5----0----5----0----5----0
101  USA 1-20-2011 3295.50
3034 EUR 30JAN2011 1876,30
101  USA 1-30-2011 2938.00
128  USA 2-5-2011  2908.74
1345 EUR 6FEB2011  3145,60
```

EuropeQ1

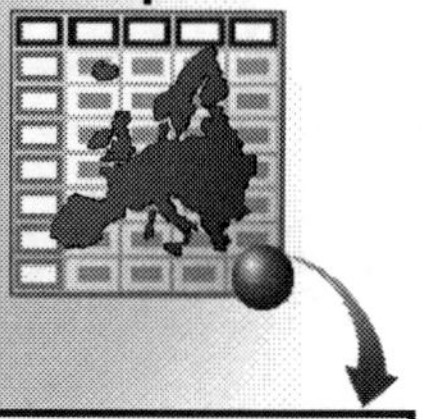

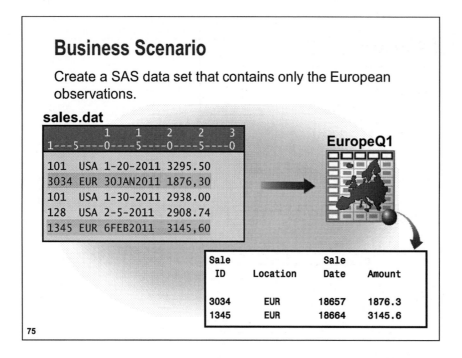

Sale ID	Location	Sale Date	Amount
3034	EUR	18657	1876.3
1345	EUR	18664	3145.6

75

4.05 Quiz

Is this the best placement for the subsetting IF statement?

```
data EuropeQ1;
   infile "&path\sales.dat";
   input SaleID $4. @6 Location $3. @;
   if Location='USA' then
      input @10 SaleDate mmddyy10.
            @20 Amount 7.;
   else if Location='EUR' then
      input @10 SaleDate date9.
            @20 Amount commax7.;
   if Location = 'EUR';
run;
```

p204d06

76

Placement of the Subsetting IF Statement

Generally, the most efficient place to put the subsetting IF statement is as soon as all the variables that are needed to evaluate the condition are assigned values.

```
data EuropeQ1;
  infile "&path\sales.dat";
  input @6 Location $3. @;
  if Location = 'EUR';
  input  @1 SaleID $4.
        @10 SaleDate date9.
        @20 Amount commax7.;
run;
```

78 p204d07

SAS releases a record held by a trailing @ when the next iteration of the DATA step begins.

Subsetting Mixed Record Types: Output

```
proc print data=EuropeQ1 noobs;
   var SaleID Location SaleDate Amount;
run;
```

PROC PRINT Output

Sale ID	Location	Sale Date	Amount
3034	EUR	18657	1876.3
1345	EUR	18664	3145.6

79

Exercises

If you restarted your SAS session since the last exercise, open and submit the **libname.sas** program found in the data folder.

Level 1

4. Reading Multiple Input Records per Observation

- The raw data file **sales2.dat** has employee information for the Australian and U.S. sales staff.
- Information for each employee is in three lines of raw data.
- The record layouts are shown below.

Line 1 layout

	Field Description	Starting Column	Length of Field	Data Type
➡	Employee ID	1	6	Numeric
	First Name	8	12	Character
➡	Last Name	21	18	Character

Line 2 layout

	Field Description	Starting Column	Length of Field	Data Type
➡	Job Title	1	20	Character
➡	Hire Date	22	10	Numeric mm/dd/yyyy
➡	Salary	33	8	Numeric for example, $100,000

Line 3 layout

Field Description	Starting Column	Length of Field	Data Type
Gender	1	1	Character
Birth Date	3	10	Numeric mm/dd/yyyy
Country	14	2	Character

a. Create a new SAS data set named **sales_staff2** that contains the fields indicated by arrows in the layout table.

b. Print **sales_staff2** and add an appropriate title.

Partial PROC PRINT Output (165 Total Observations)

```
                    Australian and US Sales Staff

      Employee_                                        Hire_
         ID       Last_Name           Job_Title         Date     Salary

       120102     Zhou              Sales Manager      12205     108255
       120103     Dawes             Sales Manager       6575      87975
       120121     Elvish            Sales Rep. II       6575      26600
       120122     Ngan              Sales Rep. II       8217      27475
       120123     Hotstone          Sales Rep. I       18901      26190
```

Level 2

5. Working with Mixed Record Types

- The raw data file **sales3.dat** has employee information for the Australian and U.S. sales staff.
- Information for each employee is in two lines of raw data.
- The record layouts are shown below.

Line 1 layout

	Field Description	Starting Column	Length of Field	Data Type
➡	Employee ID	1	6	Numeric
	First Name	8	12	Character
➡	Last Name	21	18	Character
	Gender	40	1	Character
➡	Job Title	43	20	Character

Line 2 layout for Australian employees

	Field Description	Starting Column	Length of Field	Data Type
➡	Salary	1	8	Numeric $100.000
➡	Country	10	2	Character
	Birth Date	13	10	Numeric dd/mm/yyyy
➡	Hire Date	24	10	Numeric dd/mm/yyyy

Line 2 layout for U.S. employees

	Field Description	Starting Column	Length of Field	Data Type
➡	Salary	1	8	Numeric $100,000
➡	Country	10	2	Character
	Birth Date	13	10	Numeric mm/dd/yyyy
➡	Hire Date	24	10	Numeric mm/dd/yyyy

a. Create two new SAS data sets, **US_sales** and **AU_sales**, that contain the fields indicated by arrows in the layout table. Write only U.S. employees to the **US_sales** data set and only Australian employees to the **AU_sales** data set. Do ***not*** include the **Country** variable in the output data sets.

> ✎ The salary and hire date values are different for Australian and U.S. employees. Be sure to use the correct informats in each INPUT statement.

b. Print both of the data sets with appropriate titles.

Partial **work. AU_sales** (63 Total Observations)

```
                          Australian Sales Staff

       Employee_                                                   Hire_
          ID        Last_Name          Job_Title          Salary    Date

        120102      Zhou             Sales Manager        108255   12205
        120103      Dawes            Sales Manager         87975    6575
        120121      Elvish           Sales Rep. II         26600    6575
        120122      Ngan             Sales Rep. II         27475    8217
        120123      Hotstone         Sales Rep. I          26190   18901
        120124      Daymond          Sales Rep. I          26480   18687
        120125      Hofmeister       Sales Rep. IV         32040    8460
```

Partial **work. US_sales** (102 Total Observations)

```
                          US Sales Staff

  Employee_                                                          Hire_
     ID        Last_Name           Job_Title                Salary    Date

   120261      Highpoint           Chief Sales Officer      243190   11535
   121018      Magolan             Sales Rep. II             27560    6575
   121019      Desanctis           Sales Rep. IV             31320   17684
   121020      Ridley              Sales Rep. IV             31750   16922
   121021      Farren              Sales Rep. IV             32985   13939
   121022      Stevens             Sales Rep. IV             32210   16833
   121023      Fuller              Sales Rep. I              26010   18748
   121024      Westlund            Sales Rep. II             26600   17653
```

4.3 Solutions

Solutions to Exercises

1. **Using Formatted Input**

```
data sales_staff;
   infile "&path\sales1.dat";
   input  @1 Employee_ID 6.
         @21 Last_Name $18.
         @43 Job_Title $20.
         @64 Salary Dollar8.
         @87 Hire_Date mmddyy10.;
run;

title 'Australian and US Sales Staff';
proc print data=sales_staff noobs;
run;
title;
```

2. **Using Formatted Input and the Subsetting IF Statement**

```
data AU_trainees US_trainees;
   drop Country;
   infile "&path\sales1.dat";
   input  @1 Employee_ID 6.
         @21 Last_Name $18.
         @43 Job_Title $20.
         @64 Salary Dollar8.
         @73 Country $2.
         @87 Hire_Date mmddyy10.;
   if Job_Title = 'Sales Rep. I';
   if Country = 'AU' then output AU_trainees;
   else if Country='US' then output US_trainees;
run;

title 'Australian Trainees';
proc print data=AU_trainees noobs;
run;

title 'US Trainees';
proc print data=US_trainees noobs;
run;
title;
```

3. **Using a Text String with Column Pointer Controls**

```
data seminar_ratings;
   infile "&path\seminar.dat";
   input Name $15.  @'Rating:' Rating 1.;
run;
```

```
title 'Names and Ratings';
proc print data=seminar_ratings;
   run;
title;
```

4. Reading Multiple Input Records per Observation

```
data sales_staff2;
   infile "&path\sales2.dat";
   input  @1 Employee_ID 6.
         @21 Last_Name $18. /
          @1 Job_Title $20.
         @22 Hire_Date mmddyy10.
         @33 Salary dollar8. /;
run;

title 'Australian and US Sales Staff';
proc print data=sales_staff2 noobs;
run;
title;
```

Alternate Solution

```
data sales_staff2;
   infile "&path\sales2.dat";
   input  @1 Employee_ID 6.
         @21 Last_Name $18.;
   input  @1 Job_Title $20.
         @22 Hire_Date mmddyy10.
         @33 Salary dollar8.;
   input;
run;
```

Alternate Solution

```
data sales_staff2;
   infile "&path\sales2.dat";
   input  @1 Employee_ID 6.
         @21 Last_Name $18.
    #2    @1 Job_Title $20.
         @22 Hire_Date mmddyy10.
         @33 Salary dollar8.
    #3    ;
run;
```

5. Working with Mixed Record Types

```
data AU_sales US_sales;
   drop Country;
   infile 'sales3.dat';
   input  @1 Employee_ID 6.
         @21 Last_Name $18.
         @43 Job_Title $20.;
   input @10 Country $2. @;
   if Country = 'AU' then do;
```

```
      input @1 Salary dollarx8.
            @24 Hire_Date ddmmyy10.;
      output AU_sales;
   end;
   else if Country = 'US' then do;
      input @1 Salary dollar8.
            @24 Hire_Date mmddyy10.;
      output US_sales;
   end;
run;

title 'Australian Sales Staff';
proc print data=AU_sales noobs;
run;

title 'US Sales Staff';
proc print data=US_sales noobs;
run;
title;
```

Solutions to Student Activities

4.02 Quiz – Correct Answer

Which style of INPUT statement specification should you choose to read the **offers.dat** raw data file?

Partial **offers.dat**

```
         1    1    2    2
1---5----0----5----0----5
104012/02/11 Outdoors15%
202010/07/11 Golf     7%
103009/22/11 Shoes   10%
103009/22/11 Clothes 10%
```

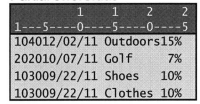

Formatted input **is the best style of INPUT statement specification to read this data.**

The offers.dat file is in fixed columns and has nonstandard data.

10

4.03 Quiz – Correct Answer

Continue writing the INPUT statement to read Offer Date. (Hint: Use the MMDDYY8. informat.)

```
input @1 Cust_type 4.
      @5 Offer_dt mmddyy8.
```

Layout: **offers.dat**

Description	Column
Customer Type	1-4
Offer Date	5-12
Item Group	14-21
Discount	22-24

Partial **offers.dat**

```
         1    1    2    2
1---5----0----5----0----5
104012/02/11 Outdoors15%
202010/07/11 Golf      7%
103009/22/11 Shoes    10%
103009/22/11 Clothes  10%
202007/08/11 Clothes  15%
203007/08/11 Clothes  25%
```

18

4.04 Quiz – Correct Answer

Using pen and paper, write an INPUT statement to read the data from the raw data file.

One answer is shown here:

```
input @1 Supplier_Code $5.
      @6 Supplier_Name $20. /
      @1 Ship_Date mmddyy8.
      @10 Amount dollar9.;
```

There are other ways to write the INPUT statement correctly.

49

4.05 Quiz – Correct Answer

Is this the best placement for the subsetting IF statement?

```
data EuropeQ1;
   infile "&path\sales.dat";
   input SaleID $4. @6 Location $3. @;
   if Location='USA' then
      input @10 SaleDate mmddyy10.
            @20 Amount 7.;
   else if Location='EUR' then
      input @10 SaleDate date9.
            @20 Amount commax7.;
   if Location = 'EUR';
run;
```

No, the subsetting IF statement should appear as early in the DATA step as possible.

77

Chapter 5 Data Transformations

5.1 Introduction **5-3**

5.2 Manipulating Character Values (Part 1) **5-8**

Exercises 5-19

5.3 Manipulating Character Values (Part 2) **5-23**

Exercises 5-39

5.4 Manipulating Numeric Values **5-43**

Exercises 5-51

5.5 Converting Variable Type **5-54**

Exercises 5-76

5.6 Solutions **5-78**

Solutions to Exercises 5-78

Solutions to Student Activities (Polls/Quizzes) 5-84

5.1 Introduction

Objectives

- Review the syntax of SAS functions.
- Introduce SAS variable lists.

3

SAS Functions

SAS provides a large library of functions for manipulating data during DATA step execution.

A SAS function is often categorized by the type of data manipulation performed:

- Array
- Character
- Date and Time
- Descriptive Statistics
- Financial
- Mathematical
- Probability
- Random Number
- Special
- State and ZIP Code
- Trigonometric

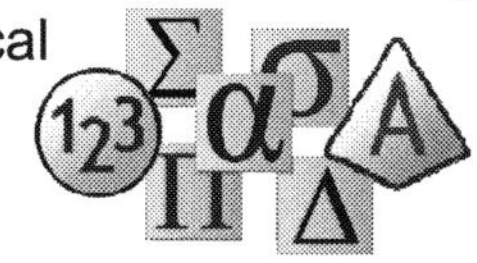

4

See SAS Help and Documentation for a complete list of functions and their syntax.

5.01 Quiz

Which SAS functions have you used?

5

Using SAS Functions (Review)

You can use functions in DATA step statements anywhere that an expression can appear.

```
data contrib;
   set orion.employee_donations;
   Total=sum(Qtr1,Qtr2,Qtr3,Qtr4);
   if Total ge 50;
run;

proc print data=contrib noobs;
   title 'Contributions $50 and Over';
   var Employee_ID Qtr1 Qtr2 Qtr3 Qtr4
   Total;
run;
```

function-name(argument-1,argument-2,...,argument-n)

6

p205d01

Using SAS Functions

Partial PROC PRINT Output (52 Total Observations)

Contributions $50 and Over

Employee_ID	Qtr1	Qtr2	Qtr3	Qtr4	Total
120267	15	15	15	15	60
120269	20	20	20	20	80
120271	20	20	20	20	80
120275	15	15	15	15	60
120660	25	25	25	25	100

7

SAS Variable Lists (Review)

An alternative method to entering variable names separately is to use a *SAS variable list*.

```
data contrib;
   set orion.employee_donations;
   Total=sum(of Qtr1-Qtr4);
   if Total ge 50;
run;
```

The keyword OF must precede the variable list.

8 p205d01

If the keyword OF is omitted from function calls that use SAS variable lists, the numbered and name range lists do not give a syntax error. Instead, the lists are interpreted as expressions. For example, **sum(Qtr1-Qtr4)** evaluates as **Qtr4** subtracted from **Qtr1**.

SAS Variable Lists: Examples

Numbered Range List

PDV

Qtr1	Qtr2	Var1	Qtr3	Qtr4

```
Total=sum(of Qtr1-Qtr4)
```

Var1 not included

Name Range List

PDV

Qtr1	Second	Q3	Fourth	Var2

```
Total=sum(of Qtr1--Fourth)
```

Var2 not included

9

SAS Variable Lists: Examples

Name Prefix List

PDV

TotJan	Qtr2	TotFeb	TotMar

```
Total=sum(of Tot:)
```

QTR2 not included

Special Name Lists

PDV

Qtr1 N	Name $	Q3 N	Fourth N

```
Total=sum(of _Numeric_)
```

Name not included

10

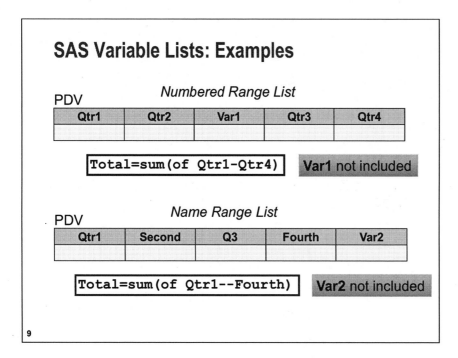

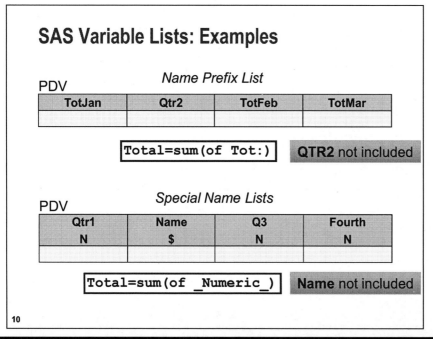

SAS Variable Lists		
Numbered range lists	**x1-x*n***	Specifies all variables from **x1** to **x*n*** inclusive. You can begin with any number and end with any number as long as you do not violate the rules for user-supplied variable names and the numbers are consecutive.
Name range lists	**x--a**	Specifies all variables ordered as they are in the program data vector, from **x** to **a** inclusive.
	x-numeric-a	Specifies all numeric variables from **x** to **a** inclusive.
	x-character-a	Specifies all character variables from **x** to **a** inclusive.

SAS Variable Lists		
Name prefix lists	**REV:**	Specifies all the variables that begin with **REV**, such as **REVJAN**, **REVFEB**, and **REVMAR**.
Special SAS name lists	**_ALL_**	Specifies all variables that are already defined in the current DATA step.
	NUMERIC	Specifies all numeric variables that are already defined in the current DATA step.
	CHARACTER	Specifies all character variables that are already defined in the current DATA step.

5.02 Quiz

Complete the assignment statement for **Total** by using a SAS variable list and the SUM function to add the values for **Year1**, **Year2**, **Year3**, and **Year4**.

PDV

Year2	Year1	Year3	Year4	Sales

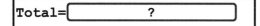

```
Total= ?
```

11

5.2 Manipulating Character Values (Part 1)

Objectives

- Use SAS functions to extract, edit, and search character values.

14

Business Scenario

A manager in the Finance Department asked for a list of all the charities that Orion Star contributes to during the year.

Partial **orion.biz_list**

Acct_ Code	Name
AEK3	ANGELA E. KEARNEY
AQI2	AQUAMISSIONS INTERNATIONAL
ATS1	A TEAM SPORTS
CBO3	CLAIRE B. OWENS
CCI2	CANCER CURES, INC.

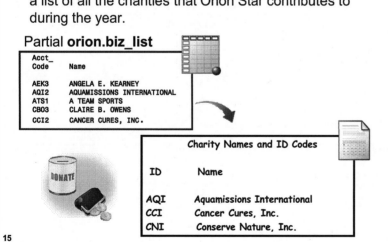

Charity Names and ID Codes

ID	Name
AQI	Aquamissions International
CCI	Cancer Cures, Inc.
CNI	Conserve Nature, Inc.

15

Business Scenario – Considerations

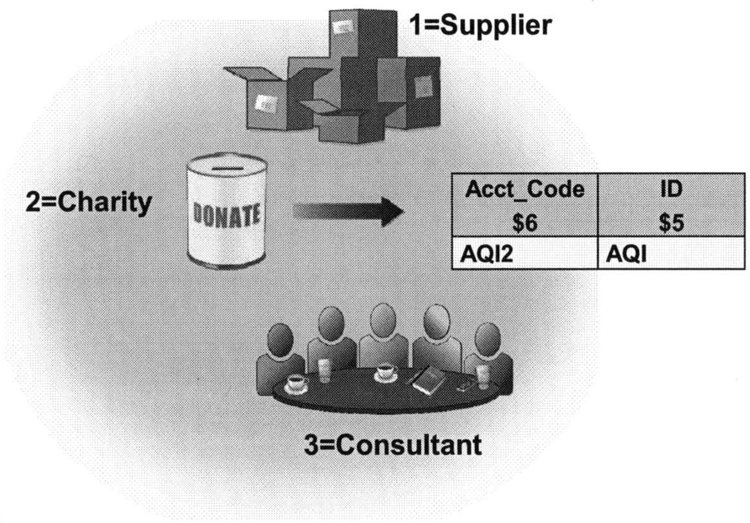

16

Create the List of Charities: Step 1

Step 1	Subset the data based on the last character of **Acct_Code**.

Partial **orion.biz list**

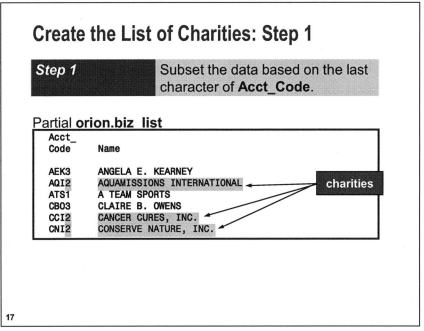

```
Acct_
Code      Name

AEK3      ANGELA E. KEARNEY
AQI2      AQUAMISSIONS INTERNATIONAL
ATS1      A TEAM SPORTS
CBO3      CLAIRE B. OWENS
CCI2      CANCER CURES, INC.
CNI2      CONSERVE NATURE, INC.
```

charities

17

SUBSTR Function (Right Side)

Extract the fourth character from the value in the **Acct_Code** variable and store it in **Org_Code**.

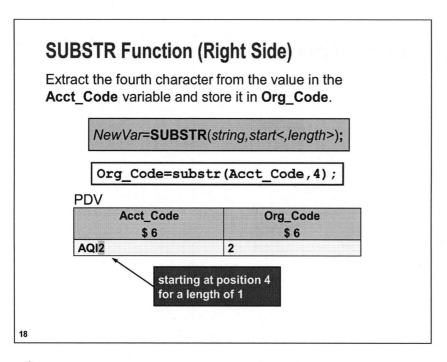

```
NewVar=SUBSTR(string,start<,length>);
```

```
Org_Code=substr(Acct_Code,4);
```

PDV

Acct_Code $ 6	Org_Code $ 6
AQI2	2

starting at position 4
for a length of 1

18

The SUBSTR function on the left side of an assignment statement is used to replace characters.

5.03 Multiple Choice Poll

Which SUBSTR function can extract the group of five numbers from the middle of the **Item_Code** value?

PDV

Item_Code $ 20
978-1-59994-397-8

a. substr(Item_Code,5,7)
b. substr(Item_Code,5)
c. substr(Item_Code,7,5)
d. substr(Item_Code,'mid',5)

19

The variable **Acct_Code** is in the output for learning purposes so that it can be easily compared to the **ID** variable. Otherwise, there is no need for it, and it could be dropped from the **charities** data set.

Create the List of Charities: Step 1

⚠ The last non-blank character in the **Acct_Code** value occurs in different positions for different observations.

Partial **orion.biz_list**

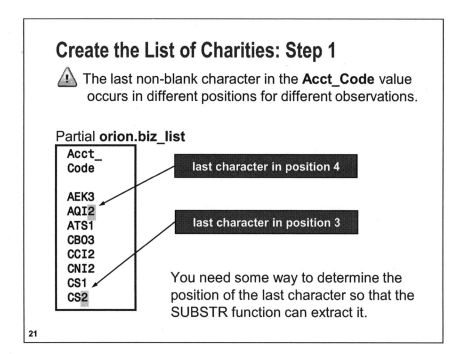

Acct_ Code
AEK3
AQI2
ATS1
CBO3
CCI2
CNI2
CS1
CS2

last character in position 4

last character in position 3

You need some way to determine the position of the last character so that the SUBSTR function can extract it.

21

LENGTH Function

The LENGTH function returns the length of a non-blank character string, excluding trailing blanks.

General form of the LENGTH function:

NewVar=**LENGTH**(*argument*);

Example:

```
Code='ABCD  ';
Last_NonBlank=length(Code);
```

PDV

Code $ 6	Last_NonBlank N 8
ABCD	4

22

Create the List of Charities: Step 1

The LENGTH function is ***nested***, or used as an argument to the SUBSTR function.

```
data charities;
   length ID $ 5;
   set orion.biz_list;
   if substr(Acct_Code,length(Acct_Code),1)='2';
   ID=substr(Acct_Code,1,length(Acct_Code)-1);
run;
```

23

p205d02

Execution: Step 1

Read the first charity observation.

```
data charities;
   length ID $ 5;
   set orion.biz_list;
   if substr(Acct_Code,length(Acct_Code),1)='2';
   ID=substr(Acct_Code,1,length(Acct_Code)-1);
run;
```

PDV

ID $ 5	Acct_Code $ 6	Name $ 30
	AQI2	AQUAMISSIONS INTERNATIONAL

24

...

Execution: Step 1

```
data charities;
   length ID $ 5;
   set orion.biz_list;
   if substr(Acct_Code,length(Acct_Code),1)='2';
   ID=substr(Acct_Code,1,length(Acct_Code)-1);
run;
```

4

PDV

ID $ 5	Acct_Code $ 6	Name $ 30
	AQI2	AQUAMISSIONS INTERNATIONAL

25 ...

Execution: Step 1

```
data charities;
   length ID $ 5;
   set orion.biz_list;
   if substr(Acct_Code,length(Acct_Code),1)='2';
   ID=substr(Acct_Code,1,length(Acct_Code)-1);
run;
```

PDV

ID $ 5	Acct_Code $ 6	Name $ 30
	AQI2	AQUAMISSIONS INTERNATIONAL

26 ...

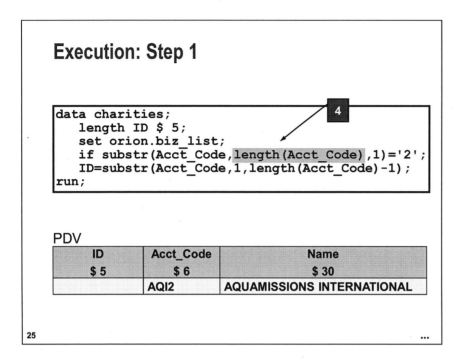

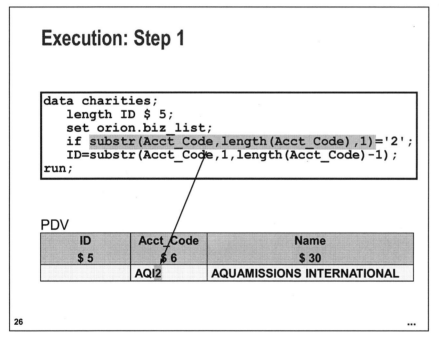

Execution: Step 1

```
data charities;
   length ID $ 5;
   set orion.biz_list;
   if substr(Acct_Code,length(Acct_Code),1)='2';
   ID=substr(Acct_Code,1,length(Acct_Code)-1);
run;
```

True

PDV

ID $ 5	Acct_Code $ 6	Name $ 30
	AQI2	AQUAMISSIONS INTERNATIONAL

27 ...

Execution: Step 1

```
data charities;
   length ID $ 5;
   set orion.biz_list;
   if substr(Acct_Code,length(Acct_Code),1)='2';
   ID=substr(Acct_Code,1,length(Acct_Code)-1);
run;
```

3

PDV

ID $ 5	Acct_Code $ 6	Name $ 30
	AQI2	AQUAMISSIONS INTERNATIONAL

28 ...

Execution: Step 1

```
data charities;
   length ID $ 5;
   set orion.biz_list;
   if substr(Acct_Code,length(Acct_Code),1)='2';
   ID=substr(Acct_Code,1,length(Acct_Code)-1);
run;
```

PDV

ID $ 5	Acct_Code $ 6	Name $ 30
	AQI2	AQUAMISSIONS INTERNATIONAL

29 ...

Execution: Step 1

```
data charities;
   length ID $ 5;
   set orion.biz_list;
   if substr(Acct_Code,length(Acct_Code),1)='2';
   ID=substr(Acct_Code,1,length(Acct_Code)-1);
run;
```

PDV

ID $ 5	Acct_Code $ 6	Name $ 30
AQI	AQI2	AQUAMISSIONS INTERNATIONAL

30 ...

Execution: Step 1

```
data charities;
   length ID $ 5;
   set orion.biz_list;
   if substr(Acct_Code,length(Acct_Code),1)='2';
   ID=substr(Acct_Code,1,length(Acct_Code)-1);
run;
```

Implicit OUTPUT;
Implicit RETURN;

PDV

ID $ 5	Acct_Code $ 6	Name $ 30
AQI	AQI2	AQUAMISSIONS INTERNATIONAL

31

Create the List of Charities: Step 1 Complete

work.charities

ID	Acct_ Code	Name
AQI	AQI2	AQUAMISSIONS INTERNATIONAL
CCI	CCI2	CANCER CURES, INC.
CNI	CNI2	CONSERVE NATURE, INC.
CS	CS2	CHILD SURVIVORS
CU	CU2	CUIDADORES LTD.
DAI	DAI2	DISASTER ASSIST, INC.
ES	ES2	EARTHSALVORS
FFC	FFC2	FARMING FOR COMMUNITIES
MI	MI2	MITLEID INTERNATIONAL
SBA	SBA2	SAVE THE BABY ANIMALS
V2	V22	VOX VICTIMAS
YYCR	YYCR2	YES, YOU CAN RECYCLE

Step 2	Transform the values in **Name** to a mix of upper and lowercase.

32

Create the List of Charities: Step 2

The name of the organization is stored as all capital letters. In the desired output, only the first letter of each word is capitalized.

Example:

Name
AQUAMISSIONS INTERNATIONAL

Change to:

Name
Aquamissions International

33

PROPCASE Function

Example:

```
Name='SURF&LINK SPORTS';
Pname=propcase(Name);
Pname2=propcase(Name,' &');
```

NewVar=**PROPCASE**(*argument <,delimiter(s)>*);

PDV

Name $ 16	Pname $ 16
SURF&LINK SPORTS	Surf&link Sports

Pname2 $ 16
Surf&Link Sports

34

5.04 Quiz

This PDV shows the current value of **Name**:

Name
HEATH*BARR*LITTLE EQUIPMENT SALES

Write an assignment statement that converts the value of **Name** to this:

Name
Heath*Barr*Little Equipment Sales

35

Completed Business Scenario

Adding an assignment statement to convert **Name** to proper case completes the **charities** data set.

```
data charities;
   length ID $ 5;
   set orion.biz_list;
   if substr(Acct_Code,length(Acct_Code),1)='2';
   ID=substr(Acct_Code,1,length(Acct_Code)-1);
   Name = propcase(Name);
run;
```

ID	Acct_ Code	Name
AQI	AQI2	Aquamissions International
CCI	CCI2	Cancer Cures, Inc.
CNI	CNI2	Conserve Nature, Inc.
CS	CS2	Child Survivors
CU	CU2	Cuidadores Ltd.

37

p205d03

Other Useful Character Functions

Function	Purpose
RIGHT(*string*)	Right-aligns a character expression.
LEFT(*string*)	Left-aligns a character expression.
UPCASE(*string*)	Converts all letters in an argument to uppercase.
LOWCASE(*string*)	Converts all letters in an argument to lowercase.
CHAR(*string,position*)	Returns a single character from a specified *position* in a character *string*.

38

The CHAR function was introduced in SAS 9.2.

5.05 Quiz

Open and submit the program file **p205a01**. Find and correct the syntax error.

p205a01.sas

```
data shoes;
   set orion.product_list;
   if substr(right(Product_Name,33,13))=
      'Running Shoes';
run;
```

Check the log for the corrected program. How many observations and variables are in the **shoes** data set?

39

Exercises

If you restarted your SAS session since the last exercise, open and submit the **libname.sas** program found in the data folder.

Level 1

1. Extracting Characters Based on Position

The data set **orion.au_salesforce** has employee data for the Sales branch in Australia.

Partial **orion.au_salesforce** (63 Total Observations, 9 Total Variables)

```
                First_
  Employee_ID   Name         Last_Name       Job_Title

       120102   Tom          Zhou           Sales Manager
       120103   Wilson       Dawes          Sales Manager
       120121   Irenie       Elvish         Sales Rep. II
       120122   Christina    Ngan           Sales Rep. II
       120123   Kimiko       Hotstone       Sales Rep. I
```

a. Orion Star wants to create user ID codes for logging on to the Australian Sales intranet site.

- Each user ID consists of the first letter of the first name, the final letter of the first name, and the first four letters of the last name.
- All these letters should be lowercase.
- As a first step to doing this, extract these letters and change their case.
- Create a new data set named **work.codes**.
- Create three new variables named **FCode1**, **FCode2**, and **LCode**. As described above, these variables should contain the following:

Variable Name	Value
FCode1	First letter of **First_Name**
FCode2	Final letter of **First_Name**
LCode	First four letters of **Last_Name**

Remember to make these new values lowercase too.

There are several ways to approach getting the final letter of **First_Name**. For one of those ways, you need to know that the length of **First_Name** is 12 characters.

b. Print the resulting data set.

- Include only the variables **First_Name**, **FCode1**, **FCode2**, **Last_Name**, and **LCode**.
- Add an appropriate title.
- Verify your output.

Partial PROC PRINT output (63 Total Observations)

```
                  Extracted Letters for User IDs

         First_
  Obs    Name        FCode1    FCode2    Last_Name      LCode

    1    Tom           t         m       Zhou           zhou
    2    Wilson        w         n       Dawes          dawe
    3    Irenie        i         e       Elvish         elvi
```

4	Christina	c	a	Ngan	ngan
5	Kimiko	k	o	Hotstone	hots

Later you see techniques that can be used to combine these letters into a single character value.

Level 2

2. Extracting Characters Based on Position

The data set **orion.newcompetitors** has data on competing retail stores that recently opened near existing Orion Star locations.

orion.newcompetitors

ID	City	Postal_ Code
AU15301W	PERTH	6002
AU12217E	SYDNEY	2000
CA 150	Toronto	M5V 3C6
CA 238	Edmonton	T5T 2B2
US 356NC	charlotte	28203
US1013CO	denver	80201
US 12CA	San diego	92139

a. Orion Star would like a data set containing only the small retail stores from these observations.

- Create a new variable, **Country**, that contains the first two characters of **ID**.
- Create a new variable, **Store_Code**, that contains the other characters from the value in **ID**. Left-justify the value so that there are no leading blanks.
- The first character in the value of **Store_Code** indicates the size of the store, and **1** is the code for a small retail store.
- Write a program to output only the small retail store observations.
  Hint: You might need to use a SUBSTR functions as part of a subsetting IF statement
- Make sure that the **City** values appear in proper case (as displayed below).

b. Print your results with an appropriate title.

Only show the columns **Store_Code**, **Country**, **City**, and **Postal_Code**.

PROC PRINT output (5 Total Observations)

New Small-Store Competitors

Store_ Code	Country	City	Postal_ Code
15301W	AU	Perth	6002
12217E	AU	Sydney	2000
150	CA	Toronto	M5V 3C6
1013CO	US	Denver	80201
12CA	US	San Diego	92139

Challenge

3. Converting U.S. Postal Codes to State Names

The data set **orion.contacts** contains a list of contacts for the U.S. charities that Orion Star donates to.

Partial **orion.contacts**

ID	Title	Name	Address1	Address2
AQI	Ms.	Farr,Sue	15 Harvey Rd.	Macon, GA 31298
CCI	Dr.	Cox,Kay B.	163 McNeil Pl.	Kern, CA 93280
CNI	Mr.	Mason,Ron	442 Glen Ave.	Miami, FL 33054
CS	Ms.	Ruth,G. H.	2491 Brady St.	Munger, MI 48747
CU	Prof.	Florentino,Helen-Ashe H.	PO Box 2253	Washington, DC 20018

a. Create a new data set named **states** that includes the variables **ID** and **Name** as well as a new variable named **Location** that shows the full name in proper case for the state that the contact is based in.

Hint: **Address2** is 24 characters long and the last item in **Address2** is always the ZIP code. Look in the online Help for character functions that use ZIP codes as arguments.

b. Print your results.

Partial PROC PRINT output (12 Total Observations)

ID	Name	Location
AQI	Farr,Sue	Georgia
CCI	Cox,Kay B.	California
CNI	Mason,Ron	Florida
CS	Ruth,G. H.	Michigan
CU	Florentino,Helen-Ashe H.	District of Columbia

5.3 Manipulating Character Values (Part 2)

Objectives

- Use SAS functions to extract, edit, and search character values.

44

Business Scenario

Create a new data set that contains data that is suitable for creating mailing labels.

Partial **orion.contacts**

ID	Title	Name	Address1	Address2
AQI	Ms.	Farr,Sue	15 Harvey Rd.	Macon, GA 31298
CCI	Dr.	Cox,Kay B.	163 McNeil Pl.	Kern, CA 93280
CNI	Mr.	Mason,Ron	442 Glen Ave.	Miami, FL 33054
CS	Ms.	Ruth,G. H.	2491 Brady St.	Munger, MI 48747

45

Create Mailing List Data

Partial **orion.contacts**

```
Title     Name

Ms.       Farr,Sue
Dr.       Cox,Kay B.
Mr.       Mason,Ron
Ms.       Ruth,G. H.
Prof.     Florentino,Helen-Ashe H
Ms.       Van Allsburg,Jan F.
Mr.       Laff,Stanley X.
Mr.       Rizen,George Q.
Dr.       Mitchell,Marc J.
Ms.       Mills,Dorothy E.
Dr.       Webb,Jonathan W.
Mr.       Keenan,Maynard J.
```

Two steps need to be accomplished:

Step 1	Separate the last name from the first and middle.
Step 2	Combine the title, the first and middle names, and last name.

46

SCAN Function: Step 1

Extract the second word of **Name**.

```
NewVar=SCAN(string,n<,charlist>);
```

```
FMName=scan(Name,2,',');
```

PDV

Name $ 16	FMName $ 200
Farr,Sue	Sue

The SCAN function returns the *n*th word of a character value.

47

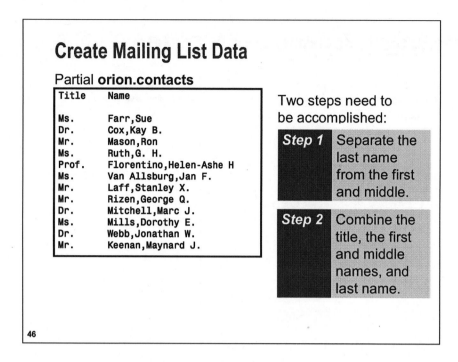

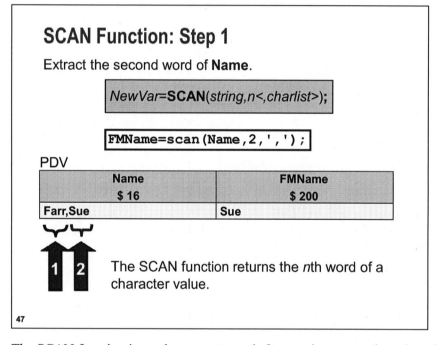

The SCAN function is used to extract words from a character value when the relative order of words is known, but their starting positions are not.

The default delimiters are as follows:

ASCII (PC, UNIX)	blank . < (+ | & ! $ *) ; - / , % ^
EBCDIC (z/OS)	blank . < (+ | & ! $ *) ; - / , % | ¢ ¬

SCAN Function: Details

When you use the SCAN function:

- A missing value is returned if there are fewer than *n* words in the string.
- If *n* is negative, the SCAN function selects the word in the character string starting from the end of string.
- The length of the created variable is 200 bytes.
- Delimiters before the first word have no effect.
- Any character or set of characters can serve as delimiters.
- Two or more contiguous delimiters are treated as a single delimiter.

48

5.06 Quiz

Consider this PDV and assignment statement:

```
Second=scan(Phrase,2,',');
```

PDV

Phrase $ 28	Second $ 200
software, hardware, services	

What value is stored in **Second**?

49

5.07 Multiple Choice Poll

What expression completes the assignment statement to correctly extract 2007 from the **Text** variable?

```
data Scan_Quiz;
   Text="New Year's Day, January 1st, 2007";
   Year=[          ?          ];
run;
```

a. scan(Text,-1);
b. scan(Text,6);
c. scan(Text,6,', ');
d. All of the above would work.

51 p205d05

Creating Mailing List Data

Using the SCAN function gives an easy way to separate the names for the mailing list.

```
data labels;
   set orion.contacts;
   length FMName LName $ 15;
   FMName=scan(Name,2,',');
   LName=scan(Name,1,',');
run;
```

Partial **labels** data set

ID	Name	Title	FMName	LName
AQI	Farr,Sue	Ms.	Sue	Farr
CCI	Cox,Kay B.	Dr.	Kay B.	Cox
CNI	Mason,Ron	Mr.	Ron	Mason
CS	Ruth,G. H.	Ms.	G. H.	Ruth

53 p205d06

CATX Function: Step 2

Combine **FMName** and **LName** to create **FullName**.

NewVar=**CATX**(*separator, string-1, … ,string-n*)

```
FullName=catx(' ',FMName,LName);
```

PDV

FMName $ 15	LName $ 15	FullName $ 200
Sue	Farr	Sue Farr

54

Other CAT Functions

There are three other CAT functions that concatenate character strings.

Function	Details
CAT(*string-1, … ,string-n*)	Does not remove leading or trailing blanks from the arguments before concatenating them.
CATS(*string-1, … ,string-n*)	Removes leading and trailing blanks from the arguments.
CATT(*string-1, … ,string-n*)	Removes trailing blanks from the arguments.

55

Example of CAT Functions

```
data test_cat;
   /* Each value has a leading and trailing blank */
   a = ' a ';
   b = ' b ';
   c = ' c ';
   cat_example=cat(a,b,c);
   catt_example=catt(a,b,c);
   cats_example=cats(a,b,c);
run;
```

Resulting Concatenated Values

cat_example	catt_example	cats_example
a b c	a b c	abc

Create Mailing List Data: Finished Program

Adding an assignment statement with the CATX function completes the program.

```
data labels;
   set orion.contacts;
   length FullName $ 35 FMName LName $ 15;
   FMName = scan(Name,2,',');
   LName = scan(Name,1,',');
   FullName = catx(' ',Title,FMName,LName);
run;
```

Partial **labels** data set

```
ID       FullName          Address1          Address2

AQI    Ms. Sue Farr      15 Harvey Rd.     Macon, GA  31298
CCI    Dr. Kay B. Cox    163 McNeil Pl.    Kern, CA  93280
CNI    Mr. Ron Mason     442 Glen Ave.     Miami, FL  33054
```

56

p205d07

Concatenation Operator

The *concatenation operator* is another way to join character strings.

General form of the concatenation operator:

NewVar=string1 !! string2;

Example: `Phone='('!!area!!') '!!Number;`

PDV

Area $ 3	Number $ 8	Phone $ 14
919	531-0000	(919) 531-0000

✎ The operator can also be written as two vertical bars (||) or two broken vertical bars (¦¦).

57

Idea Exchange

Would the SUBSTR function be appropriate to separate the contact's name into two parts based on the position of the comma?

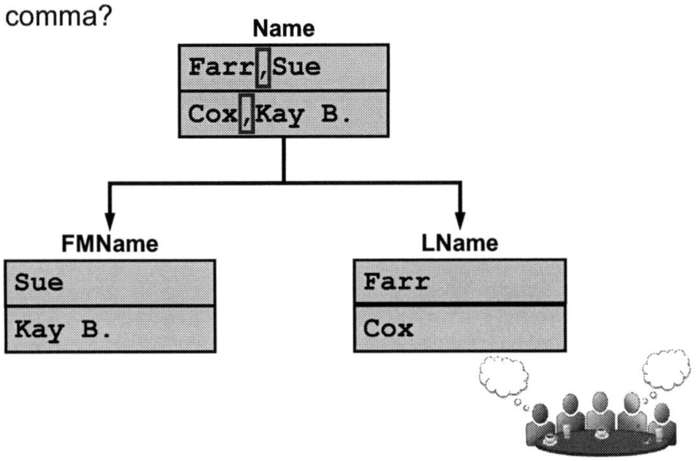

58

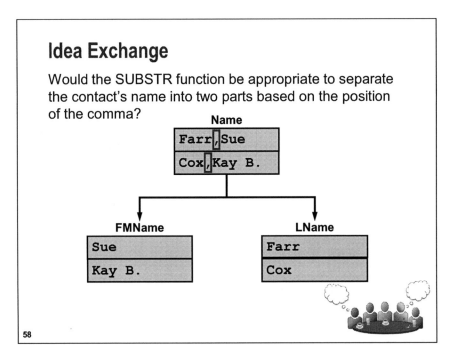

Business Scenario: Data Cleanup

The Internet Sales Group accidentally used the wrong data files for the Orion Star Catalog website.

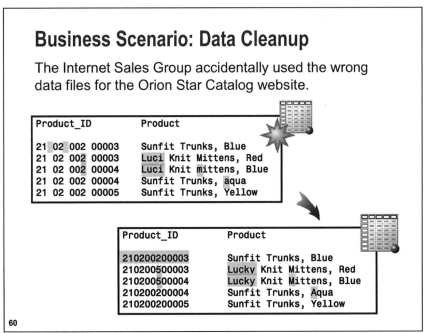

```
Product_ID          Product

21 02 002 00003     Sunfit Trunks, Blue
21 02 002 00003     Luci Knit Mittens, Red
21 02 002 00004     Luci Knit mittens, Blue
21 02 002 00004     Sunfit Trunks, aqua
21 02 002 00005     Sunfit Trunks, Yellow
```

```
Product_ID          Product

210200200003        Sunfit Trunks, Blue
210200500003        Lucky Knit Mittens, Red
210200500004        Lucky Knit Mittens, Blue
210200200004        Sunfit Trunks, Aqua
210200200005        Sunfit Trunks, Yellow
```

60

Data Cleanup: Step 1

The first step in creating the **correct** data set is to do the following:

1. Find the observations with **Mittens** as part of the **Product** value.
2. Change the middle characters of the **Product_ID** values for those observations.

```
Product_ID          Product

21 02 002 00003     Luci Knit Mittens, Red
```

```
21 02 005 00003     Luci Knit Mittens, Red
```

61

Data Cleanup: Step 1

Use the SUBSTR and FIND functions to change incorrect product IDs for mittens.

Position=**FIND**(*string,substring*<*,modifiers,startpos*>);

```
data correct;
   set orion.clean_up;
   if find(Product,'Mittens','I')>0 then do;
      substr(Product_ID,9,1)='5';
   end;
run;

proc print data=correct noobs;
run;
```

62

p205d09

FIND Function

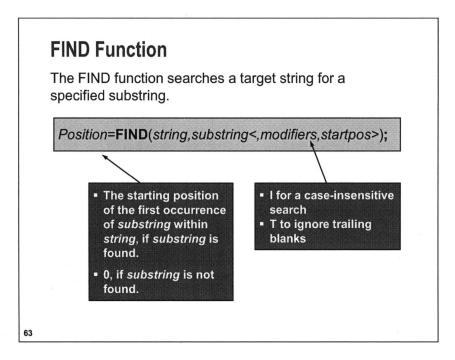

The FIND function searches a target string for a specified substring.

Position=**FIND**(*string,substring<,modifiers,startpos>*);

- The starting position of the first occurrence of *substring* within *string*, if *substring* is found.
- 0, if *substring* is not found.

- I for a case-insensitive search
- T to ignore trailing blanks

63

More on modifiers and the *startpos* value:

- A modifier can be the value I or T. These two values can be combined in either order and in either case. If this argument is omitted, the search is case sensitive and trailing blanks are considered.
- The *startpos* value not only specifies the position at which the search should start but also the direction of the search. A positive value indicates a forward (right) search. A negative value indicates a backward (left) search. If this argument is omitted, the search starts at position 1 and moves forward.
- These two optional arguments can be in either order (that is, *startpos* can precede *modifier*).

FIND Function

```
data find;
   Text='AUSTRALIA, DENMARK, US';
   Pos1=find(Text,'US');
   Pos2=find(Text,' US');
   Pos3=find(Text,'us');
   Pos4=find(Text,'us','I');
   Pos5=find(Text,'us','I',10);
run;
```

PDV

Pos1 N 8

What value does SAS assign to **Pos1**?

64 ...

FIND Function

```
data find;
   Text='AUSTRALIA, DENMARK, US';
   Pos1=find(Text,'US');
   Pos2=find(Text,' US');
   Pos3=find(Text,'us');
   Pos4=find(Text,'us','I');
   Pos5=find(Text,'us','I',10);
run;
```

2

PDV

Pos1 N 8
2

65

...

FIND Function

```
data find;
   Text='AUSTRALIA, DENMARK, US';
   Pos1=find(Text,'US');
   Pos2=find(Text,' US');
   Pos3=find(Text,'us');
   Pos4=find(Text,'us','I');
   Pos5=find(Text,'us','I',10);
run;
```

20

PDV

Pos1 N 8	Pos2 N 8
2	20

66

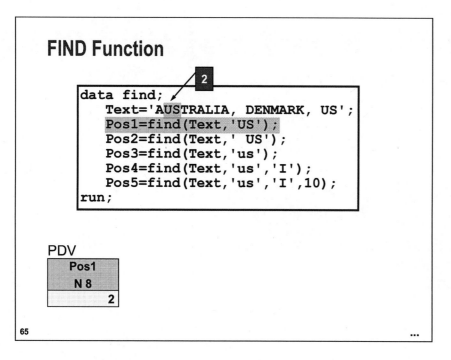

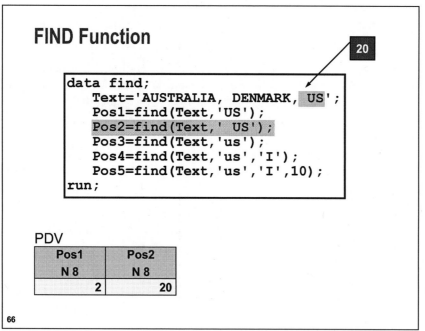

5.08 Quiz

Complete the PDV for the values for **Pos3** and **Pos4**.

```
data find;
   Text='AUSTRALIA, DENMARK, US';
   Pos1=find(Text,'US');
   Pos2=find(Text,' US');
   Pos3=find(Text,'us');
   Pos4=find(Text,'us','I');
   Pos5=find(Text,'us','I',10);
run;
```

PDV

Pos1 N 8	Pos2 N 8	Pos3 N 8	Pos4 N 8
2	20		

67

FIND Function

21

```
data find;
   Text='AUSTRALIA, DENMARK, US';
   Pos1=find(Text,'US');
   Pos2=find(Text,' US');
   Pos3=find(Text,'us');
   Pos4=find(Text,'us','I');
   Pos5=find(Text,'us','I',10);
run;
```

PDV

Pos1 N 8	Pos2 N 8	Pos3 N 8	Pos4 N 8	Pos5 N 8
2	20	0	2	21

69

Data Cleanup: Step 1

Use the SUBSTR and FIND functions to change incorrect product IDs for mittens.

SUBSTR(*string,start<,length>*)=*value*;

```
data correct;
   set orion.clean_up;
   if find(Product,'Mittens','I')>0 then do;
      substr(Product_ID,9,1)='5';
   end;
run;

proc print data=correct noobs;
run;
```

70 p205d09

SUBSTR Function (Left Side)

This form of the SUBSTR function (left side of assignment statement) replaces characters in a character variable.

Example: Replace two characters starting at position 11.

11

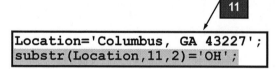

```
Location='Columbus, GA 43227';
substr(Location,11,2)='OH';
```

PDV

Location $ 18
Columbus, OH 43227

71

Data Cleanup: Step 1

```
data correct;
  set orion.clean_up;
  if find(Product,'Mittens','I')>0 then do;
     substr(Product_ID,9,1)='5';
  end;
run;
```

Product_ID	Product	Order_ID
21 02 002 00003	Sunfit Trunks, Blue	1231986335
21 02 005 00003	Luci Knit Mittens, Red	1232003930
21 02 005 00004	Luci Knit mittens, blue	1232007693
21 02 002 00004	Sunfit Trunks, aqua	1232007700
21 02 002 00005	Sunfit Trunks, Yellow	1232087464

72 p205d09

Data Cleanup: Step 2

The next step is to change the error **Luci** to **Lucky**.

Product_ID	Product	Order_ID
21 02 002 00003	Sunfit Trunks, Blue	1231986335
21 02 005 00003	Luci Knit Mittens, Red	1232003930
21 02 005 00004	Luci Knit mittens, blue	1232007693

Product_ID	Product	Order_ID
21 02 002 00003	Sunfit Trunks, Blue	1231986335
21 02 005 00003	Lucky Knit Mittens, Red	1232003930
21 02 005 00004	Lucky Knit mittens, blue	1232007693

73

Data Cleanup: Step 2

Use the TRANWRD function to replace all occurrences of **Luci** with **Lucky**.

```
data correct;
   set orion.clean_up;
   if find(Product,'Mittens','I') > 0 then do;
      substr(Product_ID,9,1)='5';
      Product=Tranwrd(Product,'Luci ','Lucky ');
   end;
run;
```

NewVar=**TRANWRD**(*source,target,replacement*);

Product_ID	Product	Order_ID
21 02 002 00003	Sunfit Trunks, Blue	1231986335
21 02 005 00003	Lucky Knit Mittens, Red	1232003930
21 02 005 00004	Lucky Knit mittens, blue	1232007693

74 p205d10

TRANWRD Function: Details

The TRANWRD function replaces or removes all occurrences of a given word (or a pattern of characters) within a character string.

NewVar=**TRANWRD**(*source,target,replacement*);

These details apply when you use the TRANWRD function:

- The TRANWRD function does not remove trailing blanks from *target* or *replacement*.
- If *NewVar* is not previously defined, it is given a length of 200.
- If the target string is not found in the source, then no replacement occurs.

75

⚠ Using the TRANWRD function to replace an existing string with a longer string might cause truncation of the resulting value if a LENGTH statement is not used.

Data Cleanup: Step 3

- Use the COMPRESS function to remove the embedded blanks from **Product_ID**.
- Use the PROPCASE function to convert all the words in **Product** to proper case.

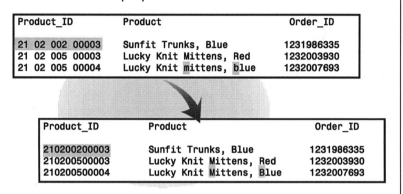

Product_ID	Product	Order_ID
21 02 002 00003	Sunfit Trunks, Blue	1231986335
21 02 005 00003	Lucky Knit Mittens, Red	1232003930
21 02 005 00004	Lucky Knit mittens, blue	1232007693

Product_ID	Product	Order_ID
210200200003	Sunfit Trunks, Blue	1231986335
210200500003	Lucky Knit Mittens, Red	1232003930
210200500004	Lucky Knit Mittens, Blue	1232007693

76

Completed Business Scenario

```
data correct;
   set orion.clean_up;
   if find(Product,'Mittens','I') > 0 then do;
      substr(Product_ID,9,1)='5';
      Product=tranwrd(Product,'Luci ','Lucky ');
   end;
   Product_ID=compress(Product_ID);
   Product=propcase(Product);
run;
```

NewVar=**COMPRESS**(*source*<,*chars*>);

Product_ID	Product	Order_ID
210200200003	Sunfit Trunks, Blue	1231986335
210200500003	Lucky Knit Mittens, Red	1232003930
210200500004	Lucky Knit Mittens, Blue	1232007693
210200200004	Sunfit Trunks, Aqua	1232007700

77

p205d11

COMPRESS Function: Example

The COMPRESS function removes the characters listed in the *chars* argument from the *source*.

```
ID='20 01-005 024';
New_ID1=compress(ID);
New_ID2=compress(ID,'-');
New_ID3=compress(ID,' -');
```

PDV

ID $ 13	New_ID1 $ 13
20 01-005 024	2001-005024

New_ID2 $ 13	New_ID3 $ 13
20 01005 024	2001005024

78

Other Functions That Remove Blanks

Function	Purpose
TRIM(*string*)	Removes trailing blanks from a character string.
STRIP(*string*)	Removes all leading and trailing blanks from a character string.
COMPBL(*string*)	Removes multiple blanks from a character string by translating each occurrence of two or more consecutive blanks into a single blank.

79

✎ The TRIMN function is similar to the TRIM function. TRIMN returns a null string (zero blanks) if the argument is blank while TRIM returns a blank.

✎ The STRIP function returns a null string if the argument is blank.

✎ By default, the length of the value returned by the COMPBL function is the same as the length of the argument.

Exercises

If you restarted your SAS session since the last exercise, open and submit the **libname.sas** program found in the data folder.

Level 1

4. Cleaning Text Data

Customer names are available in a data set named **orion.customers_ex5**:

Customer_ID	Name	Country	Gender	Birth_Date
000-000-00-0004	KVARNIQ, James	US	M	27Jun1978
Silver000-000-00-0005	STEPHANO, Sandrina	US	F	9-Jul1983
000-000-00-0009	KRAHL, Cornelia	DE	F	27Feb1978
platinum000-000-00-0010	BALLINGER, Karen	US	F	18Oct1988
000-000-00-0011	WALLSTAB, Elke	DE	F	16Aug1978
Silver000-000-00-0012	BLACK, David	US	M	12Apr1973

Use this data set to create a new data set named **names** that contains each customer's name in this format:

Mr. John B. Smith

Ms. Jane Doe

a. Write a program to create the **names** data set.

- The **names** data set should contain only three variables: **New_Name**, **Name**, and **Gender**.
- The **New_Name** variable should contain the customer's name in the new format.
  - – Female names should be preceded by the honorific title Ms.
  - – Male names should be preceded by the honorific title Mr.

b. Print the **names** data set.

c. Verify that your conversion efforts were successful.

Partial PROC PRINT Output (77 Total Observations)

```
Obs    New_Name                 Name                   Gender
  1    Mr. James Kvarniq        KVARNIQ, James           M
  2    Ms. Sandrina Stephano    STEPHANO, Sandrina       F
  3    Ms. Cornelia Krahl       KRAHL, Cornelia          F
  4    Ms. Karen Ballinger      BALLINGER, Karen         F
  5    Ms. Elke Wallstab        WALLSTAB, Elke           F
```

5. (Optional) Searching for and Replacing Character Values

- As in the previous exercise, the data set **orion.customers_ex5** contains information about Orion Star customers.
- Customers who are frequent purchasers are tagged as *Silver*, *Gold*, or *Platinum*, which appears at the beginning of their **Customer_ID** value.
- Due to updates in how Orion Star designates **Customer_ID** values, the existing values need to be modified. Any four-digit string in **Customer_ID** should be replaced by **-15-** in the output data sets, An example is **-00-**.

a. Create three output data sets: **work.silver**, **work.gold**, and **work.platinum**.

- Search **Customer_ID** for the values *Silver*, *Gold*, and *Platinum* and write them to the respective data set when they are found.
- You should get 17 observations in **work.silver**, two in **work.gold**, and five in **work.platinum**.
- Keep the variables **Customer_ID**, **Name**, and **Country** in all data sets.

b. Print the data sets with appropriate titles.

c. Confirm that any **-00-** is replaced by **-15-**.

Hint: Make sure that your searches are not case sensitive.

Partial PROC PRINT Output (17 Total Observations)

```
                    Silver-Level Customers

         Customer_ID              Name                   Country

     Silver000-000-15-0005    STEPHANO, Sandrina         US
     Silver000-000-15-0012    BLACK, David               US
     Silver000-000-15-0024    KLEM, Robyn                US
```

PROC PRINT Output (2 Total Observations)

```
                    Gold-Level Customers

        Customer_ID              Name            Country

     Gold000-000-15-0027    MCCLUNEY, Cynthia      US
     Gold000-000-07-0201    BORWICK, Angel         CA
```

PROC PRINT Output (5 Total Observations)

```
                    Platinum-Level Customers

          Customer_ID              Name                   Country

     platinum000-000-15-0010    BALLINGER, Karen            US
     platinum000-000-15-0031    MARTINEZ, Cynthia           US
     platinum000-000-15-0171    BOWERMAN, Robert            AU
     platinum000-000-15-2806    VAN DEN BERG, Raedene       ZA
     platinum000-000-07-0100    YEARGAN, Wilma              CA
```

Level 2

6. Searching Character Values and Explicit Output

- The data set **orion.employee_donations** contains information about charity contributions from Orion Star employees.
- Each employee is allowed to list either one or two charities, which are shown in the **Recipients** variable.

Partial **orion.employee_donations** (124 Total Observations, 7 Total Variables)

```
Employee_ID    Recipients

     120265    Mitleid International 90%, Save the Baby Animals 10%
     120267    Disaster Assist, Inc. 80%, Cancer Cures, Inc. 20%
     120269    Cancer Cures, Inc. 10%, Cuidadores Ltd. 90%
     120270    AquaMissions International 10%, Child Survivors 90%
     120271    Cuidadores Ltd. 80%, Mitleid International 20%
```

Some charity names have a comma in them.

a. Use explicit output to create a data set named **work.split**.

- The data set has one observation for each combination of employee and charity to which he donated.
- Some employees made two contributions. Therefore, they have two observations in the output data set. These employees contain a % character in the value of **Recipients**.

  Store the position where the % character is found in a variable named **PctLoc**. This can make subsequent coding easier.

- Create a variable named **Charity** with the name and percent contribution of the appropriate charity.
- Read only the first 10 observations from **orion.employee_donations** to test your program.

b. Modify the program to read the entire **orion.employee_donations** data set.

- Print only the columns **Employee_ID** and **Charity**.
- Add an appropriate title.

Partial PROC PRINT Output (212 Total Observations)

```
Charity Contributions for each Employee

Employee_ID    Charity

     120265    Mitleid International 90%
     120265    Save the Baby Animals 10%
     120267    Disaster Assist, Inc. 80%
     120267    Cancer Cures, Inc. 20%
     120269    Cancer Cures, Inc. 10%
```

Challenge

7. Using Character Functions with the Input Buffer

- The raw data file **supply.dat** contains information about supplier IDs (up to five characters), supplier names (up to 30 characters), and the country from which that supplier ships (two characters).

Partial **supply.dat** (52 rows total)

```
                                                   50 Scandinavian Clothing A/S NO
109 Petterson AB SE
316 Prime Sports Ltd GB
755 Top Sports DK
772 AllSeasons Outdoor Clothing US
798 Sportico ES
```

- The keyword _INFILE_, when SAS reads from a raw data file, enables you to treat the contents of the input buffer as one long character string. This can sometimes be helpful, given the wide variety of character functions in SAS.
- Blanks appear both as delimiters and inside supplier names.

Remember that both the SCAN and FIND functions can process backward through strings. See SAS Help and Documentation for more details about how to do this.

a. Create a data set named **work.supplier**.

- Use list input to obtain values for **Supplier_ID**.
- Use character functions and the _INFILE_ statement to get values for **Supplier_Name** and **Country**.

b. Print the data set with an appropriate title.

Partial PROC PRINT Output (52 Total Observations)

```
                              Supplier Information

                 Supplier_
                    ID          Supplier_Name                     Country

                   50           Scandinavian Clothing A/S           NO
                   109          Petterson AB                        SE
                   316          Prime Sports Ltd                    GB
                   755          Top Sports                          DK
                   772          AllSeasons Outdoor Clothing         US
```

5.4 Manipulating Numeric Values

Objectives

- Use SAS functions to truncate numeric values.
- Use SAS functions to compute descriptive statistics of numeric values.

82

Business Scenario

When investigating the many numeric functions that exist in SAS, you find truncation functions that you would like to investigate further.

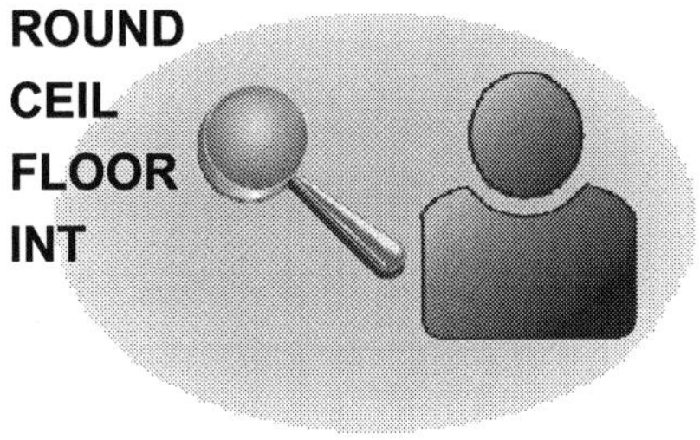

83

ROUND Function

The ROUND function returns a value rounded to the nearest multiple of *rounding unit*.

```
data truncate;
   NewVar1=round(12.12);
   NewVar2=round(42.65,.1);
   NewVar3=round(-6.478);
   NewVar4=round(96.47,10);
run;
```

NewVar=**ROUND**(*argument*<,*rounding-unit*>);

PDV

NewVar1 N 8	NewVar2 N 8	NewVar3 N 8	NewVar4 N 8
12	42.7	-6	100

84

ROUND Function

```
data truncate;
   NewVar5=round(12.69,.25);
   NewVar6=round(42.65,.5);
run;
```

Round to the nearest multiple of .25

PDV

NewVar5 N 8	NewVar6 N 8
12.75	.

85 ...

ROUND Function

```
data truncate;
   NewVar5=round(12.69,.25);
   NewVar6=round(42.65,.5);
run;
```

Round to the nearest multiple of .5

PDV

NewVar5 N 8	NewVar6 N 8
12.75	42.5

86

CEIL Function

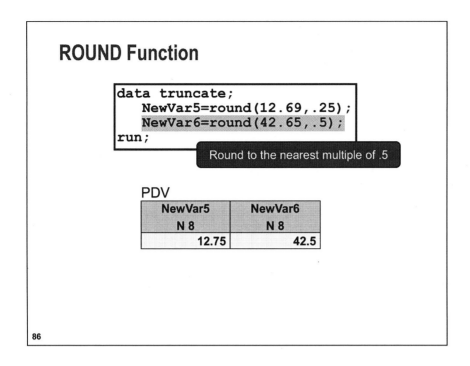

The CEIL function returns the smallest integer greater than or equal to the argument.

NewVar=**CEIL**(*argument*);

```
x=ceil(4.4);
```

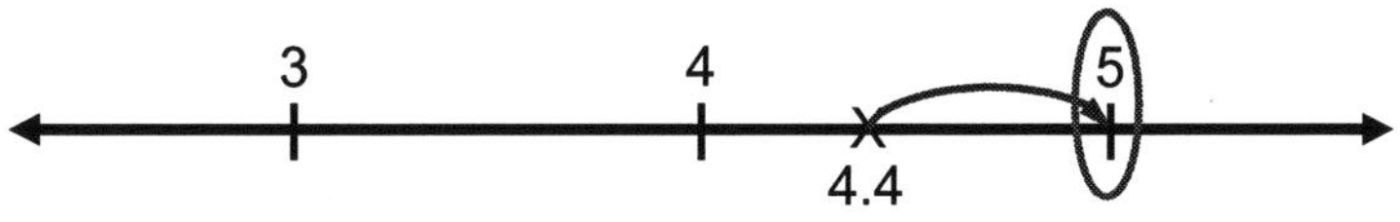

87

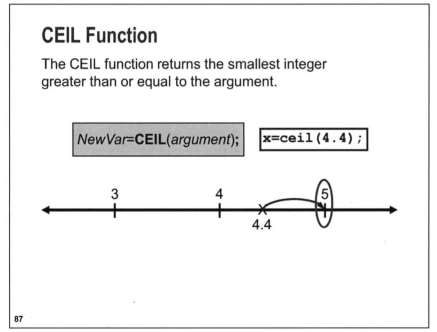

The value of *argument* is numeric.

FLOOR Function

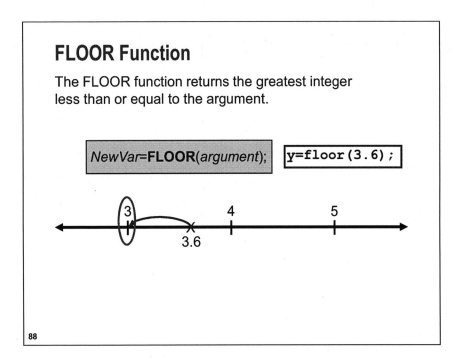

The FLOOR function returns the greatest integer less than or equal to the argument.

NewVar=**FLOOR**(*argument*);

```
y=floor(3.6);
```

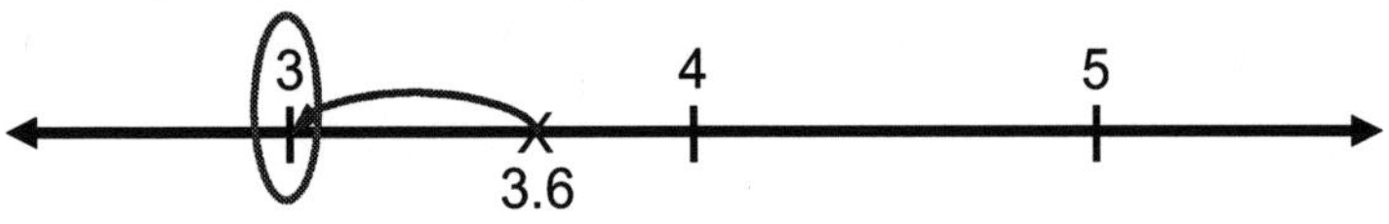

88

The value of *argument* is numeric.

INT Function

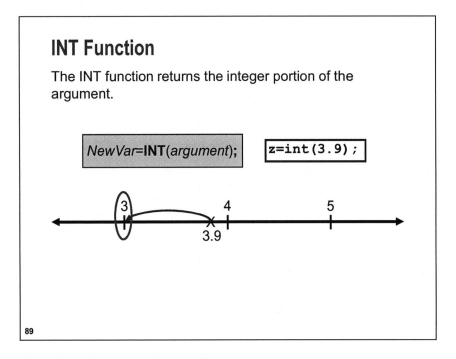

The INT function returns the integer portion of the argument.

NewVar=**INT**(*argument*);

```
z=int(3.9);
```

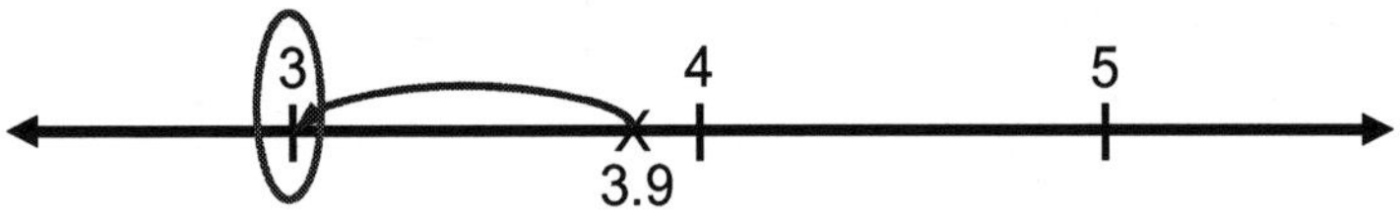

89

The value of *argument* is numeric.

Setup for the Poll

In this program, the values returned from the FLOOR and INT functions are the same.

```
data truncate;
   Var1=6.478;
   CeilVar1=ceil(Var1);
   FloorVar1=floor(Var1);
   IntVar1=int(Var1);
run;
```

PDV

Var1	CeilVar1	FloorVar1	IntVar1
6.478	7	6	6

90

5.09 Poll

Given the same value as an argument, do the INT and the FLOOR functions always return the same result?

❍ Yes

❍ No

91

Truncation Functions

Compare the values from the CEIL, FLOOR, and INT functions with a negative argument.

```
data truncate;
   Var1=-6.478;
   CeilVar1=ceil(Var1);
   FloorVar1=floor(Var1);
   IntVar1=int(Var1);
run;
```

PDV

Var1	CeilVar1	FloorVar1	IntVar1
-6.478	-6	-7	-6

93

For values greater than or equal to *0*, the FLOOR and INT functions return the same value. For values less than *0*, the CEIL and INT functions return the same value.

Business Scenario

Analysts want to calculate statistics to summarize and average each employee's quarterly contributions for the year.

Partial **orion.employee_donations**

Obs	Employee_ID	Qtr1	Qtr2	Qtr3	Qtr4
1	120265	.	.	.	25
2	120267	15	15	15	15
3	120269	20	20	20	20
4	120270	20	10	5	.

Partial **donation_stats**

Employee_ID	Total	Avg QT	Num Qt
120265	25	25	1
120267	60	15	4
120269	80	20	4
120270	35	12	3

95

Descriptive Statistics Functions

Descriptive statistic functions are used to calculate the values needed for **donation_stats**.

Function	Returns
SUM	Sum of arguments
MEAN	Average of arguments
MIN	Smallest value from arguments
MAX	Largest value from arguments
N	Count of nonmissing arguments
NMISS	Count of missing numeric arguments
CMISS	Count of missing numeric or character arguments

96

The CMISS function is new in SAS 9.2.

Descriptive Statistics Functions

```
data descript;
   Var1=12;
   Var2=.;
   Var3=7;
   Var4=5;
   SumVars=sum(Var1,Var2,Var3,Var4);
   AvgVars=mean(of Var1-Var4);
   MissVars=cmiss(of Var1-Var4);
run;
```

PDV

Var1	Var2	Var3	Var4
12	.	7	5

SumVars	AvgVars	MissVars
24	.	.

97

p205d12

...

Descriptive Statistics Functions

```
data descript;
   Var1=12;
   Var2=.;
   Var3=7;
   Var4=5;
   SumVars=sum(Var1,Var2,Var3,Var4);
   AvgVars=mean(of Var1-Var4);
   MissVars=cmiss(of Var1-Var4);
run;
```

PDV

Var1	Var2	Var3	Var4
12	.	7	5

SumVars	AvgVars	MissVars
24	8	.

98

...

Descriptive Statistics Functions

```
data descript;
   Var1=12;
   Var2=.;
   Var3=7;
   Var4=5;
   SumVars=sum(Var1,Var2,Var3,Var4);
   AvgVars=mean(of Var1-Var4);
   MissVars=cmiss(of Var1-Var4);
run;
```

PDV

Var1	Var2	Var3	Var4
12	.	7	5

SumVars	AvgVars	MissVars
24	8	1

99

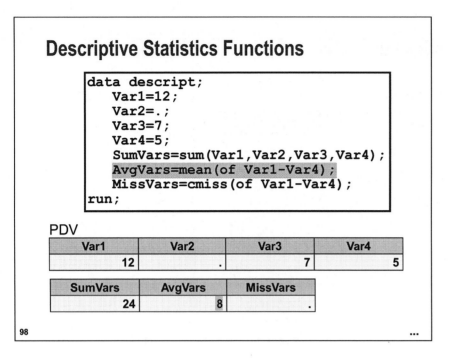

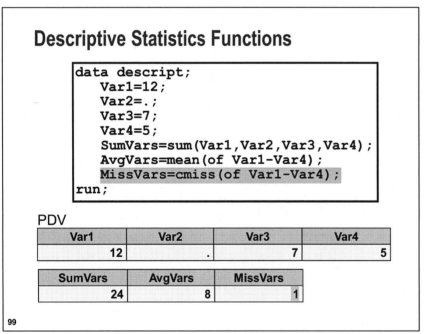

5.10 Multiple Choice Poll

Ord1, **Ord2**, and **Ord3** are variables that contain the sale amounts of the last three orders from all customers who have three orders or more. Which of the following expressions can calculate the total of the two largest orders?

a. sum(max(of Ord1-Ord3),max(of Ord1-Ord3))
b. sum(of Ord1-Ord3)-min(of Ord1-Ord3)
c. max(of Ord1-Ord3) + min(of Ord1-Ord3)
d. none of the above

100

Completed Business Scenario Program

Use the SUM, MEAN, and N functions to calculate the donation statistics.

```
data donation_stats;
   set orion.employee_donations;
   keep Employee_ID Total AvgQT NumQT;
   Total=sum(of Qtr1-Qtr4);
   AvgQT=round(Mean(of Qtr1-Qtr4));
   NumQt=n(of Qtr1-Qtr4);
run;

proc print data=donation_stats noobs;
   var Employee_ID Total AvgQt NumQt;
run
```

Employee_ID	Total	Avg QT	Num Qt
120265	25	25	1
120267	60	15	4
120269	80	20	4
...			

102

p205d13

Exercises

If you restarted your SAS session since the last exercise, open and submit the **libname.sas** program found in the data folder.

Level 1

8. Calculating Statistics and Rounding

The data set **orion.orders_midyear** contains an observation for each customer, with the total retail value of the customer's monthly orders for the first half of the year.

Partial Listing of **orion.orders_midyear** (24 Total Observations)

Customer_ID	month1	month2	month3	month4	month5	month6
5	213.1	.	478.0	525.80	394.35	191.79
10	188.1	414.09	2876.9	3164.59	2373.44	169.29
11	78.2	.	.	.	.	70.38
12	135.6	.	117.6	129.36	97.02	122.04
18	.	.	29.4	32.34	24.26	.
24	93.0	265.80	.	.	.	83.70
27	310.7	782.90	.	.	.	279.63
31	1484.3	293.30	.	.	.	1335.87
34	642.5	.	86.3	94.93	71.20	578.25

a. Create a data set named **work.sale_stats** with three new variables for all months in which the customer placed an order.

- The variable **MonthAvg** should contain the average.
- The variable **MonthMax** should contain the maximum.
- The variable **MonthSum** should contain the sum of values.
- Round **MonthAvg** to the nearest integer.

✎ Most SAS descriptive statistics functions automatically ignore missing values.

b. Print the variables **Customer_ID**, **MonthAvg**, **MonthMax**, and **MonthSum**. Add an appropriate title.

Partial PROC PRINT Output (24 Total Observations)

Statistics on Months in which the Customer Placed an Order

Customer_ID	Month Avg	Month Max	Month Sum
5	361	525.80	1803.04
10	1531	3164.59	9186.41
11	74	78.20	148.58
12	120	135.60	601.62
18	29	32.34	86.00

Level 2

There is no level 2 exercise for this section.

Challenge

9. Calculating Statistics for Missing, Median, and Highest Values

The data set **orion.orders_midyear** contains an observation for each customer, with the total retail value of the customer's monthly orders for the first half of the year.

Partial **orion.orders_midyear** (24 Total Observations)

Customer_ID	month1	month2	month3	month4	month5	month6
5	213.1	.	478.0	525.80	394.35	191.79
10	188.1	414.09	2876.9	3164.59	2373.44	169.29
11	78.2	.	.	.	.	70.38
12	135.6	.	117.6	129.36	97.02	122.04
18	.	.	29.4	32.34	24.26	.

a. Orion Star wants to look at information about the median order and the top two months' orders, but only for frequent customers.

- Create a data set named **work.freqcustomers** that contains the requested statistics.
- Frequent customers are defined to be those who placed an order in at least five of the six months.

b. Print your results with an appropriate title.

> The *median* of a set of values is the middle or central value. For example, the median of {1, 200, 3} is the value 3. If the set has an even number of values, the median is the midpoint between the two middle values.

> Consult the SAS documentation as needed to learn more about functions that can generate the desired results. It might be particularly useful to look at "Functions and CALL Routines by Category" in *SAS Language Dictionary*.

Partial PROC PRINT Output (9 Total Observations)

Month Statistics on Frequent Customers

Customer_ID	month1	month2	month3	month4	month5	month6	Month_ Median	Month_ Highest	Month_ 2nd Highest
5	213.10	.	478.0	525.80	394.35	191.790	394.35	525.80	478.00
10	188.10	414.09	2876.9	3164.59	2373.44	169.290	1393.77	3164.59	2876.90
12	135.60	.	117.6	129.36	97.02	122.040	122.04	135.60	129.36
34	642.50	.	86.3	94.93	71.20	578.250	94.93	642.50	578.25
41	134.00	119.20	313.0	344.30	258.23	120.600	196.11	344.30	313.00

5.5 Converting Variable Type

Objectives

- Explain the automatic conversion that SAS uses to convert values between data types.
- Explicitly convert values between data types.

106

Business Scenario: Convert HR Data

The data set **orion.convert** was created with data types and variable names that must be changed for future reporting and analysis.

Partial existing **orion.convert** data set

ID	GrossPay	Code	Hired
A	A	123	A

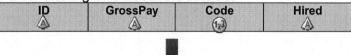

Partial converted **work.hrdata** data set

EmpID	GrossPay	Phone	HireDate
123	123	A	123

107

Data Conversion

Data types can be converted two ways:

- ***automatically*** by enabling SAS to do it for you
- ***explicitly*** with these functions:

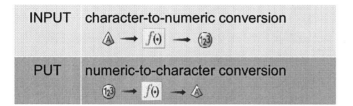

INPUT	character-to-numeric conversion 
PUT	numeric-to-character conversion 

108

Automatic Character-to-Numeric Conversion

What happens when the character values of **ID** are used in an arithmetic expression?

```
data hrdata;
   keep EmpID;
   set orion.convert;
   EmpID=ID + 11000;
run;
```

orion.convert

ID $ 5	GrossPay $ 6	Code N 8	Mobile $ 8	Hired $ 10
36	52,000	303	393-0956	04/13/2008
48	32,000	919	770-8292	08/25/2010
52	49,000	301	449-5239	06/08/2009

109 p205d14

Automatic Character-to-Numeric Conversion

Partial Log

```
28   data hrdata;
29      keep EmpID;
30      set orion.convert;
31      EmpID=ID + 11000;
32   run;

NOTE: Character values have been converted to numeric values at
the places given by:
      (Line):(Column).
      31:11
NOTE: There were 3 observations read from the data set
ORION.CONVERT.
NOTE: The data set WORK.HRDATA has 3 observations and 1
variables.
```

110

Automatic Character-to-Numeric Conversion

```
proc print data=hrdata noobs;
run;
```

PROC PRINT Output

```
       EmpID

       11036
       11048
       11052
```

The automatic conversion worked great for **ID**. Now see what happens with **GrossPay**.

111

Automatic Character-to-Numeric Conversion

What happens when the character values of **GrossPay** are used in an arithmetic expression?

```
data hrdata;
   keep GrossPay Bonus;
   set orion.convert;
   Bonus=GrossPay * .10;
run;
```

orion.convert

ID $ 5	GrossPay $ 6	Code N 8	Mobile $ 8	Hired $ 10
36	52,000	303	393-0956	04/13/2008
48	32,000	919	770-8292	08/25/2010
52	49,000	301	449-5239	06/08/2009

112 p205d15

Automatic Character-to-Numeric Conversion

```
proc print data=hrdata noobs;
run;
```

PROC PRINT Output

```
Gross
Pay        Bonus

52,000       .
32,000       .
49,000       .
```

Why did the automatic conversion not work for the values of **GrossPay**?

113

Automatic Character-to-Numeric Conversion

SAS automatically converts a character value to a numeric value when the character value is used in a numeric context, such as the following:

- assignment to a numeric variable
- an arithmetic operation
- logical comparison with a numeric value
- a function that takes numeric arguments

The WHERE statement and the WHERE= data set option do not perform any automatic conversion in comparisons.

114

Automatic Character-to-Numeric Conversion

The automatic conversion

- uses the *w.* informat
- produces a numeric missing value from a character value that does not conform to standard numeric notation.

115

Automatic Character-to-Numeric Conversion

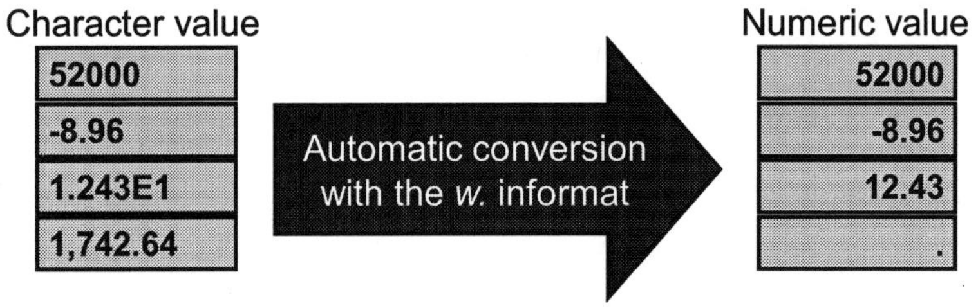

- The values in **GrossPay** contain commas, which cannot be converted by the *w.* informat, so **GrossPay** is assigned a missing value.
- To explicitly convert the values in **GrossPay**, use the INPUT function.

116

INPUT Function

The INPUT function returns the value produced when the source is read with a specified informat.

NumVar=**INPUT**(*source*,*informat*);

```
data conversions;
   CVar1='32000';
   CVar2='32.000';
   CVar3='03may2008';
   CVar4='030508';
   NVar1=input(CVar1,5.);
   NVar2=input(CVar2,commax6.);
   NVar3=input(CVar3,date9.);
   NVar4=input(CVar4,ddmmyy6.);
run;
```

117 p205d16

If you use the INPUT function to create a variable not previously defined, the type and length of the variable is defined by the informat.

INPUT Function

```
proc contents data=conversions;
run;
```

Partial PROC CONTENTS Output

Alphabetic List of Variables and Attributes

#	Variable	Type	Len
1	CVar1	Char	5
2	CVar2	Char	6
3	CVar3	Char	9
4	CVar4	Char	6
5	NVar1	Num	8
6	NVar2	Num	8
7	NVar3	Num	8
8	NVar4	Num	8

118

INPUT Function

```
proc print data=conversions noobs;
run;
```

PROC PRINT Output

CVar1	CVar2	CVar3	CVar4	NVar1	NVar2	NVar3	NVar4
32000	32.000	03may2008	030508	32000	32000	17655	17655

119

5.11 Quiz

Fill in the missing expression in the DATA step below. The expression should calculate **TotalValue** by multiplying **SharePrice** by **MyShares**.

```
data Input_Quiz;
   SharePrice="$130.25";
   MyShares=125;
   TotalValue=            ?
run;
```

120 p205d17

Explicit Character-to-Numeric Conversion

Continue with the business scenario by creating the variables **EmpID**, **Bonus**, and **HireDate**.

Use the INPUT function to explicitly convert character values to numeric.

```
data hrdata;
   keep EmpID GrossPay Bonus HireDate;
   set orion.convert;
   EmpID=input(ID,5.)+11000;
   Bonus=input(GrossPay,comma6.)*.10;
   HireDate=input(Hired,mmddyy10.);
run;
```

122 p205d18

Explicit Character-to-Numeric Conversion

```
proc print data=hrdata noobs;
   var EmpID GrossPay Bonus HireDate;
run;
```

PROC PRINT Output

SAS date values

EmpID	Gross Pay	Bonus	Hire Date
11036	52,000	5200	17635
11048	32,000	3200	18499
11052	49,000	4900	18056

123

Explicit Character-to-Numeric Conversion

```
proc print data=hrdata noobs;
   var EmpID GrossPay Bonus HireDate;
   format HireDate mmddyy10.;
run;
```

PROC PRINT Output

EmpID	Gross Pay	Bonus	HireDate
11036	52,000	5200	04/13/2008
11048	32,000	3200	08/25/2010
11052	49,000	4900	06/08/2009

What data type is **GrossPay**?

124

Converting a Variable to Another Data Type

```
proc contents data=hrdata;
run;
```

Partial PROC CONTENTS Output

```
Alphabetic List of Variables and Attributes

   #    Variable    Type    Len

   3    Bonus       Num       8
   2    EmpID       Num       8
   1    GrossPay    Char      6
   4    HireDate    Num       8
```

How can you convert **GrossPay** to a numeric variable with the same name?

125

5.12 Quiz

Does this statement convert **GrossPay** to numeric?

```
GrossPay=input(GrossPay,comma6.);
```

Open and run the program **p205a02**. Did **GrossPay** become a numeric variable?

126

Converting a Variable to Another Data Type

```
GrossPay=input(GrossPay,comma6.);
```

⚠ This assignment statement does ***not*** change **GrossPay** from a character variable to a numeric variable.

A variable is character or numeric. After the variable's type is established, it cannot be changed.

By following three steps, you can create a new variable with the same name and a different type.

128

Converting a Variable to Another Data Type

Step 1 Use the RENAME= data set option to rename.

```
data hrdata;
   set orion.convert(rename=(GrossPay=
                             CharGross));
run;
```

SAS-data-set(**RENAME=**(*old-name=new-name*))

129

old-name specifies the variable that you want to rename.

new-name specifies the new name of the variable. It must be a valid SAS name.

The new name of the variable that you want to convert is arbitrary. In this example, the existing variable is renamed **CharGross** to emphasize that a character variable is being converted.

To rename more than one variable from the same data set, separate the variables that you want to rename with a space. For example, to rename not only **GrossPay**, but also **ID**, use the following statement:

```
set orion.convert(rename=(GrossPay=CharGross ID=IDNum));
```

Converting a Variable to Another Data Type

Step 2 Use the INPUT function in an assignment statement to create a new variable with the original name of the variable that you renamed.

```
data hrdata;
   set orion.convert(rename=(GrossPay=
                              CharGross));
   GrossPay=input(CharGross,comma6.);
run;
```

130

Converting a Variable to Another Data Type

Step 3 Use a DROP= data set option in the DATA statement to exclude the original variable from the output SAS data set.

```
data hrdata(drop=CharGross);
   set orion.convert(rename=(GrossPay=
                              CharGross));
   GrossPay=input(CharGross,comma6.);
run;
```

The compilation for this program shows the PDV being created with a numeric **GrossPay** variable.

131 p205d19

Converting a Variable: Compilation

```
data hrdata(drop=CharGross);
   set orion.convert(rename=(GrossPay=
                             CharGross));
   GrossPay=input(CharGross,comma6.);
run;
```

Partial PDV

ID $ 5	CharGross $ 6	Hired $ 7

132 ...

Converting a Variable: Compilation

```
data hrdata(drop=CharGross);
   set orion.convert(rename=(GrossPay=
                             CharGross));
   GrossPay=input(CharGross,comma6.);
run;
```

Partial PDV

ID $ 5	CharGross $ 6	Hired $ 7	GrossPay N 8

133 ...

Converting a Variable: Compilation

```
data hrdata(drop=CharGross);
   set orion.convert(rename=(GrossPay=
                              CharGross));
   GrossPay=input(CharGross,comma6.);
run;
```

Partial PDV

ID $ 5	CharGross (D) $ 6	Hired $ 7	GrossPay N 8

134

Business Scenario: Continued

The **orion.convert** data set contains a numeric variable **Code** (area code) and a character variable **Mobile** (mobile telephone number).

orion.convert

ID $ 5	GrossPay $ 6	Code N 8	Mobile $ 8	Hired $ 10
36	52,000	303	393-0956	04/13/2008
48	32,000	919	770-8292	08/25/2010
52	49,000	301	449-5239	06/08/2009

136

Business Scenario: Continued

Create a character variable, **Phone**, that contains the area code in parentheses followed by the mobile telephone number.

orion.convert

ID $ 5	GrossPay $ 6	Code N 8	Mobile $ 8	Hired $ 10
36	52,000	303	393-0956	04/13/2008
48	32,000	919	770-8292	08/25/2010
52	49,000	301	449-5239	06/08/2009

Phone $ 14
(303) 393-0956
(919) 770-8292
(301)449-5239

137

Automatic Numeric-to-Character Conversion

For the first try at creating the **Phone** variable, let SAS handle the conversion automatically.

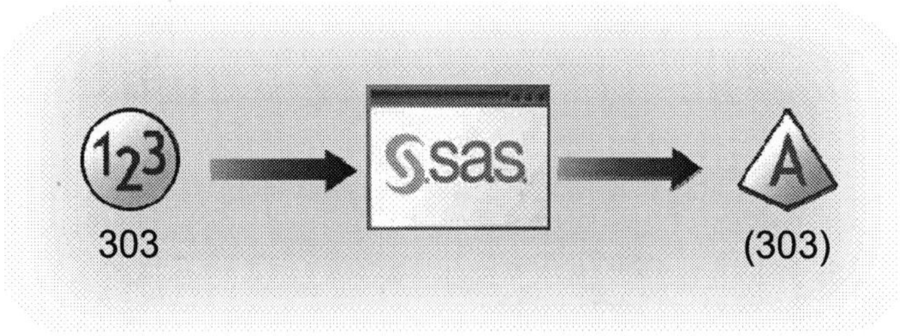

138

Automatic Numeric-to-Character Conversion

Partial **orion.convert**

Code N 8	Mobile $ 8
303	393-0956
919	770-8292
301	449-5239

```
data hrdata;
   keep Phone Code Mobile;
   set orion.convert;
   Phone='(' !! Code !! ') ' !! Mobile;
run;
```

SAS converts the numeric values in **Code** into character values automatically.

139 p205d20

Automatic Numeric-to-Character Conversion

Partial Log

```
14   data hrdata;
15      keep Phone Code Mobile;
16      set orion.convert;
17      Phone='(' !! Code !! ') ' !! Mobile;
18   run;

NOTE: Numeric values have been converted to character values
    at the places given by:
      (Line):(Column).
      17:16
NOTE: There were 3 observations read from the data set
    ORION.CONVERT.
NOTE: The data set WORK.HRDATA has 3 observations and 3
    variables.
```

140

Automatic Numeric-to-Character Conversion

```
proc print data=hrdata noobs;
run;
```

PROC PRINT Output

```
Code    Mobile                Phone

 303    393-0956    (          303) 393-0956
 919    770-8292    (          919) 770-8292
 301    449-5239    (          301) 449-5239
```

Why does SAS insert the extra blanks before the area code?

141

Automatic Numeric-to-Character Conversion

SAS converts a numeric value to a character value automatically when the numeric value is used in a character context, such as

- assignment to a character variable
- a concatenation operation
- a function that accepts character arguments.

142

The WHERE statement and the WHERE= data set option do not perform any automatic conversion in comparisons.

Automatic Numeric-to-Character Conversion

The automatic conversion

- uses the BEST12. format
- right-aligns the resulting character value.

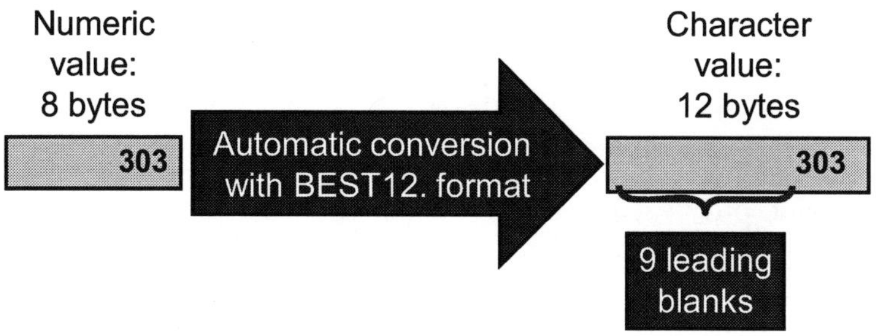

143

Automatic Numeric-to-Character Conversion

```
data hrdata;
   keep Phone Code Mobile;
   set orion.convert;
   Phone='(' !! Code !! ') ' !! Mobile;
run;
```

Partial PDV

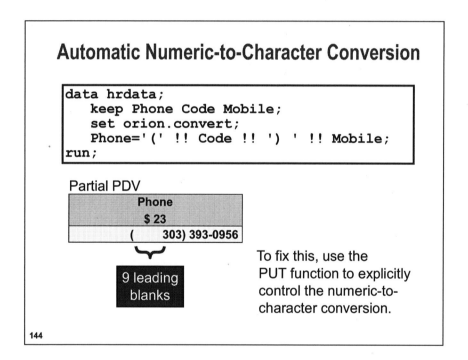

Phone $ 23
(303) 393-0956

9 leading blanks

To fix this, use the PUT function to explicitly control the numeric-to-character conversion.

144

Explicit Numeric-to-Character Conversion

The PUT function writes values with a specific format.

```
data hrdata;
   keep Phone Code Mobile;
   set orion.convert;
   Phone='(' !! put(Code,3.) !! ') '
          !! Mobile;
run;
```

CharVar=**PUT**(*source*,*format*);

The PUT function returns the value produced when *source* is written with *format*.

145 p205d22

source identifies the SAS variable or constant whose value you want to reformat. This argument can be character or numeric.

format contains the SAS format that you want applied to the variable or constant that is specified in the source. It must agree with the source in type.

The PUT function always returns a character string.

Numeric formats right-align the results. Character formats left-align the results.

If you use the PUT function to create a variable not previously defined, it creates a character variable with a length equal to the format width.

No conversion messages are written to the log by the PUT function.

Explicit Numeric-to-Character Conversion

```
proc print data=hrdata noobs;
run;
```

PROC PRINT Output

```
        Code    Mobile            Phone

         303    393-0956    (303) 393-0956
         919    770-8292    (919) 770-8292
         301    449-5239    (301) 449-5239
```

146

PUT Function: Example

This DATA step shows examples of the PUT function.

```
data conversion;
   NVar1=614;
   NVar2=55000;
   NVar3=366;
   CVar1=put(NVar1,3.);
   CVar2=put(NVar2,dollar7.);
   CVar3=put(NVar3,date9.);
run;
```

147

p205d21

PUT Function: Example

```
proc contents data=conversion varnum;
run;
```

The VARNUM option in the PROC CONTENTS statement prints a list of the variables by their logical position in the data set.

Partial PROC CONTENTS Output

Variables in Creation Order

#	Variable	Type	Len
1	NVar1	Num	8
2	NVar2	Num	8
3	NVar3	Num	8
4	CVar1	Char	3
5	CVar2	Char	7
6	CVar3	Char	9

148

PUT Function: Example

```
proc print data=conversion noobs;
run;
```

PROC PRINT Output

NVar1	NVar2	NVar3	CVar1	CVar2	CVar3
614	55000	366	614	$55,000	01JAN1961

149

CAT Functions and Numeric Conversion

The CAT family of functions converts any numeric argument to a character string by using the BEST12. format and then removing any leading blanks. No note is written to the log.

This assignment statement using CAT:

```
Phone=cat('(',Code,') ',Mobile);
```

gives equivalent results to this statement:

```
Phone='(' !! put(Code,3.) !! ') ' !! Mobile;
```

Now you can write the complete SAS program to convert the personnel data.

150

Convert HR Data: Complete Program

```
data hrdata;
   keep EmpID GrossPay Bonus Phone HireDate;
   set orion.convert(rename=(GrossPay=
                             CharGross));
   EmpID=input(ID,5.)+11000;
   GrossPay=input(CharGross,comma6.);
   Bonus=GrossPay*.10;
   HireDate=input(Hired,mmddyy10.);
   Phone=cat('(',Code,') ',Mobile);
run;

proc print data=hrdata noobs;
   var EmpID GrossPay Bonus Phone HireDate;
   format HireDate mmddyy10.;
run;
```

151 p205d23

Convert HR Data: Complete Program

PROC PRINT Output

EmpID	Gross Pay	Bonus	Phone	HireDate
11036	52000	5200	(303) 393-0956	04/13/2008
11048	32000	3200	(919) 770-8292	08/25/2010
11052	49000	4900	(301) 449-5239	06/08/2009

152

Exercises

If you restarted your SAS session since the last exercise, open and submit the **libname.sas** program found in the data folder.

Level 1

10. Using the PUT and INPUT Functions

The data set **orion.shipped** contains details about each product shipped to one of Orion Star's retail outlets in 2007.

Partial **orion.shipped**

Product_ID	Ship_Date	Quantity	Price
240800200021	05JAN2011	2	$42.45
240800200035	04JAN2011	6	$12.15
240200100225	04JAN2011	2	$77.85
210200500002	09JAN2011	3	$5.70

Partial PROC CONTENTS Output for **orion.shipped**

Variables in Creation Order

#	Variable	Type	Len	Format
1	Product_ID	Num	8	
2	Ship_Date	Num	8	DATE9.
3	Quantity	Num	8	
4	Price	Char	7	

An analyst at Orion Star has written a SAS program to calculate the total price of the items shipped and create a comment that includes the ship date. Unfortunately, the SAS program is giving unexpected results.

a. Open and submit the program **p205e10.sas**.

b. View the unexpected results.

Partial PROC PRINT Output (148 Total Observations)

Product_ID	Ship_Date	Quantity	Price	Comment	Total
240800200021	05JAN2011	2	$42.45	Shipped on 18632	.
240800200035	04JAN2011	6	$12.15	Shipped on 18631	.
240200100225	04JAN2011	2	$77.85	Shipped on 18631	.
210200500002	09JAN2011	3	$5.70	Shipped on 18636	.

c. Modify the program to generate the expected results.

Partial PROC PRINT Output

Product_ID	Ship_Date	Quantity	Price	Comment	Total
240800200021	05JAN2011	2	$42.45	Shipped on 01/05/2011	$84.90
240800200035	04JAN2011	6	$12.15	Shipped on 01/04/2011	$72.90
240200100225	04JAN2011	2	$77.85	Shipped on 01/04/2011	$155.70
210200500002	09JAN2011	3	$5.70	Shipped on 01/09/2011	$17.10

- Look above at the PROC CONTENTS output for **orion.shipped**.
- Notice that **Ship_Date** is numeric with a permanently assigned DATE9. format. It needs to be converted into a character value using the MMDDYY10. format.
- Notice that **Price** is character. It needs to be converted into a numeric value using the COMMA7. or DOLLAR7. informat.
- Use functions to convert the values of **Ship_Date** and **Price** to get the desired results.

Level 2

11. Changing a Variable's Data Type

The data set **orion.US_newhire** contains information about newly hired employees.

Partial **orion.US_newhire**

ID	Telephone	Birthday
120-012-40-4928	5467887	05DEC1972
120-012-83-3816	6888321	03MAY1969
120-341-44-0781	9418123	23NOV1976
120-423-01-7721	7839191	28JUN1971

Partial PROC CONTENTS Output of **orion.US_newhire**

Variables in Creation Order

#	Variable	Type	Len
1	ID	Char	15
2	Telephone	Num	8
3	Birthday	Char	9

a. Create a new data set from **orion.US_newhire**.
   - Name the new data set **US_converted**.
   - Remove the embedded hyphens in **ID**.
   - Convert **ID** to a numeric value.
   - Convert **Telephone** to character and place a – (hyphen or dash) between the third and fourth digits.
   - Convert **Birthday** to a SAS date value.

b. Print **US_converted** with an appropriate title and use PROC CONTENTS to check the variables types.

Partial **US_converted** (10 Total Observations)

```
                          US New Hires

                 ID          Telephone    Birthday

            120012404928     546-7887       4722
            120012833816     688-8321       3410
            120341440781     941-8123       6171
            120423017721     783-9191       4196
```

Partial PROC CONTENTS Output

```
   Variables in Creation Order

 #    Variable     Type    Len

 1    ID           Num       8
 2    Telephone    Char      8
 3    Birthday     Num       8
```

5.6 Solutions

Solutions to Exercises

1. Extracting Characters Based on Position

```
data work.codes;
   set orion.au_salesforce;
   length FCode1 FCode2 $ 1 LCode $ 4;
   FCode1=lowcase(substr(First_Name,1,1));
   FCode2=lowcase(substr(First_Name,length(First_Name),1));
   LCode=lowcase(substr(Last_Name,1,4));
run;

title 'Extracted Letters for User IDs';
proc print data=work.codes;
   var First_Name FCode1 FCode2 Last_Name LCode;
run;
title;
```

Alternate Solution

```
data work.codes;
   set orion.au_salesforce;
   length FCode1 FCode2 $ 1 LCode $ 4;
   FCode1=lowcase(substr(First_Name,1,1));
   FCode2=lowcase(substr(right(First_Name),12,1));
   /* Note 12 is the variable length of First_Name */
   LCode=lowcase(substr(Last_Name,1,4));
run;

title 'Extracted Letters for User IDs';
proc print data=work.codes;
   var First_Name FCode1 FCode2 Last_Name LCode;
run;
title;
```

2. Extracting Characters Based on Position

```
data work.small;
   set orion.newcompetitors;
   Country = substr(ID,1,2);
   Store_Code=left(substr(ID,3));
   if substr(Store_Code,1,1) = '1';
   City=propcase(City);
run;

title 'New Small-Store Competitors';
proc print data=work.small noobs;
   var Store_Code Country City Postal_Code;
run;
title;
```

3. Converting U.S. Postal Codes to State Names

```
data states;
   set orion.contacts;
   keep ID Name Location;
   Location = zipnamel(substr(right(address2),20,5));
run;

proc print data=states noobs;
run;
```

4. Cleaning Text Data

```
data names;
   length New_Name $50
          FMnames $30
          Last $30;
   set orion.customers_ex5;
   FMnames = scan(Name,2,',');
   Last = propcase(scan(Name,1,','));
   if Gender="F" then New_Name=CATX(' ','Ms.',FMNames,Last);
   else if Gender="M" then New_Name=CATX(' ','Mr.',FMNames,Last);
```

```
   keep New_Name Name Gender;
run;

proc print data=names;
run;
```

5. **(Optional) Searching for and Replacing Character Values**

```
data work.silver work.gold work.platinum;
   set orion.customers_ex5;
   Customer_ID=tranwrd(Customer_ID,'-00-','-15-');
   if find(Customer_ID,'Silver','I') > 0 then
     output work.silver;
   else if find(Customer_ID,'Gold','I') > 0 then
     output work.gold;
   else if find(Customer_ID,'Platinum','I') > 0 then
     output work.platinum;
   keep Name Customer_ID Country;
run;

title 'Silver-Level Customers';
proc print data=work.silver noobs;
run;

title 'Gold-Level Customers';
proc print data=work.gold noobs;
run;

title 'Platinum-Level Customers';
proc print data=work.platinum noobs;
run;
title;
```

6. **Searching Character Values and Explicit Output**

```
data work.split;
   set orion.employee_donations (obs=10);
   PctLoc=find(Recipients,'%');
   /* Position in which the first '%' occurs */
   if PctLoc > 0 then do;
     Charity=substr(Recipients,1,PctLoc);
     output;
     Charity=substr(Recipients,PctLoc+3);
     output;
   end;
   /* If '%' was found, then there's more than one recipient */
   /* Use PctLoc+3 for the '%, ' before the second charity */
   else do;
     Charity=trim(Recipients)!!' 100%';
     output;
   end;
   drop PctLoc Recipients;
run;
```

```
proc print data=work.split noobs;
   var Employee_ID Charity;
run;

data work.split;
   set orion.employee_donations;
   PctLoc=find(Recipients,'%');
   /* Position in which the first '%' occurs */
   if PctLoc > 0 then do;
     Charity=substr(Recipients,1,PctLoc);
     output;
     Charity=substr(Recipients,PctLoc+3);
     output;
   end;
   /* If '%' was found, then there's more than one recipient */
   /* Use PctLoc+3 for the '%, ' before the second charity */
   else do;
     Charity=trim(Recipients)!!' 100%';
     output;
   end;
   drop PctLoc Recipients;
run;

title 'Charity Contributions for each Employee';
proc print data=work.split noobs;
   var Employee_ID Charity;
run;
title;
```

Alternate Solution

```
  /* Use SCAN with '%' as a delimiter */

data work.split;
   set orion.employee_donations;
   PctLoc=find(Recipients,'%');
   /* Position in which the first '%' occurs */
   if PctLoc > 0 then do;
     Charity=scan(Recipients,1,'%')!!'%';
     output;
     Charity=substr(scan(Recipients,2,'%')!!'%',3);
     output;
   end;
   /* Because '%' is the delimiter, we must concatenate
      a '%' to the character string after the SCAN */
   else do;
     Charity=trim(Recipients)!!' 100%';
     output;
   end;
   drop PctLoc Recipients ;
run;
```

```
title 'Charity Contributions for each Employee';
proc print data=work.split noobs;
   var Employee_ID Charity;
run;
title;
```

7. **Using Character Functions with the Input Buffer**

```
data work.supplier;
   length Supplier_ID $ 5 Supplier_Name $ 30 Country $ 2;
   infile 'supply.dat';
   input Supplier_ID $;
   Country=scan(_INFILE_,-1,' ');
   StartCol=find(_INFILE_,' ');
   EndCol=find(_INFILE_,' ',-999);
   /* Everything between these first and last blanks is
   the supplier name. */
   Supplier_Name=substr(_INFILE_,StartCol+1,EndCol-StartCol);
   /* Knowing where the last blank is, Country could have
   also been created using SUBSTR. */
   drop StartCol EndCol;
run;

title 'Supplier Information';
proc print data=work.supplier noobs;
run;
title;
```

8. **Calculating Statistics and Rounding**

```
data work.sale_stats;
   set orion.orders_midyear;
   MonthAvg=round(mean(of month1-month6));
   MonthMax=max(of month1-month6);
   MonthSum=sum(of month1-month6);
run;

title 'Statistics on Months in which the Customer Placed an Order';
proc print data=work.sale_stats noobs;
   var Customer_ID MonthAvg MonthMax MonthSum;
run;
title;
```

9. **Calculating Statistics for Missing, Median, and Highest Values**

```
data work.freqcustomers;
   set orion.orders_midyear;
   if n(of month1-month6) >= 5;
   /* Alternative: if nmiss(of month1-month6) <= 1; */
   Month_Median=median(of month1-month6);
   Month_Highest=largest(1,of month1-month6);
   Month_2ndHighest=largest(2,of month1-month6);
run;
```

```
title 'Month Statistics on Frequent Customers';
proc print data=work.freqcustomers noobs;
run;
title;
```

10. Using the PUT and INPUT Functions

```
data shipping_notes;
   set orion.shipped;
   length Comment $ 21;
   Comment=cat('Shipped on ',put(Ship_Date,mmddyy10.));
   Total=Quantity * input(Price,comma7.);
run;

proc print data=shipping_notes noobs;
   format Total dollar7.2;
run;
```

11. Changing a Variable's Data Type

```
data US_converted (drop=cID nTelephone cBirthday);
   set orion.US_newhire
       (rename=(ID=cID Telephone=nTelephone
               Birthday=cBirthday));
   ID=input(compress(cID,'-'),15.);
   length Telephone $ 8;
   Telephone=cat(substr(put(nTelephone,7.),1,3),
             '-',substr(put(nTelephone,7.),4));
   Birthday = input(cBirthday,date9.);
run;

title 'US New Hires';
proc print data=US_converted noobs;
run;
title;

proc contents data=US_converted varnum;
run;
```

Solutions to Student Activities (Polls/Quizzes)

5.02 Quiz – Correct Answer

Any of these assignment statements would give the correct value for **Total**.

PDV

Year2	Year1	Year3	Year4	Sales

```
Total=sum(of Year1-Year4);

Total=sum(of Year2--Year4);

Total=sum(of Year:);
```

12

5.03 Multiple Choice Poll – Correct Answer

Which SUBSTR function can extract the group of five numbers from the middle of the **Item_Code** value?

PDV

Item_Code $ 20
978-1-59994-397-8

a. substr(Item_Code,5,7)
b. substr(Item_Code,5)
c. substr(Item_Code,7,5)
d. substr(Item_Code,'mid',5)

20

5.04 Quiz – Correct Answer

This PDV shows the current value of **Name**:

Name
HEATH*BARR*LITTLE EQUIPMENT SALES

Write an assignment statement that converts the value of **Name** to this:

Name
Heath*Barr*Little Equipment Sales

```
Name = propcase(Name,' *');
```

The second argument to the PROPCASE function must list all the characters to use as delimiters. In this example, the space and * both need to be listed.

36

5.05 Quiz – Correct Answer

Misplaced parentheses are some of the most common syntax errors with functions.

correctly placed

Corrected **p205a01.sas**

```
data shoes;
  set orion.product_list;
  if substr(right(Product_Name),33,13)=
       'Running Shoes';
run;
```

After running the corrected program, the shoes data set has eight observations and five variables.

40 **P205a01s**

5.06 Quiz – Correct Answer

PDV

Phrase $ 28	Second $ 200
software, hardware, services	hardware

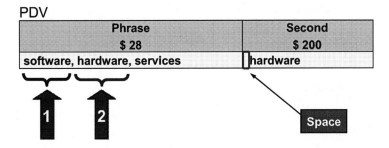

Add a blank to the delimiter list as shown below to extract the second word of **Phrase** without the leading space.

```
Second=scan(Phrase,2,', ');
```

50

5.07 Multiple Choice Poll – Correct Answer

What expression completes the assignment statement to correctly extract 2007 from the **Text** variable?

```
data Scan_Quiz;
   Text="New Year's Day, January 1st, 2007";
   Year=[              ?              ];
run;
```

a. scan(Text,-1);
b. scan(Text,6);
c. scan(Text,6,', ');
(d.) All of the above would work.

52

5.08 Quiz – Correct Answer

Complete the PDV for the values for **Pos3** and **Pos4**.

```
data find;
   Text='AUSTRALIA, DENMARK, US';
   Pos1=find(Text,'US');
   Pos2=find(Text,' US');
   Pos3=find(Text,'us');
   Pos4=find(Text,'us','I');
   Pos5=find(Text,'us','I',10);
run;
```

PDV

Pos1 N 8	Pos2 N 8	Pos3 N 8	Pos4 N 8
2	20	0	2

68

5.09 Poll – Correct Answer

Given the same value as an argument, do the INT and the FLOOR functions always return the same result?

❍ Yes

◉ No

⚠ **The INT and the FLOOR functions give different results if the argument value is negative.**

92

5.10 Multiple Choice Poll – Correct Answer

Ord1, **Ord2**, and **Ord3** are variables that contain the sale amounts of the last three orders from all customers who have three orders or more. Which of the following expressions can calculate the total of the two largest orders?

a. sum(max(of Ord1-Ord3),max(of Ord1-Ord3))
b. sum(of Ord1-Ord3)-min(of Ord1-Ord3)
c. max(of Ord1-Ord3) + min(of Ord1-Ord3)
d. none of the above

Adding the amount from all three orders and then subtracting the amount of the smallest order leaves the sum of the two largest orders.

101

5.11 Quiz – Correct Answer

Fill in the missing expression in the DATA step below. The expression should calculate **TotalValue** by multiplying **SharePrice** by **MyShares**.

```
data Input_Quiz;
   SharePrice="$130.25";
   MyShares=125;
   TotalValue=input(SharePrice,comma7.)*
                   MyShares;
run;
```

121 p205d17

For the curious, the value stored in **TotalValue** is 16281.25.

5.12 Quiz – Correct Answer

Does this statement convert **GrossPay** to numeric?

```
GrossPay=input(GrossPay,comma6.);
```

Open and run the program **p205a02**. Did **GrossPay** become a numeric variable?

No, GrossPay remains a character variable.

127

Chapter 6 Debugging Techniques

6.1 Using the PUTLOG Statement 6-3

Demonstration: Determining Logic Errors 6-8

Exercises 6-12

6.2 Solutions 6-12

Solutions to Exercises 6-12

Solutions to Student Activities (Polls/Quizzes) 6-13

6.1 Using the PUTLOG Statement

Objectives

- Use the PUTLOG statement in the DATA step to help identify logic errors.

2

Business Scenario

A mailing list application at Orion Star is not working properly. Use debugging techniques to identify and correct the problem.

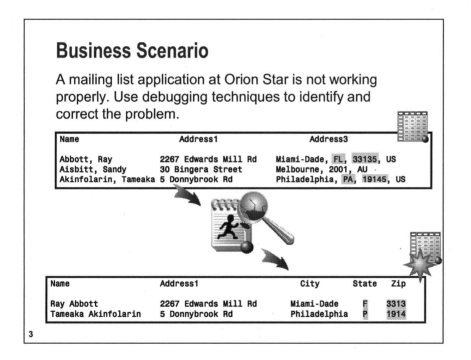

Name	Address1	Address3
Abbott, Ray	2267 Edwards Mill Rd	Miami-Dade, FL, 33135, US
Aisbitt, Sandy	30 Bingera Street	Melbourne, 2001, AU
Akinfolarin, Tameaka	5 Donnybrook Rd	Philadelphia, PA, 19145, US

Name	Address1	City	State	Zip
Ray Abbott	2267 Edwards Mill Rd	Miami-Dade	F	3313
Tameaka Akinfolarin	5 Donnybrook Rd	Philadelphia	P	1914

3

Logic Errors

A *logic error* occurs when the program statements follow the rules and execute but the results are not correct.

No notes are written to the log, so logic errors are often difficult to detect.

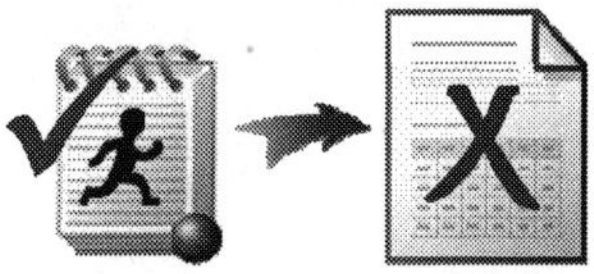

This section focuses on identifying ***logic*** errors.

4

Program and Partial Output

```
data us_mailing;
   set orion.mailing_list;
   drop Address3;
   length City $ 25 State $ 2 Zip $ 5;
   if find(Address3,'US');
   Name=catx(' ',
             scan(Name,2,','),
             scan(Name,1,','));
   City=scan(Address3,1,',');
   State=scan(address3,2,',');
   Zip=scan(Address3,3,',');
run;
```

Name	Address1	City	State	Zip
Ray Abbott	2267 Edwards Mill Rd	Miami-Dade	F	3313
Tameaka Akinfolarin	5 Donnybrook Rd	Philadelphia	P	1914
Salley Amos	3524 Calico Ct	San Diego	C	9211
Rose Anger	744 Chapwith Rd	Philadelphia	P	1914
David Anstey	939 Hilltop Needmore Rd	Miami-Dade	F	3315

5

PUTLOG Statement

The PUTLOG statement can be used in the DATA step to display

- the value(s) of one or more variables
- messages in the log.

PUTLOG *<specifications>*;

```
data us_mailing;
   set orion.mailing_list;
   drop Address3;
   length City $ 25 State $ 2 Zip $ 5;
   if find(Address3,'US');
   putlog 'Found US';
   Name=catx(' ',scan(Name,2,','),
                 scan(Name,1,','));
   City=scan(Address3,1,',');
   State=scan(address3,2,',');
   Zip=scan(Address3,3,',');
run;
```

6

The PUTLOG statement can be used to write to the SAS log in both batch and interactive modes. The PUT statement can also be used for this purpose. In addition, the PUT statement is used to write to an external file. If an external file is open for output, steps must be taken to ensure that debugging messages are written to the SAS log and not to the external file. See SAS documentation for more information about the PUT statement.

Using PUTLOG to Write the Value of a Variable

To write the name and value of a variable to the log, use this form of the PUTLOG statement:

PUTLOG *variable-name=*;

For example, if the value of the variable **City** is *San Diego*, the statement

```
putlog City=;
```

writes **City=San Diego** to the log.

7

Using PUTLOG to Write Formatted Values

To write the formatted value of a variable to the log, use this form of the PUTLOG statement:

PUTLOG *variable-name format-namew.*;

For example, if the value of the variable **City** is *Philadelphia* with a leading space, the statement

```
putlog City $quote22.;
```

writes " **Philadelphia**" to the log.

⚠ The value of *w* should be wide enough to display the value of the variable and the quotation marks.

8

✎ The format $QUOTE*w*. writes a character value in double quotation marks and preserves any leading spaces.

Using PUTLOG to Write Values of All Variables

To write the current contents of the program data vector (PDV) to the log, use this form of the PUTLOG statement:

PUTLOG _ALL_;

Partial SAS Log

```
Name=Abbott, Ray Address1=2267 Edwards Mill Rd Address3=Miami-
Dade, FL, 33135, US City=  State=  Zip=  _ERROR_=0 _N_=1
Name=Aisbitt, Sandy Address1=30 Bingera Street
Address3=Melbourne, 2001, AU City=  State=  Zip=  _ERROR_=0
_N_=2
Name=Akinfolarin, Tameaka Address1=5 Donnybrook Rd
Address3=Philadelphia, PA, 19145, US City=  State=  Zip=
_ERROR_=0 _N_=3
```

9

Special Variables

The temporary variables **_N_** and **_ERROR_** can be helpful when you debug a DATA step.

Variable	Description	Debugging Use
_N_	The number of times that the DATA step iterated	Display debugging messages for some number of iterations of the DATA step
ERROR	Initialized to 0, set to 1 when an error occurs	Display debugging messages when an error occurs.

10

6.01 Quiz

Open the file **p206a02**. Insert statements to display the values of **_N_** and **_ERROR_** in the first three iterations of the DATA step. Submit and view the log.

```
data _null_;
   set orion.donate;
run;
```

11 p206a02

Processing at the End of a DATA Step

The END= option creates a temporary variable that acts as an end-of-file indicator.

- The option can be used in SET and INFILE statements.
- The variable is initialized to 0 and is set to 1 when the last observation or record is read.

```
data work.donate;
   set orion.donate end=last;
   <additional SAS statements>
   if last=1 then do;
      <additional SAS statements>
   end;
run;
```

SET *SAS-data-set* **END=***variable <options>*;

13

Using PUTLOG with Conditional Logic

The program below displays a message in the log on the first iteration of the DATA step, and displays the contents of the PDV in the last iteration of the DATA step.

```
data _null_;
   set orion.donate end=lastObs;
   if _n_=1 then
      putlog 'First iteration';
   if lastObs then do;
      putlog 'Final values of variables:';
      putlog _all_;
   end;
run;
```

Partial SAS Log

```
First iteration
Final values of variables:
lastObs=1 Employee_ID=12447 Qtr=4 Amount=35 _ERROR_=0 _N_=16
```

14 p206d01

Determining Logic Errors

p206d02

This demonstration shows how to detect and correct logic errors using the PUTLOG statement.

1. Open and submit **p206d02**.

```
data us_mailing;
```

```
   set orion.mailing_list;
   drop Address3;
   length City $ 25 State $ 2 Zip $ 5;
   if find(Address3,'US') > 0;
   Name=catx(' ',scan(Name,2,','),scan(Name,1,','));
   City=scan(Address3,1,',');
   State=scan(address3,2,',');
   Zip=scan(Address3,3,',');
run;

proc print data=us_mailing noobs;
   title 'Current Output from Program';
run;
title;
```

Partial PROC PRINT Output

```
                          Current Output from Program

    Name                       Address1                   City           State    Zip

    Ray Abbott                 2267 Edwards Mill Rd       Miami-Dade       F      3313
    Tameaka Akinfolarin        5 Donnybrook Rd            Philadelphia     P      1914
    Salley Amos                3524 Calico Ct             San Diego        C      9211
    Rose Anger                 744 Chapwith Rd            Philadelphia     P      1914
    David Anstey               939 Hilltop Needmore Rd    Miami-Dade       F      3315
```

The values for **State** and **Zip** are incorrect. The SAS log does not contain any errors or warnings.

2. Insert PUTLOG statements to determine which statements execute, and to display the values of **_n_**, **State**, and **Zip**. Use the OBS= data set option to process only 10 observations.

```
data us_mailing;
   set orion.mailing_list (obs=10);
   drop Address3;
   length City $ 25 State $ 2 Zip $ 5;
   putlog _n_=;
   putlog "Looking for country";
   if find(Address3,'US') > 0;
   putlog "Found US";
   Name=catx(' ',scan(Name,2,','),scan(Name,1,','));
   City=scan(Address3,1,',');
   State=scan(address3,2,',');
   Zip=scan(Address3,3,',');
   putlog State= Zip=;

run;
```

3. Submit the code. The output from the PUTLOG statements appears in the log. The **US** observations are recognized, but the values of **State** and **Zip** are incorrect.

Partial SAS Log

```
_N_=1
Looking for country
Found US
```

```
State=F Zip=3313
_N_=2
Looking for country
_N_=3
Looking for country
Found US
State=P Zip=1914
```

4. Use the $QUOTE*w*. format in the PUTLOG statements to further examine the values of **State** and **Zip**.

   By default, the PUTLOG statement writes character values with the standard character format $*w*., where *w* is the length of the character variable. The standard character format left-justifies the value and removes leading blanks.

   The $QUOTE*w*. format writes the value enclosed in double quotation marks and preserves leading blanks. The closing quotation mark is displayed after the last non-blank character, so trailing blanks are not displayed.

```
data us_mailing;
   set orion.mailing_list (obs=10);
   drop Address3;
   length City $ 25 State $ 2 Zip $ 5;
   putlog _n_=;
   putlog "Looking for country";
   if find(Address3,'US') > 0;
   putlog "Found US";
   Name=catx(' ',scan(Name,2,','),scan(Name,1,','));
   City=scan(Address3,1,',');
   State=scan(address3,2,',');
   putlog state $quote4.;
   Zip=scan(Address3,3,',');
   putlog Zip $quote7.;
run;
```

5. Submit the code. The log shows that each value of **State** and **Zip** contains a leading blank.

   Partial SAS Log

```
_N_=1
Looking for country
Found US
" F"
" 3313"
_N_=2
Looking for country
_N_=3
Looking for country
Found US
" P"
" 1914"
```

6. Use the LEFT function to remove leading blanks from **State** and **Zip**.

```
data us_mailing (obs=5);
   set orion.mailing_list (obs=10);
   drop Address3;
```

```
   length City $ 25 State $ 2 Zip $ 5;
   putlog _n_=;
   putlog "Looking for country";
   if find(Address3,'US') > 0;
   putlog "Found US";
   Name=catx(' ',scan(Name,2,','),scan(Name,1,','));
   City=scan(Address3,1,',');
   State=left(scan(address3,2,','));
   putlog state $quote4.;
   Zip=left(scan(Address3,3,','));
   putlog Zip $quote7.;
run;
```

7. Submit the code and check the log. The values of **State** and **Zip** are correct.

Partial SAS Log

```
_N_=1
Looking for country
Found US
"FL"
"33135"
_N_=2
Looking for country
_N_=3
Looking for country
Found US
"PA"
"19145"
```

8. Remove the OBS= option and the PUTLOG statements. Submit the code and check the log and output.

```
data us_mailing;
   set orion.mailing_list;
   drop Address3;
   length City $ 25 State $ 2 Zip $ 5;
   if find(Address3,'US') > 0;
   Name=catx(' ',scan(Name,2,','),scan(Name,1,','));
   City=scan(Address3,1,',');
   State=left(scan(address3,2,','));
   Zip=left(scan(Address3,3,','));
run;

proc print data=work.us_mailing noobs;
   title 'Corrected Output';
run;
```

Partial PROC PRINT Output (311 Total Observations)

Corrected Output

Name	Address1	City	State	Zip
Ray Abbott	2267 Edwards Mill Rd	Miami-Dade	FL	33135
Tameaka Akinfolarin	5 Donnybrook Rd	Philadelphia	PA	19145

Salley Amos	3524 Calico Ct	San Diego	CA	92116
Rose Anger	744 Chapwith Rd	Philadelphia	PA	19142
David Anstey	939 Hilltop Needmore Rd	Miami-Dade	FL	33157

Exercises

If you restarted your SAS session since the last exercise, open and submit the **libname.sas** program found in the data folder.

Level 1

1. Debugging with the PUTLOG Statement

a. Open and submit **p206e01**.

b. Compare your results to the correct output below. Notice that your output is different. There are no error or warning messages in the log.

Partial PROC PRINT Output (37 Total Observations)

Obs	Customer_ID	Total_ Sales
1	5	691.10
2	10	3479.09
3	11	78.20
4	12	253.20
5	18	29.40

c. Insert PUTLOG statements to check program flow, display values of variables, and so on to identify the error (or errors).

d. Correct the error (or errors), resubmit the program, and verify your results.

6.2 Solutions

Solutions to Exercises

1. Debugging with the PUTLOG Statement

```
data customers;
   set orion.order_summary;
   by Customer_ID;
   if first.Customer_ID=1 then TotSales=0;
   putlog TotSales= Sale_Amt=;
   Total_Sales+Sale_Amt;
   putlog Total_Sales=;
   if last.Customer_ID=1;
   keep Customer_ID Total_Sales;
run;
```

```
data customers;
   set orion.order_summary;
   by Customer_ID;
   if first.Customer_ID=1 then Total_Sales=0;
   Total_Sales+Sale_Amt;
   if last.Customer_ID=1;
   keep Customer_ID Total_Sales;
run;

proc print data=customers;
run;
```

Solutions to Student Activities (Polls/Quizzes)

6.01 Quiz – Correct Answer

Open the file **p206a02**. Insert statements to display the values of **_N_** and **_ERROR_** in the first three iterations of the DATA step.

Solution

```
data _null_;
   set orion.donate;
   if _n_ <= 3 then
      putlog _n_= _error_=;
run;
```

Alternate Solution

```
data _null_;
   set orion.donate (obs=3);
   putlog _n_= _error_=;
run;
```

Partial SAS Log

```
_N_=1 _ERROR_=0
_N_=2 _ERROR_=0
_N_=3 _ERROR_=0
```

Use **_N_** to execute PUTLOG on the first three iterations of the DATA step, or use OBS= to process only three observations.

12

p206a02s

Chapter 7 Processing Data Iteratively

7.1 DO Loop Processing 7-3

Exercises 7-16

7.2 Conditional DO Loop Processing 7-17

Exercises 7-28

7.3 SAS Array Processing 7-30

Exercises 7-40

7.4 Using SAS Arrays 7-44

Exercises 7-59

7.5 Solutions 7-61

Solutions to Exercises 7-61

Solutions to Student Activities (Polls/Quizzes) 7-66

7.1 DO Loop Processing

Objectives

- Explain iterative DO loops.
- Use DO loops to eliminate redundant code and repetitive calculations.

3

Business Scenario

An Orion Star employee wants to compare the interest for **yearly** versus **quarterly** compounding on a $50,000 investment made for one year at 4.5 percent interest.

How much money does the employee accrue in each situation?

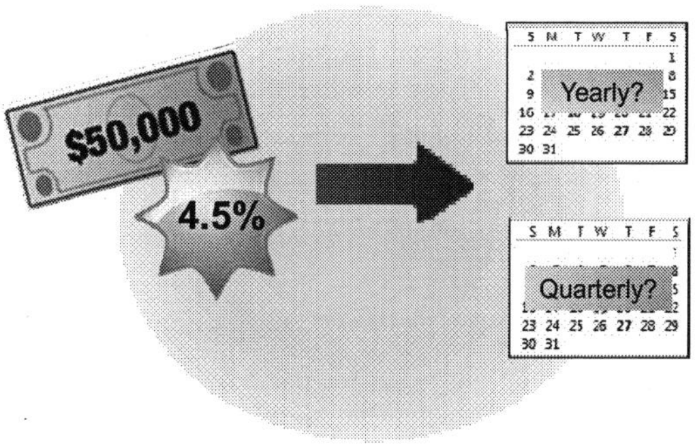

4

Repetitive Coding

```
data compound;
   Amount=50000;
   Rate=.045;
   Yearly=Amount*Rate;
   Quarterly+((Quarterly+Amount)*Rate/4);
   Quarterly+((Quarterly+Amount)*Rate/4);
   Quarterly+((Quarterly+Amount)*Rate/4);
   Quarterly+((Quarterly+Amount)*Rate/4);
run;
proc print data=compound noobs;
run;
```

Amount	Rate	Yearly	Quarterly
50000	0.045	2250	2288.25

5

p207d01

Repetitive Coding

What if the employee wants to determine annual and quarterly compounded interest for a period of 20 years (80 quarters)?

```
data compound;
   Amount=50000;
   Rate=.045;
   Yearly +(Yearly+Amount)*Rate;
   .
   .        (20x)
   .
   Yearly +(Yearly+Amount)*Rate;
   Quarterly+((Quarterly+Amount)*Rate/4);
   .
   .        (80x)
   .
   Quarterly+((Quarterly+Amount)*Rate/4);
run;
```

6

DO Loop Processing

Use DO loops to perform the repetitive calculations.

```
data compound(drop=i);
   Amount=50000;
   Rate=.045;
   do i=1 to 20;
      Yearly +(Yearly+Amount)*Rate;
   end;
   do i=1 to 80;
      Quarterly+((Quarterly+Amount)*Rate/4);
   end;
run;
```

DO *index-variable=start* **TO** *stop* <**BY** *increment*>;
    iterated SAS statements…
END;

7

p207d02

Iterative DO Statement

The values of *start*, *stop*, and *increment*

- must be numbers or expressions that yield numbers
- are established before executing the loop
- if omitted, *increment* defaults to 1.

Details of *index-variable*:

- The *index-variable* is written to the output data set by default.
- At the termination of the loop, the value of *index-variable* is one *increment* beyond the *stop* value.

8

start specifies the initial value of the index variable.

stop specifies the ending value of the index variable.

increment specifies a positive or negative number to control the incrementing of *index-variable.*

✎ Changes to the values of *stop* or *increment* made within the DO loop do not affect the number of iterations.

7.01 Quiz

What are the final values of the index variables after the following DO statements execute?

The final value is highlighted.

```
do i=1 to 5;
   ...
end;                        1 2 3 4 5 6

do j=2 to 8 by 2;
   ...
end;

do k=10 to 2 by -2;
   ...
end;
```

9

Sample DO Loops with Item Lists

- The DO loop is executed once for each item in the list.
- The list must be comma separated.

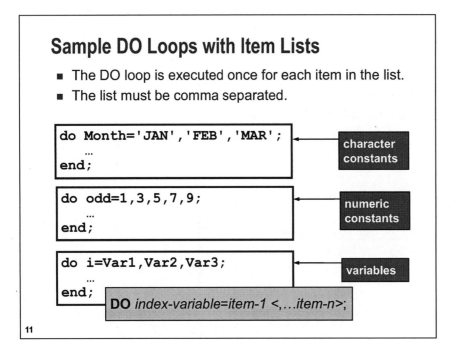

```
do Month='JAN','FEB','MAR';
   ...
end;
```

character constants

```
do odd=1,3,5,7,9;
   ...
end;
```

numeric constants

```
do i=Var1,Var2,Var3;
   ...
end;
```

variables

DO *index-variable=item-1* <,...*item-n*>;

11

Enclose character constants in quotation marks.

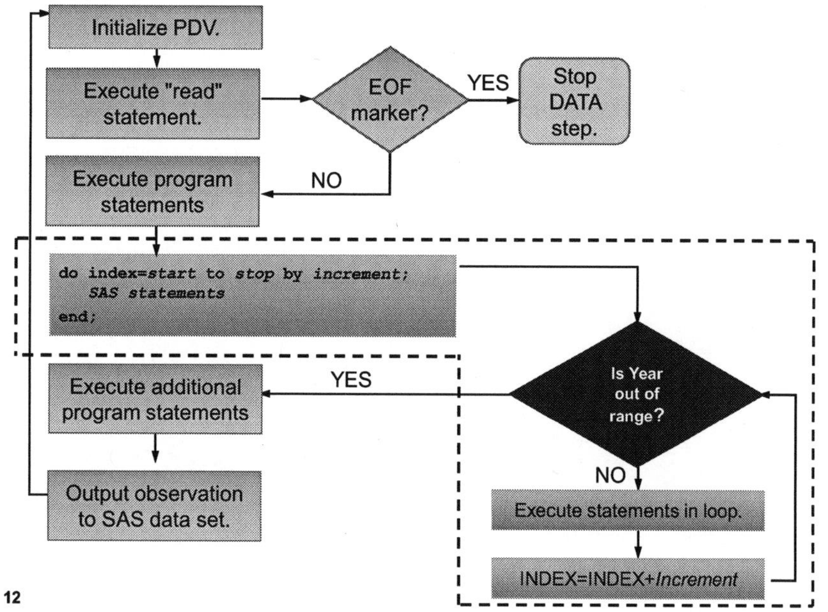

12

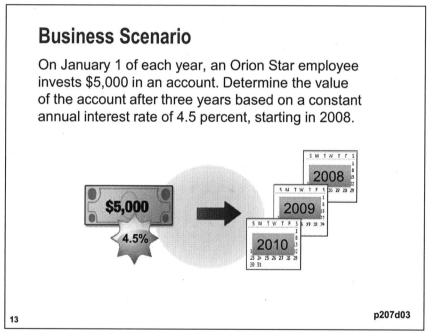

Business Scenario

On January 1 of each year, an Orion Star employee invests $5,000 in an account. Determine the value of the account after three years based on a constant annual interest rate of 4.5 percent, starting in 2008.

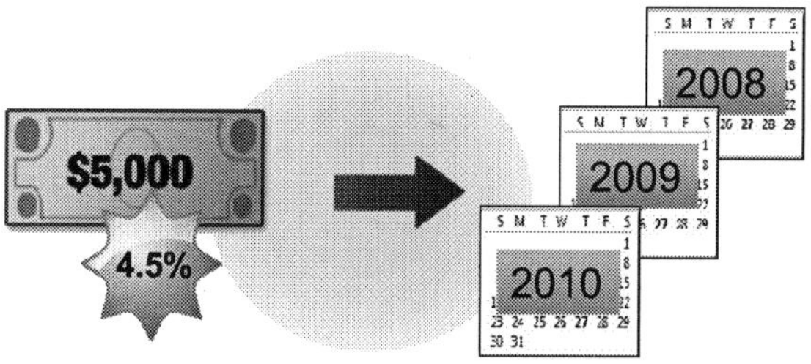

13 p207d03

Execution: Performing Repetitive Calculations

```
data invest;
   do Year=2008 to 2010;
      Capital+5000;
      Capital+(Capital*.045);
   end;
run;
```

Initialize PDV

PDV

Year	Capital	_N_
.	0	1

Capital is used in a sum statement, so it is initialized to zero automatically and retained.

14

...

Execution: Performing Repetitive Calculations

```
data invest;
   do Year=2008 to 2010;
      Capital+5000;
      Capital+(Capital*.045);
   end;
run;
```

Is Year out of range?

PDV

Year	Capital	_N_
2008	0	1

15

...

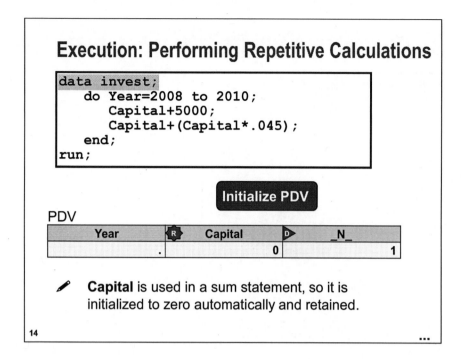

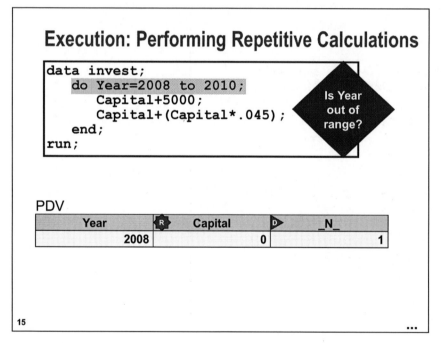

Execution: Performing Repetitive Calculations

```
data invest;
   do Year=2008 to 2010;
      Capital+5000;
      Capital+(Capital*.045);
   end;
run;
```

0 + 5000

PDV

Year	Capital	_N_
2008	5000	1

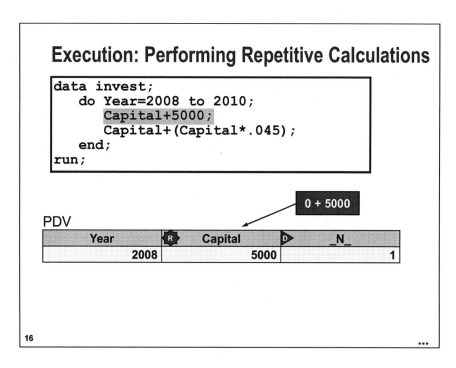

16 ...

Execution: Performing Repetitive Calculations

```
data invest;
   do Year=2008 to 2010;
      Capital+5000;
      Capital+(Capital*.045);
   end;
run;
```

5000 + (5000 * .045)

PDV

Year	Capital	_N_
2008	5225	1

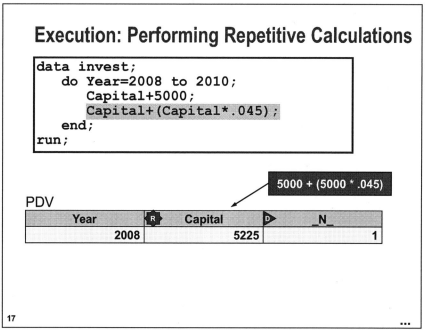

17 ...

Execution: Performing Repetitive Calculations

```
data invest;
   do Year=2008 to 2010;
      Capital+5000;
      Capital+(Capital*.045);
   end;
run;
```

Year + 1

PDV

Year	Capital	_N_
2009	5225	1

18 ...

Execution: Performing Repetitive Calculations

```
data invest;
   do Year=2008 to 2010;
      Capital+5000;
      Capital+(Capital*.045);
   end;
run;
```

Is Year out of range?

PDV

Year	Capital	_N_
2009	5225	1

19 ...

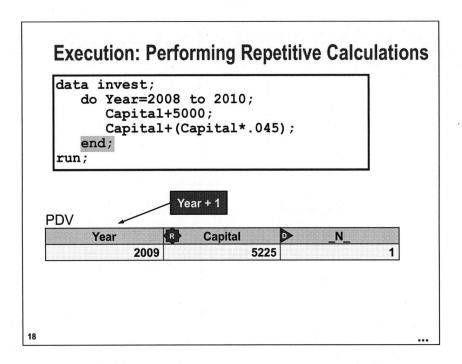

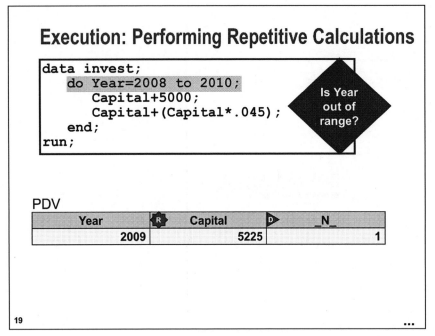

Execution: Performing Repetitive Calculations

```
data invest;
   do Year=2008 to 2010;
      Capital+5000;
      Capital+(Capital*.045);
   end;
run;
```

5225 + 5000

PDV

Year	Capital	_N_
2009	10225	1

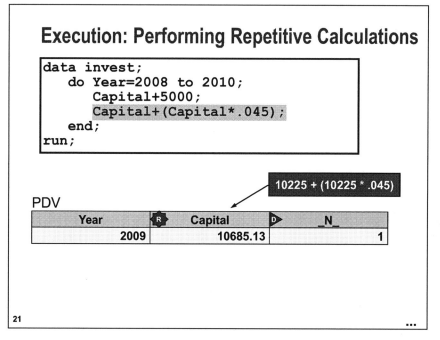

20 ...

Execution: Performing Repetitive Calculations

```
data invest;
   do Year=2008 to 2010;
      Capital+5000;
      Capital+(Capital*.045);
   end;
run;
```

10225 + (10225 * .045)

PDV

Year	Capital	_N_
2009	10685.13	1

21 ...

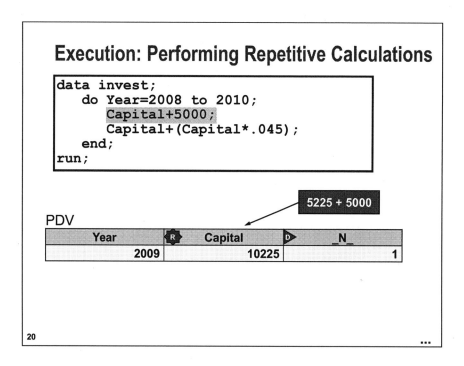

Execution: Performing Repetitive Calculations

```
data invest;
   do Year=2008 to 2010;
      Capital+5000;
      Capital+(Capital*.045);
   end;
run;
```

Year + 1

PDV

Year	Capital	_N_
2010	10685.13	1

22

...

Execution: Performing Repetitive Calculations

```
data invest;
   do Year=2008 to 2010;
      Capital+5000;
      Capital+(Capital*.045);
   end;
run;
```

Is Year out of range?

PDV

Year	Capital	_N_
2010	10685.13	1

23

...

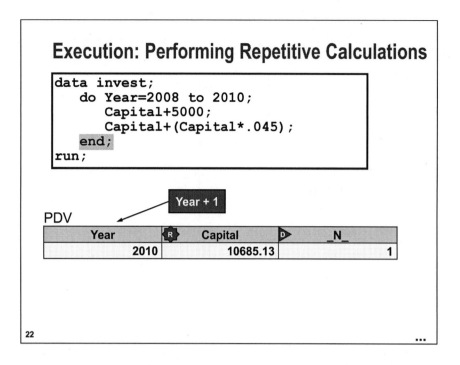

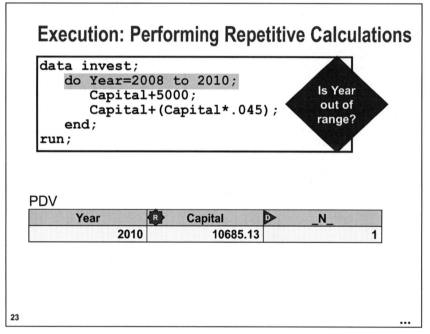

Execution: Performing Repetitive Calculations

```
data invest;
   do Year=2008 to 2010;
      Capital+5000;
      Capital+(Capital*.045);
   end;
run;
```

10685.13 + 5000

PDV

Year	Capital	_N_
2010	15685.13	1

24 ...

Execution: Performing Repetitive Calculations

```
data invest;
   do Year=2008 to 2010;
      Capital+5000;
      Capital+(Capital*.045);
   end;
run;
```

15685.13 + (15685.13 * .045)

PDV

Year	Capital	_N_
2010	16390.96	1

25 ...

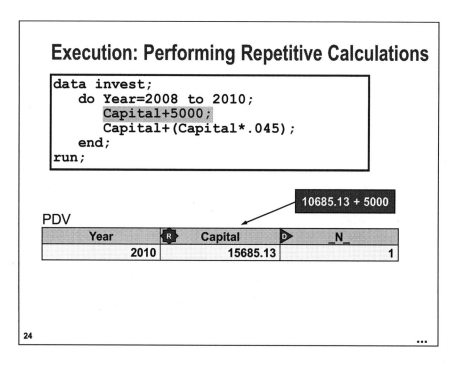

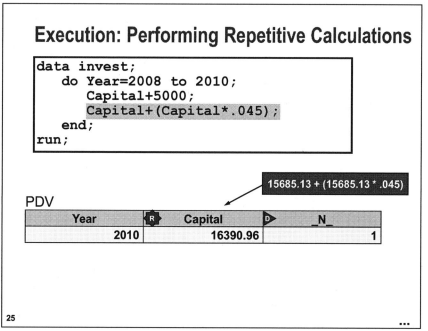

Execution: Performing Repetitive Calculations

```
data invest;
   do Year=2008 to 2010;
      Capital+5000;
      Capital+(Capital*.045);
   end;
run;
```

Year + 1

PDV

Year	Capital	_N_
2011	16390.96	1

26

...

Execution: Performing Repetitive Calculations

```
data invest;
   do Year=2008 to 2010;
      Capital+5000;
      Capital+(Capital*.045);
   end;
run;
```

Is Year out of range?

PDV

Year	Capital	_N_
2011	16390.96	1

27

...

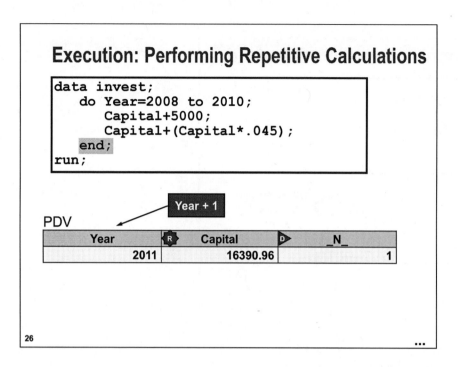

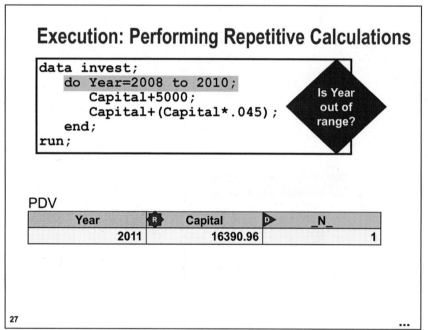

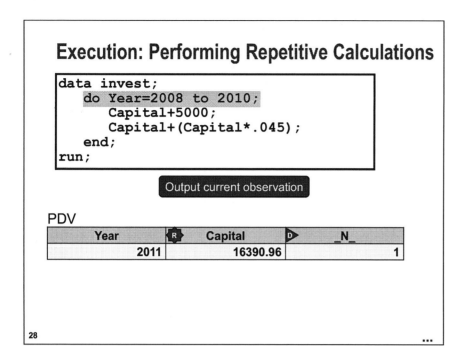

Execution: Performing Repetitive Calculations

```
data invest;
   do Year=2008 to 2010;
      Capital+5000;
      Capital+(Capital*.045);
   end;
run;
```

Output current observation

PDV

Year	R Capital	D _N_
2011	16390.96	1

28

...

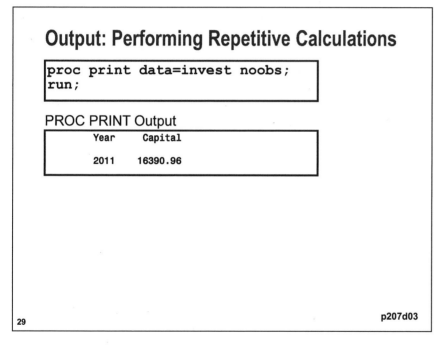

Output: Performing Repetitive Calculations

```
proc print data=invest noobs;
run;
```

PROC PRINT Output

```
Year    Capital

2011   16390.96
```

29

p207d03

7.02 Quiz

How can you generate a separate observation for each year?

```
data invest;
   do Year=2008 to 2010;
      Capital+5000;
      Capital+(Capital*.045);
   end;
run;
proc print data=invest noobs;
run;
```

30 p207a01

Exercises

If you restarted your SAS session since the last exercise, open and submit the **libname.sas** program found in the data folder.

Level 1

1. Performing Computations with DO Loops

The Orion Star Payroll Department must project total employee costs (wages, retirement benefits, and medical benefits) through future years, based on assumed increases.

a. Open the file **p207e01** and make the following changes:

- Insert a DO loop containing statements to calculate the estimated values of **Wages**, **Retire**, and **Medical**.

  – Use **Start** and **Stop** to control the values of the index variable, **Year**.

- Assume the estimated annual increase shown in the table below. For example, to calculate **Wages**, use this formula:

  wages = wages * 1.06;

Variable	Current Value	Estimated Annual Increase
Wages	$12,874,000	6.0%
Retire	1,765,000	1.4%
Medical	649,000	9.5%

- Create another variable, **Total_Cost**, as the sum of that year's **Wages**, **Retire**, and **Medical** values.
- Output one observation for each year. Your report should contain 10 observations.

b. Print and verify your results.

Partial PROC PRINT Output (10 Total Observations)

Obs	Year	Wages	Retire	Medical	Total_Cost
1	2013	13,646,440.00	1,789,710.00	710,655.00	16,146,805.00
2	2014	14,465,226.40	1,814,765.94	778,167.23	17,058,159.57
3	2015	15,333,139.98	1,840,172.66	852,093.11	18,025,405.76
4	2016	16,253,128.38	1,865,935.08	933,041.96	19,052,105.42
5	2017	17,228,316.09	1,892,058.17	1,021,680.94	20,142,055.20

The results above were generated on February 14, 2012. Your values for **Year** might differ.

7.2 Conditional DO Loop Processing

Objectives

- Use conditional DO loops.
- Use nested DO loops.

34

Business Scenario

Recall the example that forecasts the growth of several departments at Orion Star. Modify the forecasting application to use a DO loop to eliminate redundant code.

Listing of **orion.growth**

Department	Total_ Employees	Increase
Administration	34	0.25
Engineering	9	0.30
IS	25	0.10
Marketing	20	0.20
Sales	201	0.30
Sales Management	11	0.10

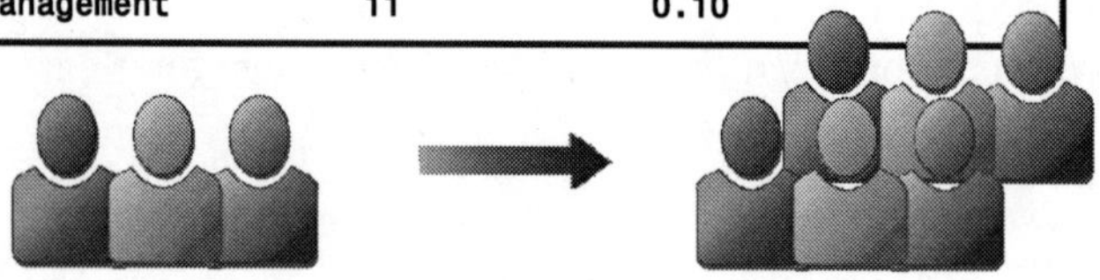

35

A Forecasting Application (Review)

```
data forecast;
   set orion.growth;
   Year=1;
   Total_Employees=Total_Employees*(1+Increase);
   output;
   Year=2;
   Total_Employees=Total_Employees*(1+Increase);
   output;
run;
proc print data=forecast noobs;
run;
```

What if you want to forecast growth over the next six years?

36 p207d04

Use a DO Loop to Reduce Redundant Code

```
data forecast;
   set orion.growth;
   do Year=1 to 6;
      Total_Employees=
         Total_Employees*(1+Increase);
      output;
   end;
run;

proc print data=forecast noobs;
run;
```

37

p207d05

Output

Partial PROC PRINT Output (36 Total Observations)

```
                      Total_
Department           Employees    Increase    Year

Administration         42.500       0.25        1
Administration         53.125       0.25        2
Administration         66.406       0.25        3
Administration         83.008       0.25        4
Administration        103.760       0.25        5
Administration        129.700       0.25        6
Engineering            11.700       0.30        1
```

38

7.03 Quiz

What stop value would you use in the DO loop to determine the number of years that it would take for the Engineering Department to exceed 75 people?

```
data forecast;
   set orion.growth;
   do Year=1 to 6;
      Total_Employees=
         Total_Employees*(1+Increase);
      output;
   end;
run;
proc print data=forecast noobs;
run;
```

39

p207d05

Business Scenario

Determine the number of years that it would take for an account to exceed $1,000,000 if $5,000 is invested annually at 4.5 percent.

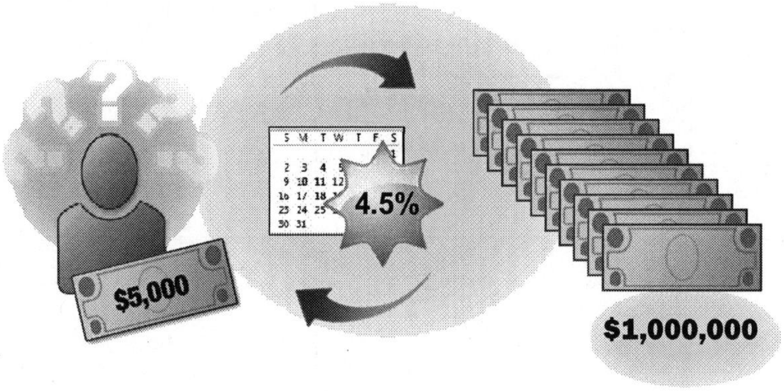

41

Conditional Iterative Processing

```
data invest;
   do until(Capital>1000000);
      Year+1;
      Capital+5000;
      Capital+(Capital*.045);
   end;
run;

proc print data=invest noobs;
   format Capital dollar14.2;
run;
```

DO UNTIL | WHILE;
<additional SAS statements>
END;

PROC PRINT Output

Capital	Year
$1,029,193.17	52

42

p207d06

DO UNTIL Statement

- The DO UNTIL statement executes statements in a DO loop repetitively until a condition is true.
- The value of expression is evaluated at the bottom of the loop.
- The statements in the loop are executed at least once.

43

DO WHILE Statement

- The DO WHILE statement executes statements in a DO loop repetitively while a condition is true.
- The value of expression is evaluated at the top of the loop.
- The statements in the loop never execute if expression is initially false.

44

7.04 Quiz

How can you generate the same result with a DO WHILE statement?

```
data invest;
   do until(Capital>1000000);
      Year+1;
      Capital+5000;
      Capital+(Capital*.045);
   end;
run;

proc print data=invest noobs;
   format capital dollar14.2;
run;
```

45 p207a02

Using DO WHILE with an Iterative DO Loop

Determine the value of the account again. Stop the loop if 30 years is reached or more than $250,000 is accumulated.

```
data invest;
   do Year=1 to 30 while(Capital<=250000);
      Capital+5000;
      Capital+(Capital*.045);
   end;
run;
proc print data=invest noobs;
   format capital dollar14.2;
run;
```

DO *index-variable=start* TO *stop* <BY *increment*> **WHILE | UNTIL** (*expression*);

PROC PRINT Output

Year	Capital
28	$264,966.67

47

p207d07

Using DO UNTIL with an Iterative DO Loop

Determine the value of the account again, but this time use a DO UNTIL statement.

```
data invest;
   do Year=1 to 30 until(Capital>250000);
      Capital+5000;
      Capital+(Capital*.045);
   end;
run;
proc print data=invest noobs;
   format capital dollar14.2;
run;
```

In a DO UNTIL loop, the condition is checked *before* the index variable is incremented.

PROC PRINT Output

Year	Capital
27	$264,966.67

48

p207d07

Business Scenario

Create one observation per year for five years, and show the earnings if you invest $5,000 per year with 4.5 percent annual interest compounded ***quarterly***.

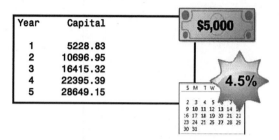

Year	Capital
1	5228.83
2	10696.95
3	16415.32
4	22395.39
5	28649.15

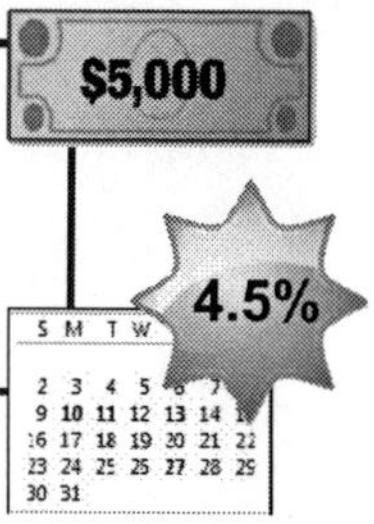

49

Nested DO Loops

DO index-variable-1=*start* TO *stop* <BY *increment*>;
  DO *index-variable-2=start* TO *stop* <BY *increment*>;
    <*additional SAS statements*>
  END;
END;

```
data invest(drop=Quarter);
   do Year=1 to 5;
      Capital+5000;
      do Quarter=1 to 4;
         Capital+(Capital*(.045/4));
      end;
      output;
   end;
run;
```

5x 4x

50 p207d08

7.05 Quiz

How can you generate one observation for each quarterly amount?

```
data invest(drop=Quarter);
   do Year=1 to 5;
      Capital+5000;
      do Quarter=1 to 4;
         Capital+(Capital*(.045/4));
      end;
      output;
   end;
run;

proc print data=invest noobs;
run;
```

51

p207a03

Business Scenario

Compare the final results of investing $5,000 a year for five years in three different banks that compound interest quarterly. Assume that each bank has a fixed interest rate, stored in the **orion.banks** data set.

Listing of **orion.banks**

Name	Rate
Carolina Bank and Trust	0.0318
State Savings Bank	0.0321
National Savings and Trust	0.0328

53

Using Nested DO Loops with a SET Statement

```
data invest(drop=Quarter Year);
   set orion.banks;
   Capital=0;
   do Year=1 to 5;
      Capital+5000;
      do Quarter=1 to 4;
         Capital+(Capital*(Rate/4));
      end;
   end;
run;
```

3x 5x 4x

There are three observations in **orion.banks**. Therefore, there are three iterations of the DATA step. **Capital** must be set to zero on each iteration of the DATA step.

54 p207d09

Execution: Nested DO Loops

```
data invest(drop=Quarter Year);
   set orion.banks;
   Capital=0;
   do Year=1 to 5;
      Capital+5000;
      do Quarter=1 to 4;
         Capital+(Capital*(Rate/4));
      end;
   end;
run;
```

First DATA step iteration

0.0318

Partial PDV

Name	Rate	_N_
Carolina Bank and Trust	**0.0318**	**1**

55 ...

Execution: Nested DO Loops

```
data invest(drop=Quarter Year);
   set orion.banks;
   Capital=0;
   do Year=1 to 5;
      Capital+5000;
      do Quarter=1 to 4;
         Capital+(Capital*(Rate/4));
      end;
   end;
run;
```

Second DATA step iteration

0.0321

Partial PDV

Name	Rate	_N_
State Savings Bank	0.0321	2

56 ...

Execution: Nested DO Loops

```
data invest(drop=Quarter Year);
   set orion.banks;
   Capital=0;
   do Year=1 to 5;
      Capital+5000;
      do Quarter=1 to 4;
         Capital+(Capital*(Rate/4));
      end;
   end;
run;
```

Third DATA step iteration

0.0328

Partial PDV

Name	Rate	_N_
National Savings and Trust	0.0328	3

57

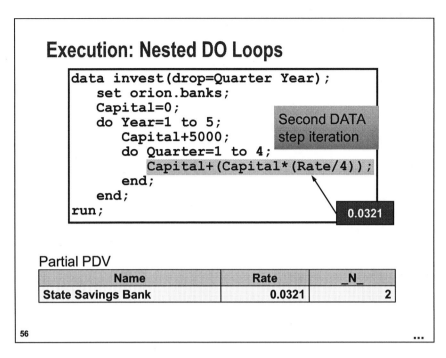

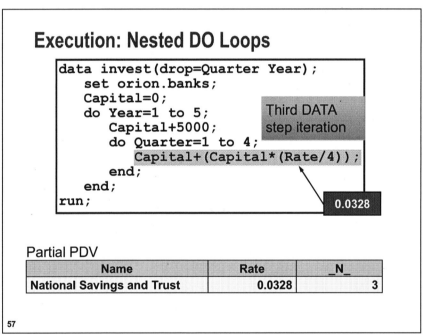

Output: Nested DO Loops

```
proc print data=invest noobs;
run;
```

PROC PRINT Output

Name	Rate	Capital
Carolina Bank and Trust	0.0318	27519.69
State Savings Bank	0.0321	27544.79
National Savings and Trust	0.0328	27603.47

58

Exercises

If you restarted your SAS session since the last exercise, open and submit the **libname.sas** program found in the data folder.

Level 1

2. Performing Computations with Conditional DO Loops

The Orion Star Payroll Department must project total employee costs (wages, retirement benefits, and medical benefits) through future years, based on assumed increases.

a. Corporate income for last year was $50,000,000. Income is projected to increase at one % per year.

Modify the previous program **p207e02** so that the DO loop stops when the year's total costs exceed the year's income.

b. Print **Year**, **Income**, and **Total_Cost** and verify that total costs exceed income after 26 observations.

PROC PRINT Output

Obs	Year	Income	Total_Cost
1	2013	50,500,000.00	16,146,805.00
2	2014	51,005,000.00	17,058,159.57
3	2015	51,515,050.00	18,025,405.76
4	2016	52,030,200.50	19,052,105.42
	...		

26	2038	64,762,815.75	67,973,189.29

The results above were generated on February 14, 2012. Your values for **Year** might differ.

Level 2

3. Using an Iterative DO Statement with a Conditional Clause

Orion's income last year was $50,000,000 and expenses totaled $38,750,000. Income is projected to increase at 1% per year and expenses are expected to increase at 2% per year.

a. Create a SAS data set named **work.expenses** that contains each year's projected income and expenses.

- Use an iterative DO statement with a conditional clause.
- Stop the loop when expenses exceed income or after 30 years, whichever comes first.

b. Print the results and format **Income** and **Expenses** with a dollar sign and two decimal places.

Hint: Recall that an iterative DO statement with a conditional clause produces different results with DO WHILE and DO UNTIL statements. The results below were generated using a DO UNTIL statement.

PROC PRINT Output

Obs	Income	Expenses	Year
1	$64,762,815.75	$64,844,951.93	26

Challenge

4. Using Other Loop Control Statements

Orion's income last year was $50,000,000 and expenses totaled $38,750,000. Income is projected to increase at 1% per year and expenses are expected to increase at 2% per year.

a. Use an iterative DO statement to calculate projected income and expenses for the next 75 years.

- Investigate SAS documentation for information about other loop control statements such as CONTINUE and LEAVE.
- Include the appropriate loop control statement (CONTINUE/LEAVE) to stop the loop when expenses exceed income.

b. Print the results and format the values of **Income** and **Expenses** with dollar signs and two decimal places.

Hint: Recall that the DO WHILE and DO UNTIL statements might produce different results.

PROC PRINT Output

Obs	Income	Expenses	Year
1	$64,762,815.75	$64,844,951.93	26

7.3 SAS Array Processing

Objectives

- Explain the concepts of SAS arrays.
- Use SAS arrays to perform repetitive calculations.

62

Array Processing

You can use arrays to simplify programs that do the following:

- perform repetitive calculations
- create many variables with the same attributes
- read data
- compare variables
- perform a table lookup

63

7.06 Quiz

Do you have experience with arrays in a programming language? If so, which languages?

64

Business Scenario

The **orion.employee_donations** data set contains quarterly contribution data for each employee. Orion management is considering a 25% matching program. Calculate each employee's quarterly contribution, including the proposed company supplement.

Partial Listing of **orion.employee_donations**

Employee_ID	Qtr1	Qtr2	Qtr3	Qtr4
120265	.	.	.	25
120267	15	15	15	15
120269	20	20	20	20
120270	20	10	5	.
120271	20	20	20	20
120272	10	10	10	10

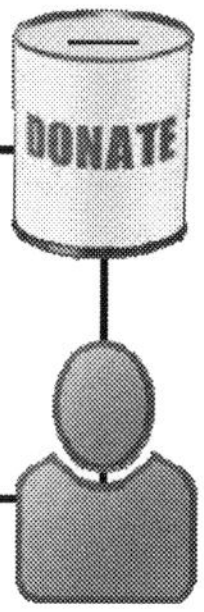

65

Performing Repetitive Calculations

```
data charity;
   set orion.employee_donations;
   keep employee_id qtr1-qtr4;
   Qtr1=Qtr1*1.25;
   Qtr2=Qtr2*1.25;
   Qtr3=Qtr3*1.25;
   Qtr4=Qtr4*1.25;
run;
proc print data=charity noobs;
run;
```

Partial PROC PRINT Output

Employee_ID	Qtr1	Qtr2	Qtr3	Qtr4
120265	.	.	.	31.25
120267	18.75	18.75	18.75	18.75
120269	25.00	25.00	25.00	25.00
120270	25.00	12.50	6.25	.

66

p207d10

Performing Repetitive Calculations

The four calculations cannot be replaced by a single calculation inside a DO loop because they are not identical.

```
data charity;
   set orion.employee_donations;
   keep employee_id qtr1-qtr4;
   Qtr1=Qtr1*1.25;
   Qtr2=Qtr2*1.25;
   Qtr3=Qtr3*1.25;
   Qtr4=Qtr4*1.25;
run;
proc print data=charity noobs;
run;
```

```
do i=1 to 4;
   ?
end;
```

A SAS array can be used to simplify this code.

67

Use Arrays to Simplify Repetitive Calculations

An array provides an alternate way to access values in the PDV, which simplifies repetitive calculations.

```
data charity;
   set orion.employee_donations;
   keep employee_id qtr1-qtr4;
   Qtr1=Qtr1*1.25;
   Qtr2=Qtr2*1.25;
   Qtr3=Qtr3*1.25;
   Qtr4=Qtr4*1.25;
run;
proc print data=charity noobs;
run;
```

An array can be used to access Qtr1-Qtr4.

PDV

Employee_ ID	Qtr1	Qtr2	Qtr3	Qtr4

68

What Is a SAS Array?

A *SAS array*

- is a temporary grouping of SAS variables that are arranged in a particular order
- is identified by an *array name*
- must contain all numeric or all character variables
- exists only for the duration of the current DATA step
- is ***not*** a variable.

69

Why Use a SAS Array?

Create an array named **Contrib** and use it to access the four numeric variables, **Qtr1 – Qtr4**.

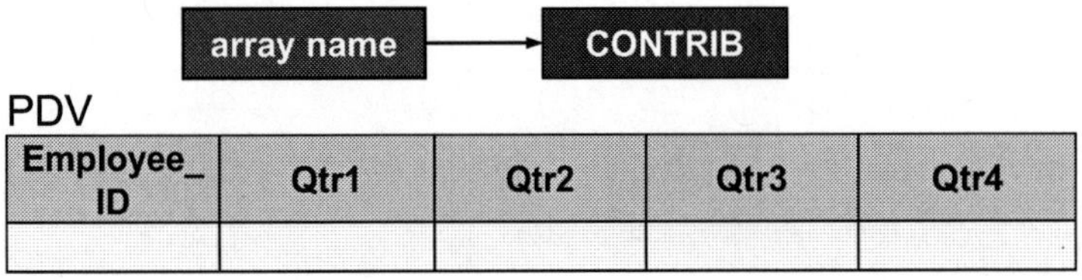

70

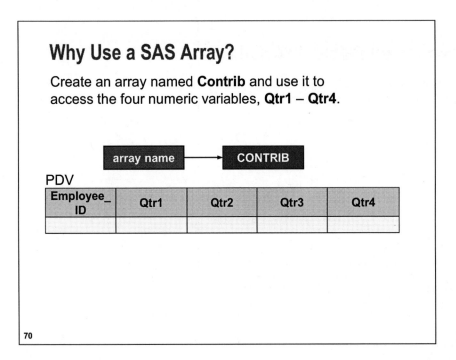

SAS arrays are different from arrays in many other programming languages. In SAS, an array is ***not*** a data structure. It is simply a convenient way of temporarily identifying a group of variables.

Array Elements

Each value in an array is called an *element.*

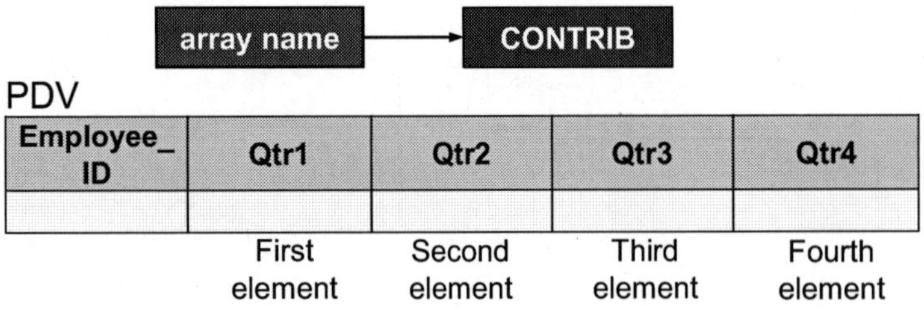

71

Referencing Array Elements

Each element is identified by a *subscript* that represents its position in the array. When you use an *array reference*, the corresponding value is substituted for the reference.

PDV

Employee_ ID	Qtr1	Qtr2	Qtr3	Qtr4

Contrib{1} Contrib{2} Contrib{3} Contrib{4}

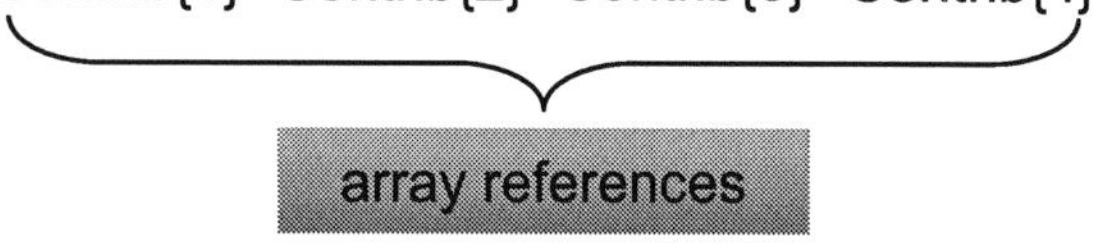

72

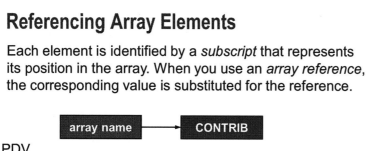

Defining an Array

The ARRAY statement is a compile-time statement that defines the elements in an array.

ARRAY *array-name {subscript}* <$> *<length>*
<array-elements>;

```
array Contrib{4} Qtr1 Qtr2 Qtr3 Qtr4;
```

PDV

Employee_ ID	Qtr1	Qtr2	Qtr3	Qtr4

Contrib{1} Contrib{2} Contrib{3} Contrib{4}

73

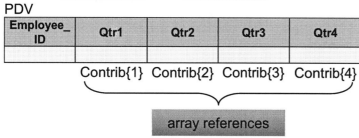

array-name	specifies the name of the array.
{subscript}	describes the number and arrangement of elements in the array by using an asterisk, a number, numbers separated by commas (for multi-dimensional arrays), a range of numbers, or an expression. The *subscript* is enclosed in braces ({}). Brackets ([]) and parentheses (()) are also allowed.
$	indicates that the elements in the array are character elements. The dollar sign is not necessary if the elements in the array were previously defined as character elements.
length	specifies the length of elements in the array that were not previously assigned a length.

array-elements names the elements that make up the array. Array elements can be listed in any order.

Array references cannot be used in compile-time statements such as LABEL, FORMAT, DROP, KEEP, or LENGTH statements.

If you use a function name as the name of the array, SAS treats parenthetical references that involve the name as array references, not function references, for the duration of the DATA step.

The four variables, **Qtr1**, **Qtr2**, **Qtr3**, and **Qtr4**, can now be referenced via the array name **Contrib**, with an appropriate subscript.

Defining an Array

An alternate syntax uses an asterisk instead of a subscript. SAS determines the subscript by counting the variables in the element list. The element list must be included.

```
array Contrib{*} Qtr1 Qtr2 Qtr3 Qtr4;
```

Subscript is 4.

Element list

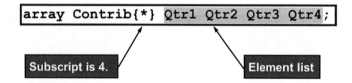

The alternate syntax is often used when the array elements are defined with a SAS variable list.

```
array Contrib{*} Qtr:;
```

74

You can use special SAS name lists to reference variables that were previously defined in the same DATA step. The _CHARACTER_ variable lists character values only. The _NUMERIC_ variable lists numeric values only.

Avoid using the _ALL_ special SAS name list to reference variables, because the elements in an array must be either all character or all numeric values.

Defining an Array

Variables that are elements of an array do not need the following:

- to have similar, related, or numbered names
- to be stored sequentially
- to be adjacent

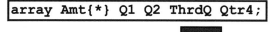

```
array Amt{*} Q1 Q2 ThrdQ Qtr4;
```

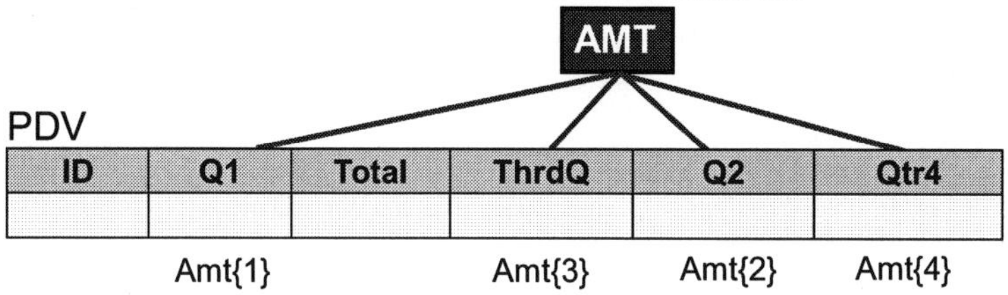

75

7.07 Quiz

Open and submit **p207a04**. View the log to determine the cause of the error.

```
data charity(keep=Employee_ID Qtr1-Qtr4);
   set orion.employee_donations;
   array Contrib1{3} Qtr1-Qtr4;
   array Contrib2{5} qtr:;
   /* additional SAS statements */
run;
```

76 p207a04

Using a DO Loop to Process an Array

```
data charity;
   set orion.employee_donations;
   keep Employee_ID Qtr1-Qtr4;
   array Contrib{4} Qtr1-Qtr4;
   do i=1 to 4;
      Contrib{i}=Contrib{i}*1.25;
   end;
run;
```

DO *index-variable*=1 TO *number-of-elements-in-array*;
<*additional SAS statements*>
END;

To reference an element, the index variable is often used as a subscript: ***array-name*{*index-variable*}**

78 p207d11

To process particular elements of an array, specify those elements as the range of the iterative DO statement.

By default, SAS includes *index-variable* in the output data set. Use a DROP or KEEP statement or the DROP= or KEEP= data set option to prevent the index variable from being written to your output data set.

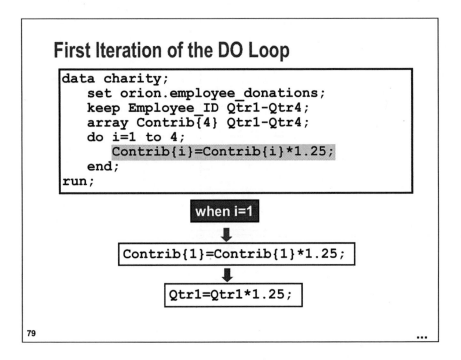

First Iteration of the DO Loop

```
data charity;
   set orion.employee_donations;
   keep Employee_ID Qtr1-Qtr4;
   array Contrib{4} Qtr1-Qtr4;
   do i=1 to 4;
      Contrib{i}=Contrib{i}*1.25;
   end;
run;
```

when i=1

⬇

```
Contrib{1}=Contrib{1}*1.25;
```

⬇

```
Qtr1=Qtr1*1.25;
```

79 ...

Second Iteration of the DO Loop

```
data charity;
   set orion.employee_donations;
   keep Employee_ID Qtr1-Qtr4;
   array Contrib{4} Qtr1-Qtr4;
   do i=1 to 4;
      Contrib{i}=Contrib{i}*1.25;
   end;
run;
```

when i=2

```
Contrib{2}=Contrib{2}*1.25;
```

```
Qtr2=Qtr2*1.25;
```

80 ...

Third Iteration of the DO Loop

```
data charity;
   set orion.employee_donations;
   keep Employee_ID Qtr1-Qtr4;
   array Contrib{4} Qtr1-Qtr4;
   do i=1 to 4;
      Contrib{i}=Contrib{i}*1.25;
   end;
run;
```

when i=3

```
Contrib{3}=Contrib{3}*1.25;
```

```
Qtr3=Qtr3*1.25;
```

81 ...

Fourth Iteration of the DO Loop

```
data charity;
   set orion.employee_donations;
   keep Employee_ID Qtr1-Qtr4;
   array Contrib{4} Qtr1-Qtr4;
   do i=1 to 4;
      Contrib{i}=Contrib{i}*1.25;
   end;
run;
```

when i=4

```
Contrib{4}=Contrib{4}*1.25;
```

```
Qtr4=Qtr4*1.25;
```

82

Output: Using a Do Loop to Process an Array

```
proc print data=charity noobs;
run;
```

Partial PROC PRINT Output

Employee_ID	Qtr1	Qtr2	Qtr3	Qtr4
120265	.	.	.	31.25
120267	18.75	18.75	18.75	18.75
120269	25.00	25.00	25.00	25.00
120270	25.00	12.50	6.25	.
120271	25.00	25.00	25.00	25.00
120272	12.50	12.50	12.50	12.50
120275	18.75	18.75	18.75	18.75
120660	31.25	31.25	31.25	31.25
120662	12.50	.	6.25	6.25

83

Exercises

If you restarted your SAS session since the last exercise, open and submit the **libname.sas** program found in the data folder.

Level 1

5. Using Arrays for Repetitive Computations

Monthly customer order data for the first half of the year is stored in the data set **orion.orders_midyear**. The Orion Star Sales manager is considering a 5% price decrease next year. The manager wants to see how such a discount would affect this year's income.

Partial **orion.orders_midyear**

Obs	Customer_ID	Month1	Month2	Month3	Month4	Month5	Month6
1	5	213.10	.	478.0	525.80	394.35	191.79
2	10	188.10	414.09	2876.9	3164.59	2373.44	169.29
3	11	78.20	.	.	.	.	70.38
4	12	135.60	.	117.6	129.36	97.02	122.04
5	18	.	.	29.4	32.34	24.26	.
6	24	93.00	265.80	.	.	.	83.70
7	27	310.70	782.90	.	.	.	279.63
8	31	1484.30	293.30	.	.	.	1335.87
9	34	642.50	.	86.3	94.93	71.20	578.25
10	41	134.00	119.20	313.0	344.30	258.23	120.60
11	45	443.88	216.20	40.2	44.22	33.17	399.49
12	49	24.80	.	.	.	.	22.32

a. Create a data set, **discount_sales**, to reflect the 5% discount.

- Create an array, **Mon**, to access **Month1** through **Month6**.
- Use a DO loop to adjust each customer's monthly data. Apply the 5% discount.

b. Print the resulting data set and verify your results.

- Add an appropriate title.
- Use the DOLLAR format for the monthly sales amounts.

Partial PROC PRINT Output (24 Total Observations)

Monthly Sales with 5% Discount

Customer_ID	Month1	Month2	Month3	Month4	Month5	Month6
5	$202.45	.	$454.10	$499.51	$374.63	$182.20
10	$178.70	$393.39	$2,733.06	$3,006.36	$2,254.77	$160.83
11	$74.29	.	.	.	.	$66.86
12	$128.82	.	$111.72	$122.89	$92.17	$115.94
18	.	.	$27.93	$30.72	$23.04	.

Level 2

6. Using Arrays for Repetitive Computations

Monthly customer order data for the first half of the year is stored in the data set **orion.orders_midyear**. Orion Star Sales management is considering a 10% price decrease during the first three months of the upcoming year. Management wants to see how such a discount would affect this year's sales.

Partial **orion.orders_midyear**

Customer_ID	Month1	Month2	Month3	Month4	Month5	Month6
5	213.10	.	478.0	525.80	394.35	191.79
10	188.10	414.09	2876.9	3164.59	2373.44	169.29
11	78.20	.	.	.	.	70.38
12	135.60	.	117.6	129.36	97.02	122.04
18	.	.	29.4	32.34	24.26	.

a. Create a data set, **special_offer**, including the 10% discount in months 1 through 3.

- Create an array, **Mon**, to access **Month1** through **Month3**.
- Use a DO loop to adjust each customer's monthly data to include the 10% discount (**Month1** through **Month3** only).
- Create three new variables:
  - **Total_Sales** – the total of current sales over the six months
  - **Projected_Sales** – the total of the adjusted sales over the six months (including the three discounted months)
  - **Difference** – the difference between **Total_Sales** and **Projected_Sales**
- Keep only the new variables: **Total_Sales**, **Projected_Sales**, and **Difference**.

b. Print the resulting data set and verify your results.

- Suppress the session start date, page number, and observation column.
- Add an appropriate title.
- Use the SUM statement to display a total for the **Difference** variable.
- Use the DOLLAR. format for all variables.

Partial PROC PRINT Output (24 Total Observations)

```
                 Total Sales with 10% Discount in First Three Months

                              Total_      Projected_
                               Sales         Sales        Difference

                           $1,803.04     $1,733.93          $69.11
                           $9,186.41     $8,838.50         $347.91
                             $148.58       $140.76           $7.82
                             $601.62       $576.30          $25.32
                               ...
                           $1,518.95     $1,467.02          $51.93
                                                        ==========
                                                         $1,550.74
```

Challenge

7. Terminating a DATA Step

Monthly order data for the first half of the year is stored in the **orion.orders_midyear** data set. This data set is updated monthly and can contain data for 1 to 12 months.

Partial **orion.orders_midyear**

Obs	Customer_ID	Month1	Month2	Month3	Month4	Month5	Month6

1	5	213.10	.	478.0	525.80	394.35	191.79
2	10	188.10	414.09	2876.9	3164.59	2373.44	169.29
3	11	78.20	.	.	.	.	70.38
4	12	135.60	.	117.6	129.36	97.02	122.04
5	18	.	.	29.4	32.34	24.26	.

a. Orion Star decided to create a Frequent Shopper Program (FSP). The company wants to invite customers who placed orders in 50% of the months to date (assuming at least three months of data exist for that year), and who spent at least $1000 since the beginning of the year.

- Open the input data set and verify that it contains at least three months of data.
- If there is less than three months, write a message to the SAS log and stop the DATA step immediately.
- If there are at least three months of data in the data set, create an array, **Mon**, to access the **Month*n*** variables, regardless of how many **Month*n*** variables exist in the data set.
  Hint: Consider using a SAS variable list to list the array elements.
- Use a DO loop to examine each customer's data to determine whether the customer qualifies for the Frequent Shopper Program.
- Create a new data set, **fsp**, that contains an observation for each qualifying customer.
- Use the report below to determine which variables to drop or keep.

Hint: Use SAS documentation to investigate the use of the STOP statement and the DIM function.

b. Print the resulting data set with an appropriate title and formats, and verify your results.

Partial PROC PRINT Output (11 Total Observations)

orion.orders_midyear: Frequent Shoppers

Obs	Customer_ID	Total_ Order_ Amount	Months_ Ordered
1	5	$1,803.04	5
2	10	$9,186.41	6
3	27	$1,373.23	3
4	31	$3,113.47	3
5	34	$1,473.18	5

c. Test your program using **orion.orders_qtr1**.

PROC PRINT Output

orion.orders_qtr1: Frequent Shoppers

Obs	Customer_ID	Total_ Order_ Amount	Months_ Ordered
1	10	$3,479.09	3
2	27	$1,093.60	2
3	31	$1,777.60	2
4	171	$1,849.99	3
5	2806	$1,506.90	3

d. Test your program using **orion.orders_two_months**.

Partial SAS Log

```
Insufficient data for Frequent Shopper Program
NOTE: There were 1 observations read from the data set ORION.ORDERS_TWO_MONTHS.
NOTE: The data set WORK.FSP has 0 observations and 3 variables.
NOTE: DATA statement used (Total process time):

1066
1067  title 'orion.orders_two_months: Frequent Shoppers ';
1068  proc print data=fsp;
1069     format total_order_amount dollar10.2;
1070  run;

NOTE: No observations in data set WORK.FSP.
```

7.4 Using SAS Arrays

Objectives

- Use arrays as arguments to SAS functions.
- Explain array functions.
- Use arrays to create new variables.
- Use arrays to perform a table lookup.

87

Using an Array as a Function Argument

The program below passes an array to the SUM function.

```
data test;
   set orion.employee_donations;
   array val{4} Qtr1-Qtr4;
   Tot1=sum(of Qtr1-Qtr4);
   Tot2=sum(of val{*});
run;
proc print data=test;
   var Employee_ID Tot1 Tot2;
run;
```

The array is passed as if it were a variable list.

Partial PROC PRINT Output

Obs	Employee_ID	Tot1	Tot2
1	120265	25	25
2	120267	60	60
3	120269	80	80

88 p207d13

DIM Function

The DIM function returns the number of elements in an array. This value is often used as the stop value in a DO loop.

```
data charity;
   set orion.employee_donations;
   keep Employee_ID Qtr1-Qtr4;
   array Contrib{*} qtr:;
   do i=1 to dim(Contrib);
      Contrib{i}=Contrib{i}*1.25;
   end;
run;
```

DIM(*array_name*)

89 p207d12

The HBOUND function returns the upper bound of an array. The LBOUND function returns the lower bound of an array. The following DO loop processes every element in an array:

```
do i=lbound(items) to hbound(items);
   *process items{i};
end;
```

In most arrays, subscripts range from 1 to *n*, where *n* is the number of elements in the array. The value 1 is a convenient lower bound. Thus, you do not need to specify the lower bound. However, specifying both bounds is useful when the array dimensions have a beginning point other than 1. For example, the following ARRAY statement defines an array of 10 elements, with subscripts that range from 5 to 14:

```
array items{5:14} n5-n14;
```

Using an Array to Create Numeric Variables

An ARRAY statement can be used to create new variables in the program data vector.

```
array Pct{4} Pct1-Pct4;
```

If **Pct1** through **Pct4** do not exist in the PDV, they are created.

This statement produces the same results:

```
array Pct{4};
```

PDV

Pct1 N 8	Pct2 N 8	Pct3 N 8	Pct4 N 8

91

Using an Array to Create Character Variables

Define an array named **Month** to create six variables to hold character values with a length of 10.

```
array Month{6} $ 10;
```

PDV

Month1 $ 10	Month2 $ 10	Month3 $ 10	Month4 $ 10	Month5 $ 10	Month6 $ 10

92

Business Scenario

Using **orion.employee_donations** as input, calculate the percentage that each quarterly contribution represents of the employee's total annual contribution. Create four new variables to hold the percentages.

Employee_ID	Qtr1	Qtr2	Qtr3	Qtr4
120265	.	.	.	25
120267	15	15	15	15

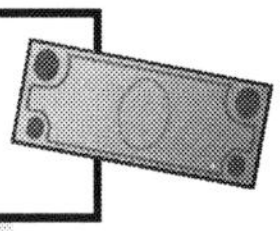

Employee_ID	Percent1	Percent2	Percent3	Percent4
120265	.	.	.	100%
120267	25%	25%	25%	25%

%

93

Creating Variables with Arrays

```
data percent(drop=i);
   set orion.employee_donations;
   array Contrib{4} Qtr1-Qtr4;
   array Percent{4};
   Total=sum(of contrib{*});
   do i=1 to 4;
      percent{i}=contrib{i}/total;
   end;
run;
```

The second ARRAY statement creates four numeric variables: **Percent1**, **Percent2**, **Percent3**, and **Percent4**.

94 p207d14

The first ARRAY statement uses the existing variables **Qtr1**, **Qtr2**, **Qtr3**, and **Qtr4**. In that ARRAY statement, a numbered range SAS variable list is used.

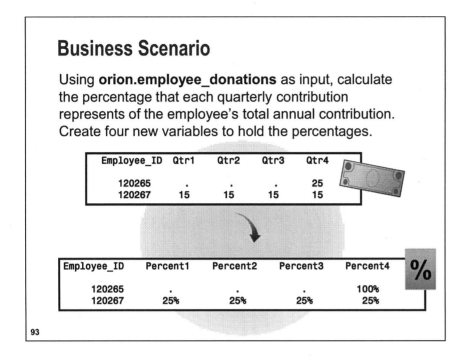

Output: Creating Variables with Arrays

```
proc print data=percent noobs;
   var Employee_ID Percent1-Percent4;
   format Percent1-Percent4 percent6.;
run;
```

Partial PROC PRINT Output (124 Total Observations)

Employee_ID	Percent1	Percent2	Percent3	Percent4
120265	.	.	.	100%
120267	25%	25%	25%	25%
120269	25%	25%	25%	25%
120270	57%	29%	14%	.
120271	25%	25%	25%	25%
120272	25%	25%	25%	25%
120275	25%	25%	25%	25%
120660	25%	25%	25%	25%
120662	50%	.	25%	25%
120663	.	.	100%	.
120668	25%	25%	25%	25%

95

The PERCENT*w.d* format multiplies values by 100, formats them in the same way as the BEST*w.d* format, and adds a percent sign (%) to the end of the formatted value. Negative values are enclosed in parentheses. The PERCENT*w.d* format provides room for a percent sign and parentheses, even if the value is not negative.

Business Scenario

Using **orion.employee_donations** as input, calculate the difference in each employee's contribution from one quarter to the next.

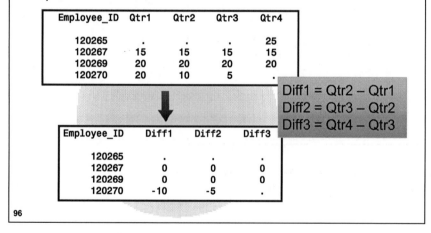

Employee_ID	Qtr1	Qtr2	Qtr3	Qtr4
120265	.	.	.	25
120267	15	15	15	15
120269	20	20	20	20
120270	20	10	5	.

Diff1 = Qtr2 – Qtr1
Diff2 = Qtr3 – Qtr2
Diff3 = Qtr4 – Qtr3

Employee_ID	Diff1	Diff2	Diff3
120265	.	.	.
120267	0	0	0
120269	0	0	0
120270	-10	-5	.

96

7.08 Quiz

How many ARRAY statements would you use to calculate the difference in each employee's contribution from one quarter to the next?

Partial **orion.employee_donations**

Employee_ID	Qtr1	Qtr2	Qtr3	Qtr4
120265	.	.	.	25
120267	15	15	15	15
120269	20	20	20	20

First difference: Qtr2 – Qtr1
Second difference: Qtr3 – Qtr2
Third difference: Qtr4 – Qtr3

97

Creating Variables with Arrays

```
data change;
   set orion.employee_donations;
   drop i;
   array Contrib{4} Qtr1-Qtr4;
   array Diff{3};
   do i=1 to 3;
      Diff{i}=Contrib{i+1}-Contrib{i};
   end;
run;
```

The **Contrib** array refers to existing variables. The **Diff** array creates three variables: **Diff1**, **Diff2**, and **Diff3**.

99 p207d15

Creating Variables with Arrays

```
data change;
   set orion.employee_donations;
   drop i;
   array Contrib{4} Qtr1-Qtr4;
   array Diff{3};
   do i=1 to 3;
      Diff{i}=Contrib{i+1}-Contrib{i};
   end;
run;
```

when i=1

```
Diff{1}=Contrib{2}-Contrib{1};
```

```
Diff1=Qtr2-Qtr1;
```

100

...

Creating Variables with Arrays

```
data change;
   set orion.employee_donations;
   drop i;
   array Contrib{4} Qtr1-Qtr4;
   array Diff{3};
   do i=1 to 3;
      Diff{i}=Contrib{i+1}-Contrib{i};
   end;
run;
```

when i=2

```
Diff{2}=Contrib{3}-Contrib{2};
```

```
Diff2=Qtr3-Qtr2;
```

101

...

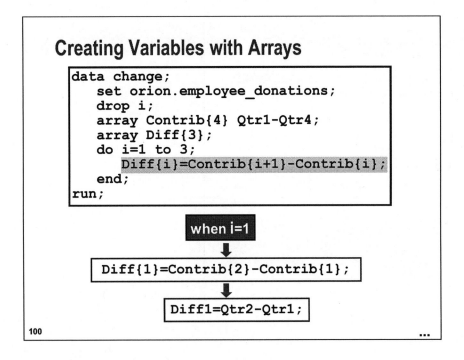

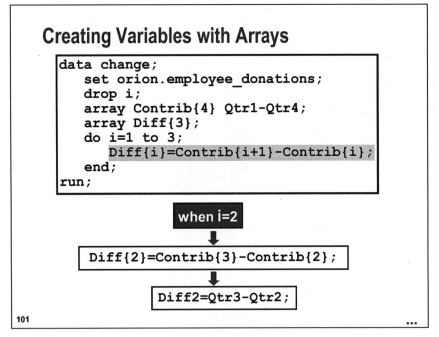

Creating Variables with Arrays

```
data change;
   set orion.employee_donations;
   drop i;
   array Contrib{4} Qtr1-Qtr4;
   array Diff{3};
   do i=1 to 3;
      Diff{i}=Contrib{i+1}-Contrib{i};
   end;
run;
```

when i=3

```
Diff{3}=Contrib{4}-Contrib{3};
```

```
Diff3=Qtr4-Qtr3;
```

102

Creating Variables with Arrays

```
proc print data=change noobs;
   var Employee_ID Diff1-Diff3;
run;
```

Partial PROC PRINT Output (124 Total Observations)

Employee_ID	Diff1	Diff2	Diff3
120265	.	.	.
120267	0	0	0
120269	0	0	0
120270	-10	-5	.
120271	0	0	0
120272	0	0	0
120275	0	0	0
120660	0	0	0
120662	.	.	0

103

Business Scenario

Determine the difference between employee contributions and the quarterly goals of $10, $20, $20, and $15. Use a lookup table to store the quarterly goals.

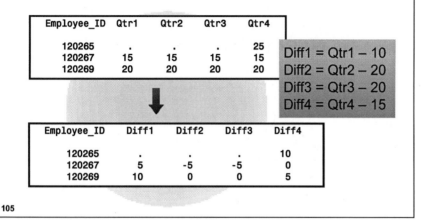

Employee_ID	Qtr1	Qtr2	Qtr3	Qtr4
120265	.	.	.	25
120267	15	15	15	15
120269	20	20	20	20

Diff1 = Qtr1 – 10
Diff2 = Qtr2 – 20
Diff3 = Qtr3 – 20
Diff4 = Qtr4 – 15

Employee_ID	Diff1	Diff2	Diff3	Diff4
120265	.	.	.	10
120267	5	-5	-5	0
120269	10	0	0	5

105

Assigning Initial Values to an Array

When the initial value list is specified, all elements behave as if they were named in a RETAIN statement. This is often used to create a *lookup table*, that is, a list of values to refer to during DATA step processing.

ARRAY *array-name* {*subscript*} <$> <*length*>
<*array-elements*> <(*initial-value-list*)>;

```
array Target{5} (50,100,125,150,200);
```

PDV

R Target1 N 8	R Target2 N 8	R Target3 N 8	R Target4 N 8	R Target5 N 8
50	100	125	150	200

106

(*initial-value-list*) lists the initial values for the corresponding array elements. The values for elements can be numbers or character strings. Character strings must be enclosed in quotation marks.

Elements and values are matched by position. If there are more array elements than initial values, the remaining array elements are assigned missing values and SAS issues a warning.

Compilation: What Variables Are Created?

```
data compare(drop=i Goal1-Goal4);
   set orion.employee_donations;
   array Contrib{4} Qtr1-Qtr4;
   array Diff{4};
   array Goal{4} (10,20,20,15);
   do i=1 to 4;
      Diff{i}=Contrib{i}-Goal{i};
   end;
run;
```

Partial PDV

Employee_ ID	Qtr1	Qtr2	Qtr3	Qtr4

107 p207d16

Compilation: What Variables Are Created?

```
data compare(drop=i Goal1-Goal4);
   set orion.employee_donations;
   array Contrib{4} Qtr1-Qtr4;
   array Diff{4};
   array Goal{4} (10,20,20,15);
   do i=1 to 4;
      Diff{i}=Contrib{i}-Goal{i};
   end;
run;
```

No variables created

Partial PDV

Employee_ ID	Qtr1	Qtr2	Qtr3	Qtr4

108 ...

Compilation: What Variables Are Created?

```
data compare(drop=i Goal1-Goal4);
   set orion.employee_donations;
   array Contrib{4} Qtr1-Qtr4;
   array Diff{4};
   array Goal{4} (10,20,20,15);
   do i=1 to 4;
      Diff{i}=Contrib{i}-Goal{i};
   end;
run;
```

Partial PDV

Employee_ ID	Qtr1	Qtr2	Qtr3	Qtr4	Diff1

Diff2	Diff3	Diff4

109

...

Compilation: What Variables Are Created?

```
data compare(drop=i Goal1-Goal4);
   set orion.employee_donations;
   array Contrib{4} Qtr1-Qtr4;
   array Diff{4};
   array Goal{4} (10,20,20,15);
   do i=1 to 4;
      Diff{i}=Contrib{i}-Goal{i};
   end;
run;
```

Partial PDV

Employee_ ID	Qtr1	Qtr2	Qtr3	Qtr4	Diff1

Diff2	Diff3	Diff4	Goal1	Goal2	Goal3	Goal4

110

...

Compilation: What Variables Are Created?

```
data compare(drop=i Goal1-Goal4);
   set orion.employee_donations;
   array Contrib{4} Qtr1-Qtr4;
   array Diff{4};
   array Goal{4} (10,20,20,15);
   do i=1 to 4;
      Diff{i}=Contrib{i}-Goal{i};
   end;
run;
```

Partial PDV

Employee_ ID	Qtr1	Qtr2	Qtr3	Qtr4	Diff1

Diff2	Diff3	Diff4	Goal1	Goal2	Goal3	Goal4	i

111 ...

Compilation: Drop Flags Are Set

```
data compare(drop=i Goal1-Goal4);
   set orion.employee_donations;
   array Contrib{4} Qtr1-Qtr4;
   array Diff{4};
   array Goal{4} (10,20,20,15);
   do i=1 to 4;
      Diff{i}=Contrib{i}-Goal{i};
   end;
run;
```

Partial PDV

Employee_ ID	Qtr1	Qtr2	Qtr3	Qtr4	Diff1

Diff2	Diff3	Diff4	D Goal1	D Goal2	D Goal3	D Goal4	D i

112 ...

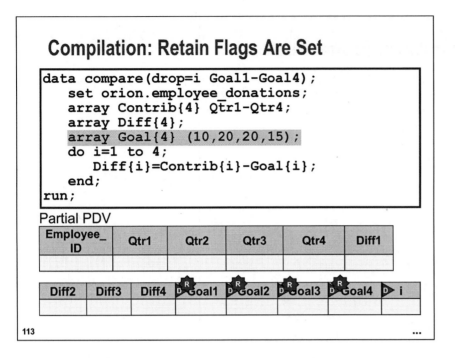

Compilation: Retain Flags Are Set

```
data compare(drop=i Goal1-Goal4);
   set orion.employee_donations;
   array Contrib{4} Qtr1-Qtr4;
   array Diff{4};
   array Goal{4} (10,20,20,15);
   do i=1 to 4;
      Diff{i}=Contrib{i}-Goal{i};
   end;
run;
```

Partial PDV

Employee_ ID	Qtr1	Qtr2	Qtr3	Qtr4	Diff1

Diff2	Diff3	Diff4	D R Goal1	D R Goal2	D R Goal3	D R Goal4	D i

113 ...

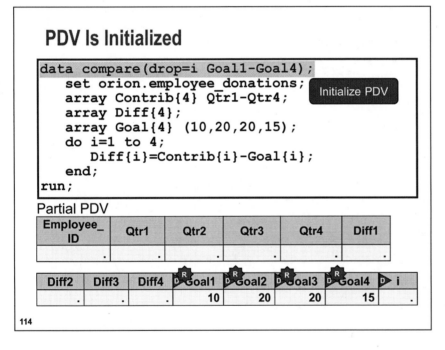

PDV Is Initialized

```
data compare(drop=i Goal1-Goal4);
   set orion.employee_donations;
   array Contrib{4} Qtr1-Qtr4;
   array Diff{4};
   array Goal{4} (10,20,20,15);
   do i=1 to 4;
      Diff{i}=Contrib{i}-Goal{i};
   end;
run;
```

Initialize PDV

Partial PDV

Employee_ ID	Qtr1	Qtr2	Qtr3	Qtr4	Diff1
.	.	.	.	.	.

Diff2	Diff3	Diff4	D R Goal1	D R Goal2	D R Goal3	D R Goal4	D i
.	.	.	10	20	20	15	.

114

Creating a Temporary Lookup Table

You can use the keyword _TEMPORARY_ in an ARRAY statement to indicate that the elements are not needed in the output data set.

```
data compare(drop=i);
   set orion.employee_donations;
   array Contrib{4} Qtr1-Qtr4;
   array Diff{4};
   array Goal{4} _temporary_ (10,20,20,15);
   do i=1 to 4;
      Diff{i}=Contrib{i}-Goal{i};
   end;
run;
```

115 p207d17

You can save memory if you do not need to access the individual array element variables by name, but the only way that you can access the array elements is by array subscripting. Arrays of temporary elements are useful when the only purpose for creating an array is to perform a calculation. To preserve the result of the calculation, assign it to a variable.

Output: Creating a Temporary Lookup Table

```
proc print data=compare noobs;
   var employee_id diff1-diff4;
run;
```

Partial PROC PRINT Output (124 Total Observations)

Employee_ID	Diff1	Diff2	Diff3	Diff4
120265	.	.	.	10
120267	5	-5	-5	0
120269	10	0	0	5
120270	10	-10	-15	.
120271	10	0	0	5

What can be done to ignore missing values?

116

The SUM Function Ignores Missing Values

The SUM function ignores missing values. It can be used to calculate the difference between the quarterly contribution and the corresponding goal.

```
data compare(drop=i);
   set orion.employee_donations;
   array Contrib{4} Qtr1-Qtr4;
   array Diff{4};
   array Goal{4} _temporary_ (10,20,20,15);
   do i=1 to 4;
      Diff{i}=sum(Contrib{i},-Goal{i});
   end;
run;
```

117 p207d18

Output: Lookup Table Application

```
proc print data=compare noobs;
   var employee_id diff1-diff4;
run;
```

Partial PROC PRINT Output (124 Total Observations)

Employee_ID	Diff1	Diff2	Diff3	Diff4
120265	-10	-20	-20	10
120267	5	-5	-5	0
120269	10	0	0	5
120270	10	-10	-15	-15
120271	10	0	0	5

The missing values were handled as if no contribution were made for that quarter.

118

7.09 Quiz

Using pencil and paper, write an ARRAY statement to define a temporary lookup table named **Country** with three elements, each two characters long. Initialize the elements to *AU*, *NZ*, and *US*. Refer to the syntax below.

ARRAY *array-name* {*subscript*} <$> <*length*>
<*array-elements*> <(*initial-value-list*)>;

119

Exercises

If you restarted your SAS session since the last exercise, open and submit the **libname.sas** program found in the data folder.

Level 1

8. Using an Array for Table Lookup

The manager of the Sales Department wants to identify preferred customers for an upcoming promotion. Use the **orion.orders_midyear** data set and a lookup table to create a new data set, **preferred_cust**.

Partial **orion.orders_midyear**

Customer_ID	Month1	Month2	Month3	Month4	Month5	Month6
5	213.10	.	478.0	525.80	394.35	191.79
10	188.10	414.09	2876.9	3164.59	2373.44	169.29
11	78.20	.	.	.	.	70.38
12	135.60	.	117.6	129.36	97.02	122.04
18	.	.	29.4	32.34	24.26	.

a. Open the file **p207e07** and make the following changes:

- Create a temporary lookup table, **Target**, to hold the target sales amount for each month:
  200, 400, 300, 100, 100, 200
- Create new variables, **Over1**, **Over2**, …,**Over6**, to hold the amount that a customer spent above the corresponding month's target.

- Use a DO loop to calculate the values of **Over1** through **Over6** when the corresponding month's sales amount exceeds the target.

  ✎ If the sales did not exceed the target for a given month, then do not perform this calculation.

- Store the sum of **Over1** through **Over6** in another new variable, **Total_Over**.
- Write an observation only if **Total_Over** is greater than 500.
- The new data set should include only **Customer_ID**, **Over1** through **Over6**, and **Total_Over**.

b. Print the new data set and verify your results.

Partial PROC PRINT Output (9 Total Observations)

Customer_ID	Over1	Over2	Over3	Over4	Over5	Over6	Total_ Over
5	13.1	.	178.0	425.80	294.35	.	911.25
10	.	14.09	2576.9	3064.59	2273.44	.	7929.02
27	110.7	382.90	.	.	.	79.63	573.23
31	1284.3	.	.	.	.	1135.87	2420.17
34	442.5	.	.	.	.	378.25	820.75

Level 2

9. Using a Character Array for Table Lookup

The Public Safety Department at Orion Star wants all employees to be aware of the new policies and procedures regarding customer incidents in their retail stores.

- Each employee must participate in web-based training and then take a multiple-choice test that consists of 10 questions.
- Each question has five choices (A through E).
- The test results from each testing session are entered into the SAS data set **orion.test_answers** as shown below.
- Each observation in **orion.test_answers** contains a single person's answers.

Partial **orion.test_answers** (15 Total Observations)

Employee_ ID	Q1	Q2	Q3	Q4	Q5	Q6	Q7	Q8	Q9	Q10
121044	A	C	C	B	D	E	D	B	B	A
120145	B	C	C		E	E	D	B	A	A
120761	A	C	C	B	D	D	E	B	B	C
120656	B	C	C	A	D	B	B	C	A	D
121107	A	C	C	B	E	E	D	B	B	A

- The correct answers for the questions are shown below:

Question:	1	2	3	4	5	6	7	8	9	10
Answer:	A	C	C	B	E	E	D	B	B	A

a. Read **orion.test_answers** and determine whether each person passed or failed the test.

- Compute a variable **Score** that contains the total correct answers for each person.

Create a temporary array for the answer key.

- If an employee scores 7 or higher, write the observation to a data set named **passed**.
- If an employee scores less than 7, write the observation to a data set named **failed**.

b. Print the **passed** data set to verify that it contains 12 observations.

Partial PROC PRINT Output (12 Total Observations)

Passed

Obs	Employee_ ID	Q1	Q2	Q3	Q4	Q5	Q6	Q7	Q8	Q9	Q10	Score
1	121044	A	C	C	B	D	E	D	B	B	A	9
2	120145	B	C	C		E	E	D	B	A	A	7
3	121107	A	C	C	B	E	E	D	B	B	A	10
4	121038	B	C	C	B	D	D	D	B	B	A	7
5	120273	C	C	C	B	E	E	E	B	B	A	8

c. Print the **failed** data set to verify that it contains three observations.

PROC PRINT Output

Failed

Obs	Employee_ ID	Q1	Q2	Q3	Q4	Q5	Q6	Q7	Q8	Q9	Q10	Score
1	120761	A	C	C	B	D	D	E	B	B	C	6
2	120656	B	C	C	A	D	B	B	C	A	D	2
3	120798		A	C	B	D	D	D	B	B	A	6

7.5 Solutions

Solutions to Exercises

1. Performing Computations with DO Loops

```
data future_expenses;
   drop start stop;
   Wages=12874000;
   Retire=1765000;
   Medical=649000;
   start=year(today())+1;
   stop=start+9;
   do Year=start to stop;
      wages = wages * 1.06;
      retire=retire*1.014;
      medical=medical *1.095;
      Total_Cost=sum(wages,retire,medical);
      output;
   end;
run;

*Alternate DATA Step Solution;
```

```
data future_expenses;
   Wages=12874000;
   Retire=1765000;
   Medical=649000;
   do Year=year(today())+1 to year(today())+10;
      wages = wages * 1.06;
      retire=retire*1.014;
      medical=medical *1.095;
      Total_Cost= sum(wages,retire,medical);
      output;
   end;
run;

proc print data=future_expenses;
   format wages retire medical total_cost comma14.2;
   var year wages retire medical total_cost;
run;
```

2. **Performing Computations with Conditional DO Loops**

```
data income_expenses;
   Wages=12874000;
   Retire=1765000;
   Medical=649000;
   Income=50000000;
   Year=year(today())+1;
   do until (Total_Cost > Income);
      wages = wages * 1.06;
      retire=retire*1.014;
      medical=medical *1.095;
      Total_Cost= sum(wages,retire,medical);
      Income=Income *1.01;
      output;
      year+1;
   end;
run;

proc print data=income_expenses;
   format total_cost income comma14.2;
   var year income total_cost;
run;
```

3. **Using an Iterative DO Loop with a Conditional Clause**

```
data expenses;
   Income= 50000000;
   Expenses = 38750000;
   do Year=1 to 30 until (Expenses > Income);
      income+(income * .01);
      expenses+(expenses * .02);
   end;
run;
```

```
proc print data=expenses;
   format income expenses dollar15.2;
run;
```

4. **Using Other Loop Control Statements**

```
data expenses;
   Income=50000000;
   Expenses =38750000;
   do Year=1 to 75;
      income +(income * .01);
      expenses+(expenses * .02);
      if expenses > income then leave;
   end;
run;

proc print data=expenses;
   format income expenses dollar14.2;
run;
```

5. **Using Arrays for Repetitive Computations**

```
data discount_sales;
   set orion.orders_midyear;
   array mon{*} month1-month6;
   drop i;
   do i=1 to 6;
      mon{i}=mon{i} *.95;
   end;
run;

title 'Monthly Sales with 5% Discount';
proc print data=discount_sales noobs;
   format month1-month6 dollar10.2;
run;
title;
```

6. **Using Arrays for Repetitive Computations**

```
data special_offer;
   set orion.orders_midyear;
   array mon{*} month1-month3;
   keep Total_Sales Projected_Sales Difference;
   Total_Sales=sum(of month1-month6);
   do i=1 to 3;
      mon{i}=mon{i} *.90;
   end;
   Projected_Sales=sum(of month1-month6);
   Difference=Total_Sales-Projected_Sales;
run;

options nodate nonumber;
title 'Total Sales with 10% Discount in First Three Months';
proc print data=special_offer noobs;
```

```
   format total_sales projected_sales difference dollar10.2;
   sum difference;
run;
title;
```

7. Terminating a DATA Step

```
data fsp;
   set orion.orders_midyear;
   keep Customer_ID Months_Ordered Total_Order_Amount;
   array amt{*} month:;
   if dim(amt) < 3 then do;
      put 'Insufficient data for Frequent Shopper Program';
      stop;
   end;
   Total_Order_Amount=0;
   Months_Ordered=0;
   do i=1 to dim(amt);
      if amt{i} ne . then Months_Ordered+1;
      Total_Order_Amount+amt{i};
   end;
   if Total_Order_Amount>1000 and Months_Ordered >= (dim(amt))/2;
run;

title 'orion.orders_midyear: Frequent Shoppers ';
proc print data=fsp;
   format total_order_amount dollar10.2;
run;
title;

data fsp;
   set orion.orders_qtr1;
   keep Customer_ID Months_Ordered Total_Order_Amount;
   array amt{*} month:;
   if dim(amt) < 3 then do;
      put 'Insufficient data for Frequent Shopper Program';
      stop;
   end;
   Total_Order_Amount=0;
   Months_Ordered=0;
   do i=1 to dim(amt);
      if amt{i} ne . then Months_Ordered+1;
      Total_Order_Amount+amt{i};
   end;
   if Total_Order_Amount>1000 and Months_Ordered >= (dim(amt))/2;
run;
title 'orion.orders_qtr1: Frequent Shoppers ';
proc print data=fsp;
   format total_order_amount dollar10.2;
run;
title;
```

```
data fsp;
   set orion.orders_two_months;
   keep Customer_ID Months_Ordered Total_Order_Amount;
   array amt{*} month:;
   if dim(amt) < 3 then do;
      put 'Insufficient data for Frequent Shopper Program';
      stop;
   end;
   Total_Order_Amount=0;
   Months_Ordered=0;
   do i=1 to dim(amt);
      if amt{i} ne . then Months_Ordered+1;
      Total_Order_Amount+amt{i};
   end;
   if Total_Order_Amount>1000 and Months_Ordered >= (dim(amt))/2;
run;
title 'orion.orders_two_months: Frequent Shoppers ';

proc print data=fsp;
   format total_order_amount dollar10.2;
run;
title;
```

8. **Using an Array for Table Lookup**

```
data preferred_cust;
   set orion.orders_midyear;
   array Mon{6} Month1-Month6;
   keep Customer_ID Over1-Over6 Total_Over;
   array Over{6};
   array Target{6} _temporary_ (200,400,300,100,100,200);
   do i=1 to 6;
      if Mon{i} > Target{i} then
         Over{i} = Mon{i} - Target{i};
   end;
   Total_Over=sum(of Over{*});
   if Total_Over > 500;
run;

proc print data=preferred_cust noobs;
run;
```

9. **Using a Character Array for Table Lookup**

```
data passed failed;
   set orion.test_answers;
   drop i;
   array Response{10} Q1-Q10;
   array Answer{10} $ 1 _temporary_ ('A','C','C','B','E',
                                     'E','D','B','B','A');
   Score=0;
   do i=1 to 10;
      if Answer{i}=Response{i} then Score+1;
```

```
   end;
   if Score ge 7 then output passed;
   else output failed;
run;

title 'Passed';
proc print data=passed;
run;
title;

title 'Failed';
proc print data=failed;
run;
title;
```

Solutions to Student Activities (Polls/Quizzes)

7.01 Quiz – Correct Answer

What are the final values of the index variables after the following DO statements execute?

The final values are highlighted.

```
do i=1 to 5;
   ...
end;                    1 2 3 4 5 6

do j=2 to 8 by 2;
   ...
end;                    2 4 6 8 10

do k=10 to 2 by -2;
   ...
end;                    10 8 6 4 2 0
```

10

7.02 Quiz – Correct Answer

How can you generate a separate observation for each year? **Place an explicit OUTPUT statement inside the DO loop.**

```
data invest;
   do Year=2008 to 2010;
      Capital+5000;
      Capital+(Capital*.045);
      output;
   end;
run;
proc print data=invest noobs;
run;
```

PROC PRINT Output

Year	Capital
2008	5225.00
2009	10685.13
2010	16390.96

There is no observation for 2011.

31 **p207a01s**

7.03 Quiz – Correct Answer

What stop value would you use in the DO loop to determine the number of years that it would take for the Engineering Department to exceed 75 people?
unknown

```
data forecast;
   set orion.growth;
   do Year=1 to 6;
      Total_Employees=
         Total_Employees*(1+Increase);
      output;
   end;
run;
proc print data=forecast noobs;
run;
```

Use *conditional iterative processing* to stop a loop when a condition is met.

40 **p207d05**

7.04 Quiz – Correct Answer

How can you generate the same result with a DO WHILE statement? **Change the DO UNTIL statement to a DO WHILE statement and modify the condition.**

```
data invest;
   do while(Capital<=1000000);
      Year+1;
      Capital+5000;
      Capital+(Capital*.045);
   end;
run;

proc print data=invest noobs;
   format capital dollar14.2;
run;
```

46

p207a02s

7.05 Quiz – Correct Answer

How can you generate one observation for each quarterly amount? **Move the OUTPUT statement to the inner loop and do not drop Quarter.**

```
data invest;
   do Year=1 to 5;
      Capital+5000;
      do Quarter=1 to 4;
         Capital+(Capital*(.045/4));
         output;
      end;
   end;
run;

proc print data=invest
run;
```

Partial PROC PRINT Output

Year	Capital	Quarter
1	5056.25	1
1	5113.13	2
1	5170.66	3
1	5228.83	4
2	10343.90	1
2	10460.27	2

52

p207a03s

7.07 Quiz – Correct Answer

Open and submit **p207a04**. View the log to determine the cause of the error. **The subscript and the number of elements in the list do not agree.**

```
data charity(keep=Employee_ID Qtr1-Qtr4);
   set orion.employee_donations;
   array Contrib1{3} Qtr1-Qtr4;
   array Contrib2{5} qtr:;
   /* additional SAS statements */
run;
```

The subscript and element list must agree.

Partial SAS Log

```
177      array Contrib1{3} Qtr1-Qtr4;
ERROR: Too many variables defined for the dimension(s) specified
for the array Contrib1.
178      array Contrib2{5} qtr:;
ERROR: Too few variables defined for the dimension(s) specified
for the array Contrib2.
```

77

7.08 Quiz – Correct Answer

How many ARRAY statements would you use to calculate the difference in each employee's contribution from one quarter to the next? **Answers can vary, but one solution is to use two arrays.**

Partial **orion.employee_donations**

Employee_ID	Qtr1	Qtr2	Qtr3	Qtr4
120265	.	.	.	25
120267	15	15	15	15
120269	20	20	20	20

First difference: Qtr2 – Qtr1
Second difference: Qtr3 – Qtr2
Third difference: Qtr4 – Qtr3

Use one array to refer to the existing variables and a second array to create the three difference variables.

98

7.09 Quiz – Correct Answer

Using pencil and paper, write an ARRAY statement to define a temporary lookup table named **Country** with three elements, each two characters long. Initialize the elements to *AU*, *NZ*, and *US*. Refer to the syntax below.

ARRAY *array-name {subscript}* <$> <*length*>
<*array-elements*> <(*initial-value-list*)>;

```
array Country{3} $ 2 _temporary_ ('AU','NZ','US');
```

120

Chapter 8 Restructuring a Data Set

8.1 Rotating with the DATA Step 8-3

Exercises 8-22

8.2 Solutions 8-24

Solutions to Exercises 8-24

Solutions to Student Activities (Polls/Quizzes) 8-26

8.1 Rotating with the DATA Step

Objectives

- Use a DATA step with arrays and DO loop processing to restructure a data set.

2

Data Set Structure

Some data sets store all the information about one entity in a single observation. For convenience, this is referred to as a *wide* data set.

Customer_ID	Qtr1	Qtr2	Qtr3	Qtr4	Method
134391	.	125	.	.	Cash
143561	150	79	67	15	Credit
158913	208	22	.	33	Credit

All information for Customer 143561 is in a single observation.

3

Data Set Structure

Other data sets have multiple observations per entity. For convenience, this is referred to as a *narrow* data set.

Customer_ID	Period	Amount
134391	Qtr2	125
143561	Qtr1	150
143561	Qtr2	79
143561	Qtr3	67
143561	Qtr4	15
158913	Qtr1	208
158913	Qtr2	22

The information for Customer 143561 is stored in four observations. Each observation represents a donation for a different quarter.

4

Business Scenario: A Frequency Report

The Orion Payroll Manager asked for a report showing the number of Orion Star employees who made charitable donations in each quarter.

Sketch of the Desired Report

Period	Frequency
Qtr1	56
Qtr2	99
Qtr3	24
Qtr4	75

The FREQ procedure can be used to generate the desired report.

5

8.01 Quiz

Which data set structure is more appropriate for using PROC FREQ to determine the number of charitable donations made in each of the four quarters (**Qtr1–Qtr4**)?

a.

Employee_ID	Qtr1	Qtr2	Qtr3	Qtr4
120265	.	.	.	25
120267	15	15	15	15
120269	20	20	20	20

b.

Employee_ID	Period	Amount
120265	Qtr4	25
120267	Qtr1	15
120267	Qtr2	15
120267	Qtr3	15
120267	Qtr4	15

6

Business Scenario: Considerations

The data set contains the needed information, but is not in the form to be analyzed easily using the FREQ procedure.

Partial **orion.employee_donations**

Employee_ID	Qtr1	Qtr2	Qtr3	Qtr4	Paid_By
120265	.	.	.	25	Cash or Check
120267	15	15	15	15	Payroll Deduction
120269	20	20	20	20	Payroll Deduction

Changing the data set from a wide to a narrow structure can simplify this task.

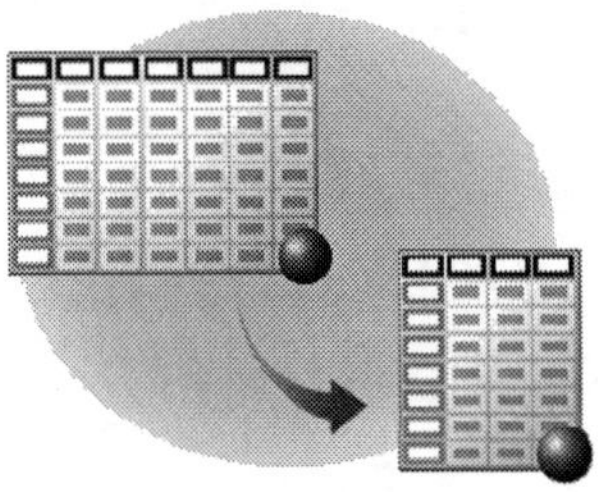

8

Business Scenario: Considerations

Restructure the input data set, and create a separate observation for each nonmissing quarterly contribution.

Employee_ID	Qtr1	Qtr2	Qtr3	Qtr4	Paid_By
120265	.	.	.	25	Cash or Check
120267	15	15	15	15	Payroll Deduction
120269	20	20	20	20	Payroll Deduction

Employee_ID	Period	Amount
120265	Qtr4	25
120267	Qtr1	15
120267	Qtr2	15
120267	Qtr3	15
120267	Qtr4	15
120269	Qtr1	20
120269	Qtr2	20
120269	Qtr3	20
120269	Qtr4	20

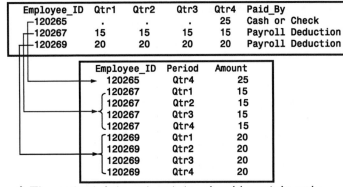

✎ The output data set, **rotate**, should contain only **Employee_ID**, **Period**, and **Amount**.

9

Rotating a SAS Data Set

The DATA step below rotates the input data set and outputs an observation if a contribution was made in a given quarter.

```
data rotate (keep=Employee_Id Period Amount);
   set orion.employee_donations
            (drop=recipients paid_by);
   array contrib{4} qtr1-qtr4;
   do i=1 to 4;
      if contrib{i} ne . then do;
         Period=cats("Qtr",i);
         Amount=contrib{i};
         output;
      end;
   end;
run;
```

Include only nonmissing values

10 p208d01

Compilation: Rotating a SAS Data Set

```
data rotate (keep=Employee_Id Period Amount);
   set orion.employee_donations
            (drop=recipients paid_by);
   array contrib{4} qtr1-qtr4;
   do i=1 to 4;
      if contrib{i} ne . then do;
         Period=cats("Qtr",i);
         Amount=contrib{i};
         output;
      end;
   end;
run;
```

PDV

Employee_ID	Qtr1	Qtr2	Qtr3	Qtr4	i	Period	Amount

work.rotate

Employee_ID	Period	Amount

11 p208d01 ...

Execution: Rotating a SAS Data Set

```
data rotate (keep=Employee_Id Period Amount);
   set orion.employee_donations
            (drop=recipients paid_by);
   array contrib{4} qtr1-qtr4;
   do i=1 to 4;
      if contrib{i} ne . then do;
         Period=cats("Qtr",i);
         Amount=contrib{i};
         output;
      end;
   end;
run;
```

Initialize PDV

PDV

Employee_ID	Qtr1	Qtr2	Qtr3	Qtr4	i	Period	Amount
.	.	.	.	.	.		.

work.rotate

Employee_ID	Period	Amount

12 ...

Execution: Rotating a SAS Data Set

```
data rotate (keep=Employee_Id Period Amount);
   set orion.employee_donations
            (drop=recipients paid_by);
   array contrib{4} qtr1-qtr4;
   do i=1 to 4;
      if contrib{i} ne . then do;
         Period=cats("Qtr",i);
         Amount=contrib{i};
         output;
      end;
   end;
run;
```

PDV

Employee_ID	Qtr1	Qtr2	Qtr3	Qtr4	i	Period	Amount
120265	.	.	.	25	1		.

work.rotate

Employee_ID	Period	Amount

13 ...

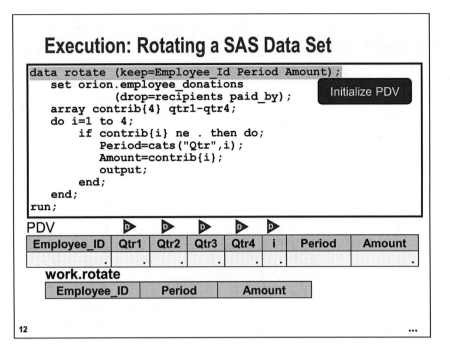

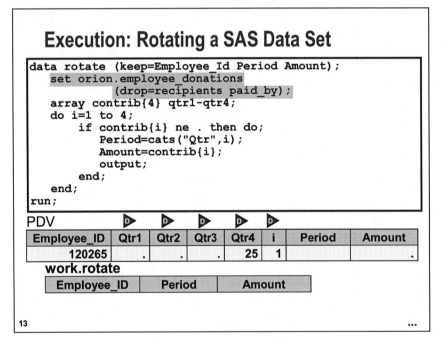

Execution: Rotating a SAS Data Set

```
data rotate (keep=Employee_Id Period Amount);
   set orion.employee_donations
          (drop=recipients paid_by);
   array contrib{4} qtr1-qtr4;
   do i=1 to 4;
      if contrib{i} ne . then do;
         Period=cats("Qtr",i);
         Amount=contrib{i};
         output;
      end;
   end;
run;
```

PDV

Employee_ID	Qtr1	Qtr2	Qtr3	Qtr4	i	Period	Amount
120265	.	.	.	25	1		.

work.rotate

Employee_ID	Period	Amount

14 ...

Execution: Rotating a SAS Data Set

```
data rotate (keep=Employee_Id Period Amount);
   set orion.employee_donations
          (drop=recipients paid_by);
   array contrib{4} qtr1-qtr4;
   do i=1 to 4;
      if contrib{i} ne . then do;
         Period=cats("Qtr",i);
         Amount=contrib{i};
         output;
      end;
   end;
run;
```

False

PDV

Employee_ID	Qtr1	Qtr2	Qtr3	Qtr4	i	Period	Amount
120265	.	.	.	25	1		.

work.rotate

Employee_ID	Period	Amount

15 ...

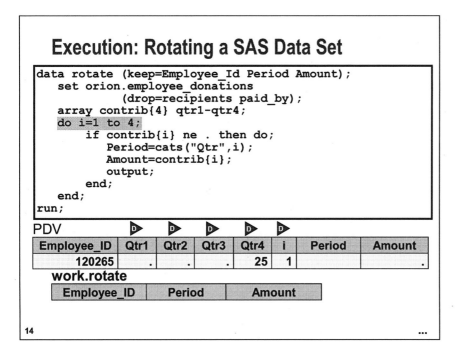

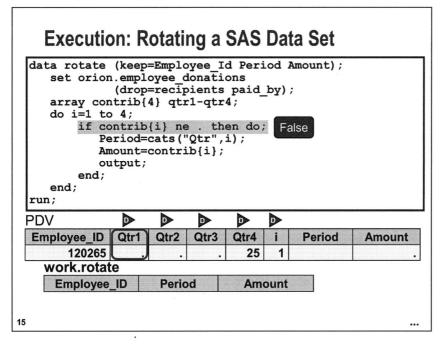

Execution: Rotating a SAS Data Set

```
data rotate (keep=Employee_Id Period Amount);
   set orion.employee_donations
          (drop=recipients paid_by);
   array contrib{4} qtr1-qtr4;
   do i=1 to 4;
      if contrib{i} ne . then do;
         Period=cats("Qtr",i);
         Amount=contrib{i};
         output;
      end;
   end;
run;
```

i+1

PDV

Employee_ID	Qtr1	Qtr2	Qtr3	Qtr4	i	Period	Amount
120265	.	.	.	25	2		.

work.rotate

Employee_ID	Period	Amount

16 ...

Execution: Rotating a SAS Data Set

```
data rotate (keep=Employee_Id Period Amount);
   set orion.employee_donations
          (drop=recipients paid_by);
   array contrib{4} qtr1-qtr4;
   do i=1 to 4;
      if contrib{i} ne . then do;
         Period=cats("Qtr",i);
         Amount=contrib{i};
         output;
      end;
   end;
run;
```

PDV

Employee_ID	Qtr1	Qtr2	Qtr3	Qtr4	i	Period	Amount
120265	.	.	.	25	2		.

work.rotate

Employee_ID	Period	Amount

17 ...

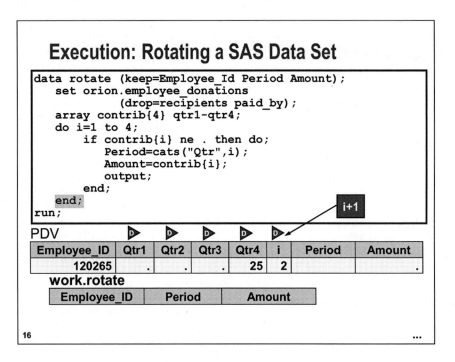

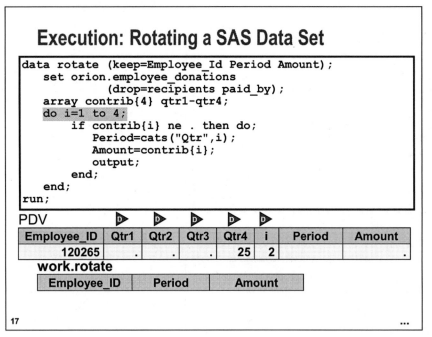

Execution: Rotating a SAS Data Set

```
data rotate (keep=Employee_Id Period Amount);
   set orion.employee_donations
          (drop=recipients paid_by);
   array contrib{4} qtr1-qtr4;
   do i=1 to 4;
      if contrib{i} ne . then do;   False
         Period=cats("Qtr",i);
         Amount=contrib{i};
         output;
      end;
   end;
run;
```

PDV

Employee_ID	Qtr1	Qtr2	Qtr3	Qtr4	i	Period	Amount
120265	.	.	.	25	2		.

work.rotate

Employee_ID	Period	Amount

18 ...

Execution: Rotating a SAS Data Set

```
data rotate (keep=Employee_Id Period Amount);
   set orion.employee_donations
          (drop=recipients paid_by);
   array contrib{4} qtr1-qtr4;
   do i=1 to 4;
      if contrib{i} ne . then do;
         Period=cats("Qtr",i);
         Amount=contrib{i};
         output;
      end;
   end;
run;
```

i+1

PDV

Employee_ID	Qtr1	Qtr2	Qtr3	Qtr4	i	Period	Amount
120265	.	.	.	25	3		.

work.rotate

Employee_ID	Period	Amount

19 ...

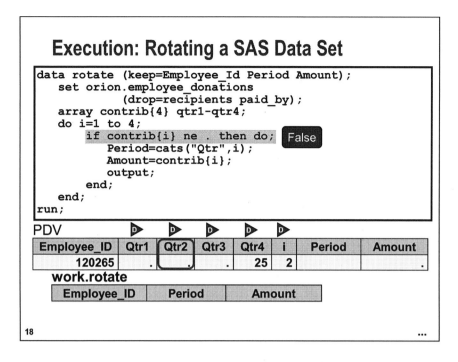

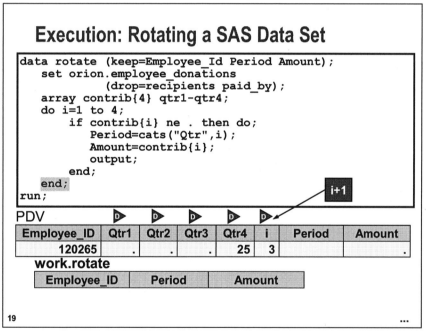

Execution: Rotating a SAS Data Set

```
data rotate (keep=Employee_Id Period Amount);
   set orion.employee_donations
         (drop=recipients paid_by);
   array contrib{4} qtr1-qtr4;
   do i=1 to 4;
      if contrib{i} ne . then do;
         Period=cats("Qtr",i);
         Amount=contrib{i};
         output;
      end;
   end;
run;
```

PDV (D: Qtr1, Qtr2, Qtr3, Qtr4, i)

Employee_ID	Qtr1	Qtr2	Qtr3	Qtr4	i	Period	Amount
120265	.	.	.	25	3		.

work.rotate

Employee_ID	Period	Amount

20 ...

Execution: Rotating a SAS Data Set

```
data rotate (keep=Employee_Id Period Amount);
   set orion.employee_donations
         (drop=recipients paid_by);
   array contrib{4} qtr1-qtr4;
   do i=1 to 4;
      if contrib{i} ne . then do;
         Period=cats("Qtr",i);
         Amount=contrib{i};
         output;
      end;
   end;
run;
```

False

PDV (D: Qtr1, Qtr2, Qtr3, Qtr4, i)

Employee_ID	Qtr1	Qtr2	Qtr3	Qtr4	i	Period	Amount
120265	.	.	.	25	3		.

work.rotate

Employee_ID	Period	Amount

21 ...

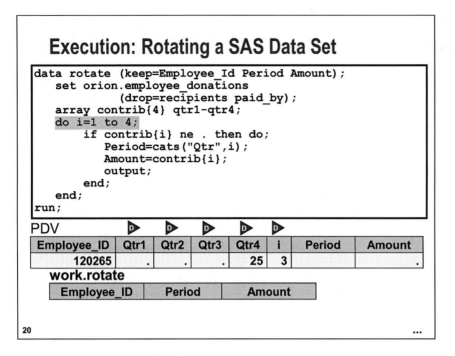

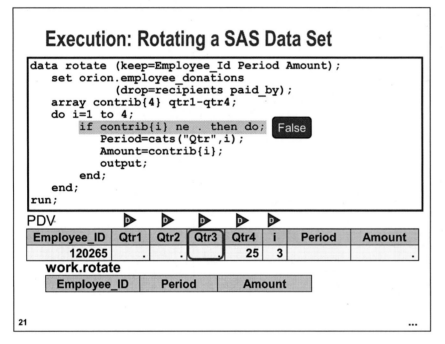

Execution: Rotating a SAS Data Set

```
data rotate (keep=Employee_Id Period Amount);
   set orion.employee_donations
          (drop=recipients paid_by);
   array contrib{4} qtr1-qtr4;
   do i=1 to 4;
      if contrib{i} ne . then do;
         Period=cats("Qtr",i);
         Amount=contrib{i};
         output;
      end;
   end;
run;
```

i+1

PDV

Employee_ID	Qtr1	Qtr2	Qtr3	Qtr4	i	Period	Amount
120265	.	.	.	25	4		.

work.rotate

Employee_ID	Period	Amount

22 ...

Execution: Rotating a SAS Data Set

```
data rotate (keep=Employee_Id Period Amount);
   set orion.employee_donations
          (drop=recipients paid_by);
   array contrib{4} qtr1-qtr4;
   do i=1 to 4;
      if contrib{i} ne . then do;
         Period=cats("Qtr",i);
         Amount=contrib{i};
         output;
      end;
   end;
run;
```

PDV

Employee_ID	Qtr1	Qtr2	Qtr3	Qtr4	i	Period	Amount
120265	.	.	.	25	4		.

work.rotate

Employee_ID	Period	Amount

23 ...

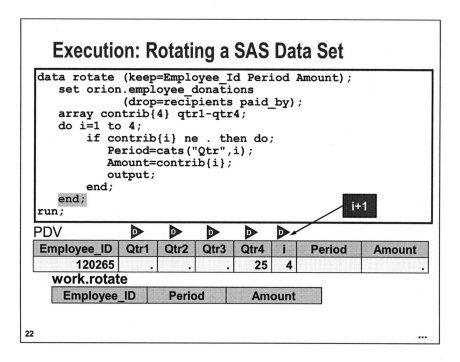

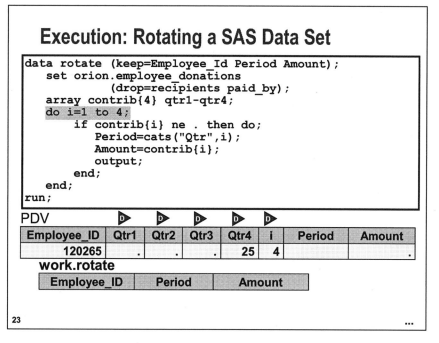

Execution: Rotating a SAS Data Set

```
data rotate (keep=Employee_Id Period Amount);
   set orion.employee_donations
          (drop=recipients paid_by);
   array contrib{4} qtr1-qtr4;
   do i=1 to 4;
      if contrib{i} ne . then do;
         Period=cats("Qtr",i);
         Amount=contrib{i};
         output;
      end;
   end;
run;
```

True

PDV

Employee_ID	Qtr1	Qtr2	Qtr3	Qtr4	i	Period	Amount
120265	.	.	.	25	4		.

work.rotate

Employee_ID	Period	Amount

24 ...

Execution: Rotating a SAS Data Set

```
data rotate (keep=Employee_Id Period Amount);
   set orion.employee_donations
          (drop=recipients paid_by);
   array contrib{4} qtr1-qtr4;
   do i=1 to 4;
      if contrib{i} ne . then do;
         Period=cats("Qtr",i);
         Amount=contrib{i};
         output;
      end;
   end;
run;
```

PDV

Employee_ID	Qtr1	Qtr2	Qtr3	Qtr4	i	Period	Amount
120265	.	.	.	25	4	Qtr4	.

work.rotate

Employee_ID	Period	Amount

25 ...

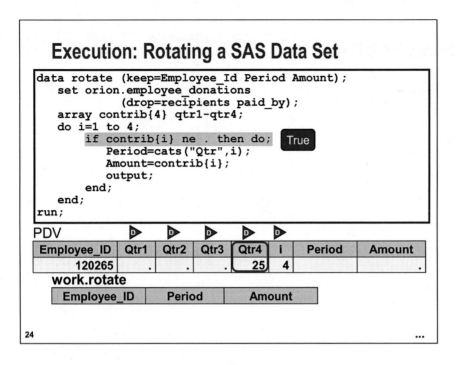

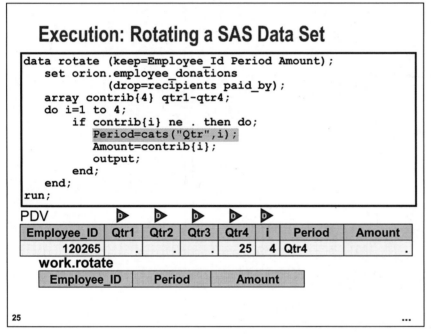

Automatic conversion occurs when you use a numeric value in character context. The functions in the CAT family remove leading and trailing blanks from numeric arguments after it formats the numeric value with the BEST12. format.

Execution: Rotating a SAS Data Set

```
data rotate (keep=Employee_Id Period Amount);
   set orion.employee_donations
          (drop=recipients paid_by);
   array contrib{4} qtr1-qtr4;
   do i=1 to 4;
       if contrib{i} ne . then do;
          Period=cats("Qtr",i);
          Amount=contrib{i};
          output;
       end;
   end;
run;
```

PDV

Employee_ID	Qtr1	Qtr2	Qtr3	Qtr4	i	Period	Amount
120265	.	.	.	25	4	Qtr4	25

work.rotate

Employee_ID	Period	Amount

26 ...

Execution: Rotating a SAS Data Set

```
data rotate (keep=Employee_Id Period amount);
   set orion.employee_donations
          (drop=recipients paid_by);
   array contrib{4} qtr1-qtr4;
   do i=1 to 4;
       if contrib{i} ne . then do;
          Period=cats("Qtr",i);
          Amount=contrib{i};
          output;
       end;
   end;
run;
```

Output current observation

PDV

Employee_ID	[illegible]	[illegible]	[illegible]	[illegible]	[illegible]	Period	Amount
120265	.	.	.	[illegible]	[illegible]	Qtr4	25

work.rotate

Employee_ID	Period	Amount
120265	Qtr4	25

27 ...

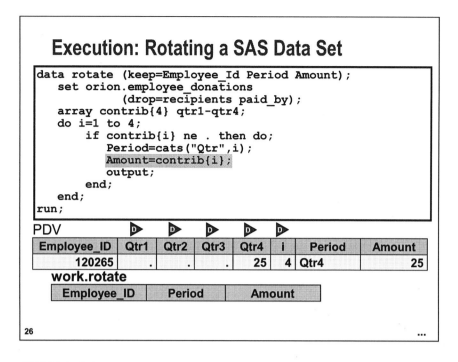

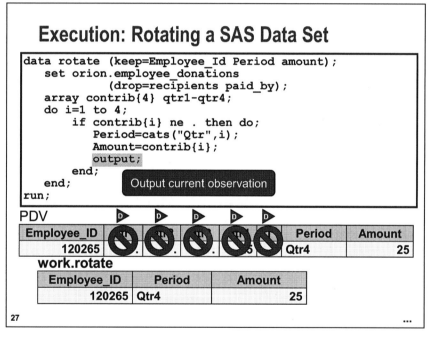

Execution: Rotating a SAS Data Set

```
data rotate (keep=Employee_Id Period Amount);
   set orion.employee_donations
         (drop=recipients paid_by);
   array contrib{4} qtr1-qtr4;
   do i=1 to 4;
      if contrib{i} ne . then do;
         Period=cats("Qtr",i);
         Amount=contrib{i};
         output;
      end;
   end;
run;
```

i+1

PDV

Employee_ID	Qtr1	Qtr2	Qtr3	Qtr4	i	Period	Amount
120265	.	.	.	25	5	Qtr4	25

work.rotate

Employee_ID	Period	Amount
120265	Qtr4	25

28 ...

Execution: Rotating a SAS Data Set

```
data rotate (keep=Employee_Id Period Amount);
   set orion.employee_donations
         (drop=recipients paid_by);
   array contrib{4} qtr1-qtr4;
   do i=1 to 4;
      if contrib{i} ne . then do;
         Period=cats("Qtr",i);
         Amount=contrib{i};
         output;
      end;
   end;
run;
```

Out of range

PDV

Employee_ID	Qtr1	Qtr2	Qtr3	Qtr4	i	Period	Amount
120265	.	.	.	25	5	Qtr4	25

work.rotate

Employee_ID	Period	Amount
120265	Qtr4	25

29 ...

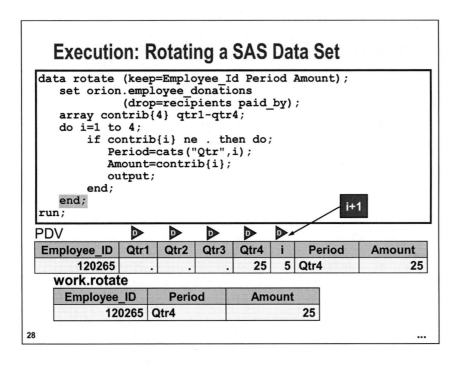

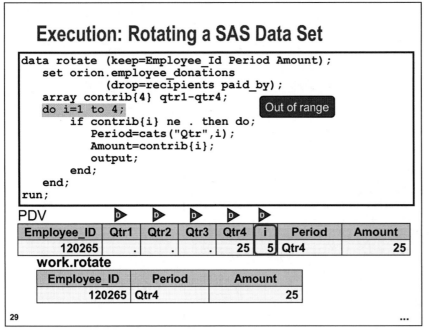

Execution: Rotating a SAS Data Set

```
data rotate (keep=Employee_Id Period Amount);
   set orion.employee_donations
          (drop=recipients paid_by);
   array contrib{4} qtr1-qtr4;
   do i=1 to 4;
      if contrib{i} ne . then do;
         Period=cats("Qtr",i);
         Amount=contrib{i};
         output;
      end;
   end;
run;
```

Implicit OUTPUT;
Implicit RETURN;

PDV

Employee_ID	Qtr1	Qtr2	Qtr3	Qtr4	i	Period	Amount
120265	.	.	.	25	5	Qtr4	25

work.rotate

Employee_ID	Period	Amount
120265	Qtr4	25

30 ...

Execution: Rotating a SAS Data Set

```
data rotate (keep=Employee_Id Period Amount);
   set orion.employee_donations
          (drop=recipients paid_by);
   array contrib{4} qtr1-qtr4;
   do i=1 to 4;
      if contrib{i} ne . then do;
         Period=cats("Qtr",i);
         Amount=contrib{i};
         output;
      end;
   end;
run;
```

Reinitialize PDV

PDV

Employee_ID	Qtr1	Qtr2	Qtr3	Qtr4	i	Period	Amount
120265	.	.	.	25	.		.

work.rotate

Employee_ID	Period	Amount
120265	Qtr4	25

31 ...

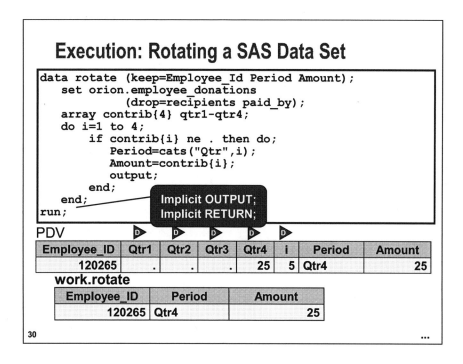

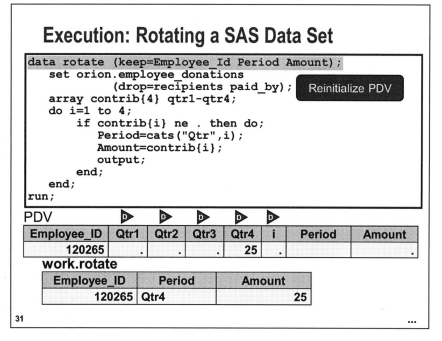

Execution: Rotating a SAS Data Set

```
data rotate (keep=Employee_Id Period Amount);
   set orion.employee_donations
            (drop=recipients paid_by);
   array contrib{4} qtr1-qtr4;
   do i=1 to 4;
      if contrib{i} ne . then do;
         Period=cats("Qtr",i);
         Amount=contrib{i};
         output;
      end;
   end;
run;
```

PDV

Employee_ID	Qtr1 D	Qtr2 D	Qtr3 D	Qtr4 D	i D	Period	Amount
120267	15	15	15	15	.		.

work.rotate

Employee_ID	Period	Amount
120265	Qtr4	25

32 ...

Execution: Rotating a SAS Data Set

```
data rotate (keep=Employee_Id Period Amount);
   set orion.employee_donations
            (drop=recipients paid_by);
   array contrib{4} qtr1-qtr4;
   do i=1 to 4;
      if contrib{i} ne . then do;
         Period=cats("Qtr",i);
         Amount=contrib{i};
         output;
      end;
   end;
run;
```

PDV

Employee_ID	Qtr1 D	Qtr2 D	Qtr3 D	Qtr4 D	i D	Period	Amount
120267	15	15	15	15	1		.

work.rotate

Employee_ID	Period	Amount
120265	Qtr4	25

33 ...

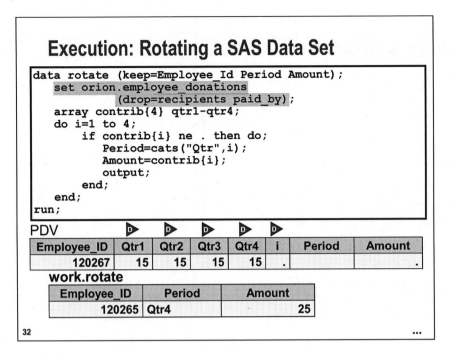

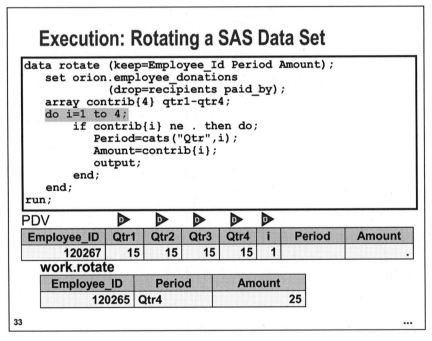

Execution: Rotating a SAS Data Set

```
data rotate (keep=Employee_Id Period Amount);
   set orion.employee_donations
            (drop=recipients paid_by);
   array contrib{4} qtr1-qtr4;
   do i=1 to 4;
      if contrib{i} ne . then do;
         Period=cats("Qtr",i);
         Amount=contrib{i};
         output;
      end;
   end;
run;
```

True

PDV

Employee_ID	Qtr1	Qtr2	Qtr3	Qtr4	i	Period	Amount
120267	15	15	15	15	1		.

work.rotate

Employee_ID	Period	Amount
120265	Qtr4	25

34 ...

Execution: Rotating a SAS Data Set

```
data rotate (keep=Employee_Id Period Amount);
   set orion.employee_donations
            (drop=recipients paid_by);
   array contrib{4} qtr1-qtr4;
   do i=1 to 4;
      if contrib{i} ne . then do;
         Period=cats("Qtr",i);
         Amount=contrib{i};
         output;
      end;
   end;
run;
```

PDV

Employee_ID	Qtr1	Qtr2	Qtr3	Qtr4	i	Period	Amount
120267	15	15	15	15	1	Qtr1	.

work.rotate

Employee_ID	Period	Amount
120265	Qtr4	25

35 ...

Execution: Rotating a SAS Data Set

```
data rotate (keep=Employee_Id Period Amount);
   set orion.employee_donations
            (drop=recipients paid_by);
   array contrib{4} qtr1-qtr4;
   do i=1 to 4;
       if contrib{i} ne . then do;
          Period=cats("Qtr",i);
          Amount=contrib{i};
          output;
       end;
   end;
run;
```

PDV

Employee_ID	Qtr1	Qtr2	Qtr3	Qtr4	i	Period	Amount
120267	15	15	15	15	1	Qtr1	15

work.rotate

Employee_ID	Period	Amount
120265	Qtr4	25

36 ...

Execution: Rotating a SAS Data Set

```
data rotate (keep=Employee_Id Period Amount);
   set orion.employee_donations
            (drop=recipients paid_by);
   array contrib{4} qtr1-qtr4;
   do i=1 to 4;
       if contrib{i} ne . then do;
          Period=cats("Qtr",i);
          Amount=contrib{i};
          output;
       end;
   end;
run;
```

Output current observation

PDV

Employee_ID	[illegible]	[illegible]	[illegible]	[illegible]	[illegible]	Period	Amount
120267	[illegible]	[illegible]	[illegible]	[illegible]	[illegible]	Qtr1	15

work.rotate

Employee_ID	Period	Amount
120265	Qtr4	25
120267	Qtr1	15

37 ...

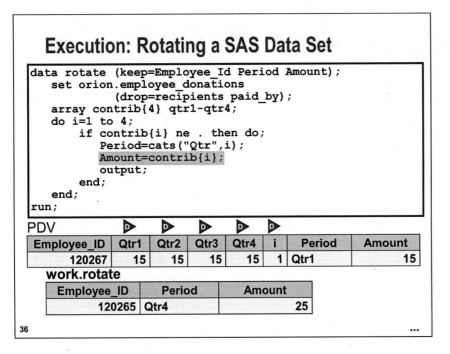

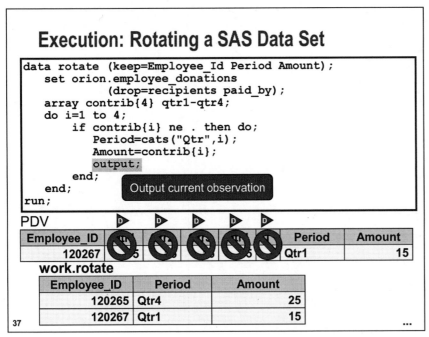

Execution: Rotating a SAS Data Set

```
data rotate (keep=Employee_Id Period Amount);
   set orion.employee_donations
          (drop=recipients paid_by);
   array contrib{4} qtr1-qtr4;
   do i=1 to 4;
      if contrib{i} ne . then do;
         Period=cats("Qtr",i);
         Amount=contrib{i};
         output;
      end;
   end;
run;
```

Continue until EOF

PDV

Employee_ID	Qtr1	Qtr2	Qtr3	Qtr4	i	Period	Amount
120267	15	15	15	15	1	Qtr1	15

work.rotate

Employee_ID	Period	Amount
120265	Qtr4	25
120267	Qtr1	15

38

Output: Rotated Data Set

```
proc print data=rotate;
run;
```

Partial PROC PRINT Output (417 Total Observations)

Obs	Employee_ID	Period	Amount
1	120265	Qtr4	25
2	120267	Qtr1	15
3	120267	Qtr2	15
4	120267	Qtr3	15
5	120267	Qtr4	15

39 p208d01

Analyzing the Rotated SAS Data Set

```
proc freq data=rotate;
   tables Period /nocum nopct;
run;
```

PROC FREQ Output

Period	Frequency
Qtr1	110
Qtr2	98
Qtr3	107
Qtr4	102

40

p208d01

Exercises

If you restarted your SAS session since the last exercise, open and submit the **libname.sas** program found in the data folder.

Level 1

1. Rotating a Data Set

The data set **orion.orders_midyear** contains an observation for each customer, with the total retail value of the customer's monthly orders for the first half of the year.

Partial Listing of **orion.orders_midyear** (24 Total Observations)

Obs	Customer_ID	Month1	Month2	Month3	Month4	Month5	Month6
1	5	213.10	.	478.0	525.80	394.35	191.79
2	10	188.10	414.09	2876.9	3164.59	2373.44	169.29
3	11	78.20	.	.	.	.	70.38
4	12	135.60	.	117.6	129.36	97.02	122.04
5	18	.	.	29.4	32.34	24.26	.

a. Rotate **orion.orders_midyear** to create an output data set, **sixmonths**, containing one observation per month for each customer.

- The data set should contain **Customer_ID**, **Month**, and **Sales**.
- Do not output an observation if the monthly total is missing.

b. Print the new data set. Verify the results.

Partial PROC PRINT Output (88 Total Observations)

Obs	Customer_ID	Month	Sales
1	5	1	213.10
2	5	3	478.00
3	5	4	525.80
4	5	5	394.35
5	5	6	191.79

Level 2

2. Rotating a Data Set and Using a Lookup Table

The data set **orion.travel_expense** contains an observation for each employee business trip and includes **Trip_ID**, **Employee_ID**, and up to five expenses, **Exp1-Exp5**. The table below shows the type of each expense:

Exp1	Airfare
Exp2	Hotel
Exp3	Meals
Exp4	Transportation
Exp5	Miscellaneous

Partial **orion.travel_expense** (10 Total Observations)

Obs	Trip_ID	Employee_ ID	Exp1	Exp2	Exp3	Exp4	Exp5
1	1044-1	121044	345.97	568.54	235.00	320.00	.
2	0145-1	120145	256.00	675.90	343.25	125.00	67.50
3	0656-1	120656	312.26	.	236.98	325.00	45.00
4	1119-1	121119	597.80	780.99	345.87	195.00	50.75
5	0812-1	120812	345.24	865.45	534.20	430.50	76.75

a. Rotate **orion.travel_expense** to create an output data set named **travel** that contains one observation per nonmissing travel expense.

- The new data set should contain the variables **Trip_ID**, **Employee_ID**, **Expense_Type**, and **Amount**.
- Use two arrays in your solution: one to refer to each of the five expenses in an observation and a second array to store the expense types as a lookup table.

b. Print the new data set.

- Format **Amount** with dollar signs, commas, and two decimal places.
- Compare your results to the partial listing below.

Partial PROC PRINT Output (44 Total Observations)

Obs	Trip_ID	Employee_ ID	Expense_Type	Amount
1	1044-1	121044	Airfare	$345.97
2	1044-1	121044	Hotel	$568.54

3	1044-1	121044	Meals	$235.00
4	1044-1	121044	Transportation	$320.00
5	0145-1	120145	Airfare	$256.00

Challenge

3. Rotating a Data Set

The data set **orion.order_summary** contains monthly order information with multiple observations for each customer.

Partial **orion.order_summary** (101 Total Observations)

Customer_ID	Order_ Month	Sale_Amt
5	5	478.00
5	6	126.80
5	9	52.50
5	12	33.80
10	3	32.60

a. Rotate **orion.order_summary** to create an output data set named **customer_orders** that contains one observation for each customer.

- Use an array in a DATA step.
- The new data set should contain **Customer_ID** and **Month1** through **Month12**.

b. Print the new data set. Verify the results.

Partial PROC PRINT Output (37 Total Observations)

Customer_ID	Month1	Month2	Month3	Month4	Month5	Month6	Month7 ...	Month 11	Month12
5	.	.	.	.	478.0	126.80	.	.	33.80
10	.	.	32.6	250.8	79.8	12.20	163.29	1894.60	143.30
11	.	.	.	.	.	.	.	.	.
12	.	117.6	.	.	.	48.40	.	.	.
18	.	29.4	.	.	.	.	.	.	.

8.2 Solutions

Solutions to Exercises

1. Rotating a Data Set

```
data sixmonths;
   set orion.orders_midyear;
   keep customer_id month sales;
   array months{6} month1-month6;
   do Month=1 to 6;
      if months{Month} ne . then do;
         Sales=months{Month};
         output;
      end;
```

```
   end;
run;

proc print data=sixmonths;
run;
```

2. Rotating a Data Set and Using a Lookup Table

```
data travel;
   set orion.travel_expense;
   keep employee_id trip_id Expense_Type amount;
   array exp{5} exp1-exp5;
   array descr{5} $ 14 _temporary_ ('Airfare', 'Hotel', 'Meals',
                              'Transportation', 'Miscellaneous');
   do i=1 to 5;
      if exp{i} ne . then do;
         Expense_Type=descr{i};
         Amount=exp{i};
         output;
      end;
   end;
run;

proc print data=travel;
   format Amount dollar8.2;
run;
```

3. Rotating a Data Set

```
data customer_orders;
   set orion.order_summary;
   retain Month1-Month12;
   array Month{12};
   by Customer_ID;
   if first.Customer_ID then call missing(of Month{*});
   Month{Order_month}=Sale_Amt;
   if last.Customer_ID;
   drop Order_Month Sale_Amt;
run;

options ls=120;
proc print data=customer_orders noobs;
run;
```

Solutions to Student Activities (Polls/Quizzes)

8.01 Quiz – Correct Answer

Which data set structure is more appropriate for using PROC FREQ to determine the number of charitable donations made in each of the four quarters (**Qtr1**–**Qtr4**)?

Proposed SAS Program

```
proc freq data=b;
   tables Period /nocum nopct;
run;
```

b.

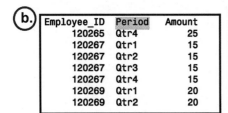

Employee_ID	Period	Amount
120265	Qtr4	25
120267	Qtr1	15
120267	Qtr2	15
120267	Qtr3	15
120267	Qtr4	15
120269	Qtr1	20
120269	Qtr2	20

PROC FREQ Output

The FREQ Procedure

Period	Frequency
Qtr1	2
Qtr2	2
Qtr3	1
Qtr4	2

7

Chapter 9 Combining SAS® Data Sets

9.1 Using Data Manipulation Techniques with Match-Merging 9-3

Demonstration: Performing a Match-Merge on Data Sets That Lack a Common Variable 9-13

Exercises 9-20

9.2 Solutions 9-24

Solutions to Exercises 9-24

Solutions to Student Activities (Polls/Quizzes) 9-25

9.1 Using Data Manipulation Techniques with Match-Merging

Objectives

- Review match-merging of SAS data sets.
- Show examples of data manipulation techniques used with match-merging.
- Show techniques to perform a match-merge for these special cases:
  - three or more SAS data sets that lack a single common variable
  - variable names that need to be altered to obtain the correct merge results.

2

Match-Merging (Review)

Match-merging combines observations from one or more SAS data sets into a single observation in a new data set, based on the values of one or more common variables.

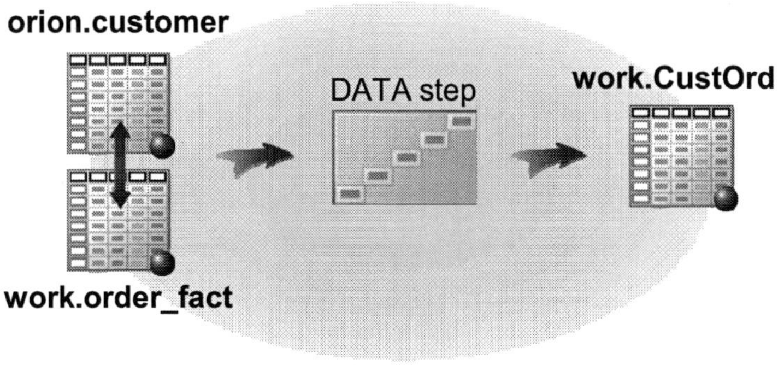

3

9.01 Multiple Choice Poll

Which statement is true concerning match-merging?

a. The MERGE statement must refer to permanent data sets.
b. The variables in the BY statement can be in only one of the data sets.
c. Only two data sets can be specified in the MERGE statement.
d. When you use the MERGE statement with the BY statement, the data must be sorted or indexed on the BY variable.

4

Match-Merging (Review)

Partial SAS Log

```
729  proc sort data=orion.order_fact
730            out=work.order_fact;
731     by Customer_ID;
732     where year(Order_Date)=2007;
733  run;

NOTE: There were 128 observations read from the data set ORION.ORDER_FACT.
      WHERE YEAR(Order_Date)=2007;
NOTE: The data set WORK.ORDER_FACT has 128 observations and 12 variables.

734
735  data CustOrd;
736     merge orion.customer
737           work.order_fact;
738     by Customer_ID;
739  run;

NOTE: There were 77 observations read from the data set ORION.CUSTOMER.
NOTE: There were 128 observations read from the data set WORK.ORDER_FACT.
NOTE: The data set WORK.CUSTORD has 163 observations and 22 variables.
```

6 p209d01

Match-Merging (Review)

Partial PROC PRINT Output

Obs	Customer_Name	Gender	Quantity	Total_Retail_ Price
152	Tommy Mcdonald	M	2	$49.00
153	Colin Byarley	M	.	.
154	Lera Knott	F	.	.
155	Wilma Yeargan	F	.	.
156	Patrick Leach	M	2	$42.40
157	Patrick Leach	M	1	$55.90
158	Portia Reynoso	F	.	.

matches

non-matches

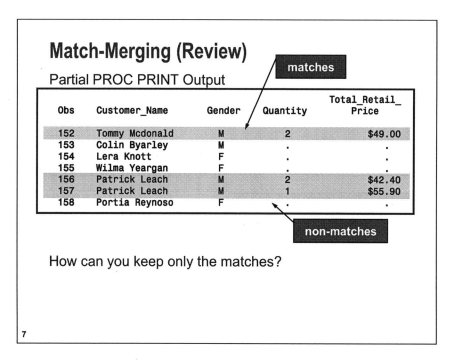

How can you keep only the matches?

7

Match-Merging (Review)

This program writes observations for matches only. The IN= data set option creates a variable that can be used to identify matches and non-matches.

```
data CustOrd;
   merge orion.customer(in=cust)
         work.order_fact(in=order);
   by Customer_ID;
   if cust=1 and order=1;
run;
```

```
NOTE: There were 77 observations read from the data set ORION.CUSTOMER.
NOTE: There were 128 observations read from the data set WORK.ORDER_FACT.
NOTE: The data set WORK.CUSTORD has 128 observations and 22 variables.
```

8 p209d01

9.02 Quiz

Write the appropriate IF statement to create the desired data set that contains only non-matches.

```
data combine;
   merge products(in=InProd) costs(in=InCost);
   by ID;
                   ?
run;
```

Products

Product	ID
XYZ Shoe	A123
ABC Coat	B456

\+

Costs

ID	Cost
B456	59.99
C789	35.75

=

Combine

Product	ID	Cost
XYZ Shoe	A123	
	C789	35.75

9

Business Scenario

A marketing manager needs three SAS data sets to help with her analysis of customers and orders.

The input SAS data sets need to be merged to create the output.

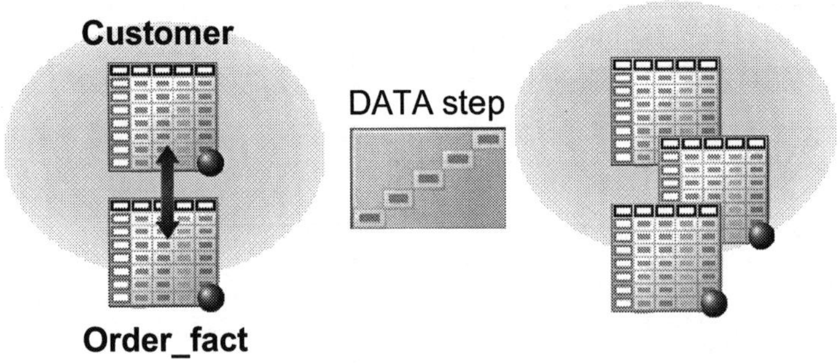

12

Business Scenario

The manager would like you to create the following SAS data sets:

- **noorders** – containing the name and birthdate of customers who have not placed an order
- **orders** – detailing orders placed including customer name, ID of the product ordered, quantity, and price
- **summary** – containing a count of orders placed by each customer

13

Using Data Manipulation Techniques

These techniques are added one at a time to show how the final solution can be built and tested in small steps.

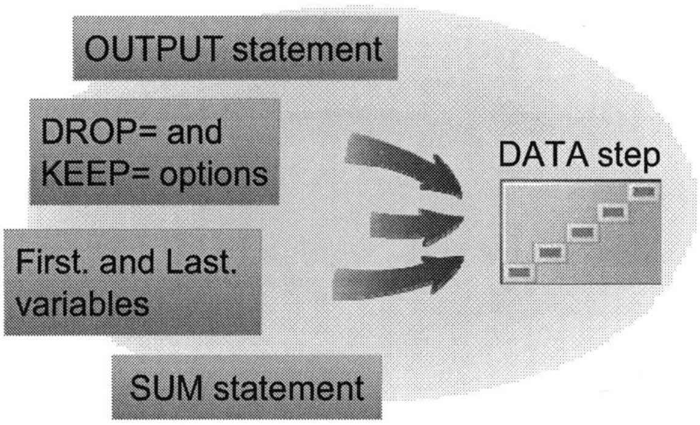

14

OUTPUT Statement

In this program, the OUTPUT statement is used to direct customers with matching orders to one data set and customers with no orders to another data set.

```
data orders noorders;
   merge orion.customer
         work.order_fact(in=order);
   by Customer_ID;
   if order=1 then output orders;
   else output noorders;
run;
```

Partial SAS Log

```
NOTE: There were 77 observations read from the data set ORION.CUSTOMER.
NOTE: There were 128 observations read from the data set WORK.ORDER_FACT.
NOTE: The data set WORK.ORDERS has 128 observations and 22 variables.
NOTE: The data set WORK.NOORDERS has 35 observations and 22 variables.
```

15

p209d02

DROP= and KEEP= Options

You can use the DROP= and KEEP= data set options to determine which variables are written to each output data set.

```
data orders(keep=Customer_Name Quantity
              Product_ID  Total_Retail_Price)
     noorders(keep=Customer_Name Birth_Date);
   merge orion.customer
         work.order_fact(in=order);
   by Customer_ID;
   if order=1 then output orders;
   else output noorders;
run;
```

Partial SAS Log

```
NOTE: The data set WORK.ORDERS has 128 observations and 4 variables.
NOTE: The data set WORK.NOORDERS has 35 observations and 2 variables.
```

16

p209d02

9.03 Quiz

What two temporary variables are created due to the BY statement?

```
data orders(keep=Customer_Name Quantity
            Product_ID Total_Retail_Price)
     noorders(keep=Customer_Name Birth_Date);
   merge orion.customer
         work.order_fact(in=order);
   by Customer_ID;
   if order=1 then output orders;
   else output noorders;
run;
```

17

First. and Last. Variables and Sum Statement

The First. and Last. variables along with the sum statement can be used to create the values for the **summary** data set.

```
data orders(keep=Customer_Name Quantity
                 Product_ID Total_Retail_Price)
     noorders(keep=Customer_Name Birth_Date)
     summary (keep=Customer_Name NumOrders);
   merge orion.customer
         work.order_fact(in=order);
   by Customer_ID;
   if order=1 then do;
      output orders;
      if first.Customer_ID then NumOrders=0;
      NumOrders+1;
      if last.Customer_ID then output summary;
   end;
   else output noorders;
run;
```

19 p209d02

Business Scenario: Final Results

The **noorders** data set contains the names and birthdates of customers who did not place an order.

Partial **noorders** (35 observations total)

Customer_Name	Birth_ Date
James Kvarniq	27JUN1978
Cornelia Krahl	27FEB1978
Karen Ballinger	18OCT1988
Robyn Klem	02JUN1963
Cynthia Mccluney	15APR1973

20

Business Scenario: Final Results

The **orders** data set contains orders, including customer name, ID of the product ordered, quantity, and price.

Partial **orders** (128 observations total)

Customer_Name	Product_ID	Quantity	Total_Retail_ Price
Sandrina Stephano	230100500026	1	$247.50
Sandrina Stephano	240100100433	1	$3.00
Sandrina Stephano	240700300002	2	$43.98
Sandrina Stephano	230100500093	2	$265.60
Sandrina Stephano	230100600030	1	$86.30
Sandrina Stephano	220101400276	2	$136.80
Sandrina Stephano	240100400044	1	$353.60
Sandrina Stephano	240100400049	1	$421.20
Elke Wallstab	230100200047	1	$72.70
David Black	220100100272	3	$68.40

21

Business Scenario: Final Results

The **summary** data set contains a count of the orders placed by each customer.

Partial **summary** (42 observations total)

Customer_Name	Number Orders
Sandrina Stephano	8
Elke Wallstab	1
David Black	5
Markus Sepke	2
Ulrich Heyde	3

22

Multiple Data Sets without a Common Variable

You can use the DATA step to merge three or more SAS data sets that lack a common variable.

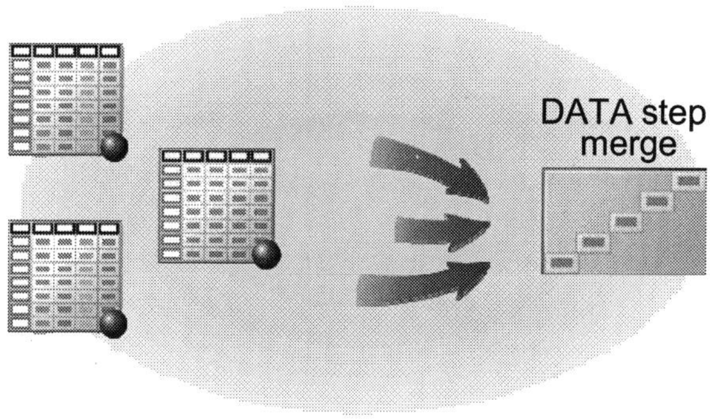

23

✎ The BY statement variables ***must*** exist on all of the data sets. If the data sets lack a common variable, more than one DATA step is required.

Multiple Data Sets without a Common Variable

The following report is created using data from three data sets:

Partial PROC PRINT Output

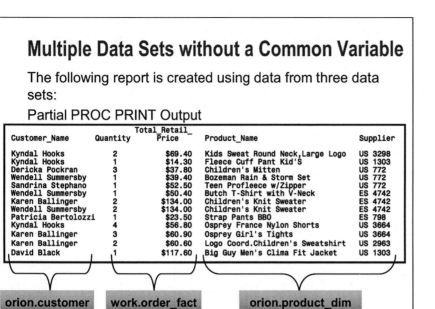

Customer_Name	Quantity	Total_Retail_ Price	Product_Name	Supplier
Kyndal Hooks	2	$69.40	Kids Sweat Round Neck,Large Logo	US 3298
Kyndal Hooks	1	$14.30	Fleece Cuff Pant Kid'S	US 1303
Dericka Pockran	3	$37.80	Children's Mitten	US 772
Wendell Summersby	1	$39.40	Bozeman Rain & Storm Set	US 772
Sandrina Stephano	1	$52.50	Teen Profleece w/Zipper	US 772
Wendell Summersby	1	$50.40	Butch T-Shirt with V-Neck	ES 4742
Karen Ballinger	2	$134.00	Children's Knit Sweater	ES 4742
Wendell Summersby	2	$134.00	Children's Knit Sweater	ES 4742
Patricia Bertolozzi	1	$23.50	Strap Pants BBO	ES 798
Kyndal Hooks	4	$56.80	Osprey France Nylon Shorts	US 3664
Karen Ballinger	3	$60.90	Osprey Girl's Tights	US 3664
Karen Ballinger	2	$60.60	Logo Coord.Children's Sweatshirt	US 2963
David Black	1	$117.60	Big Guy Men's Clima Fit Jacket	US 1303

orion.customer | work.order_fact | orion.product_dim

24

9.04 Quiz

Any number of data sets can be merged in a single DATA step. However, the data sets must have a common variable and be sorted by that variable.

Do the following data sets have a common variable?

orion.customer	work.order_fact	orion.product_dim
Customer_ID	Customer_ID	Product_ID
Country	Employee_ID	Product_Line
Gender	Street_ID	Product_Category
Personal_ID	Order_Date	Product_Group
Customer_Name	Delivery_Date	Product_Name
Customer_FirstName	Order_ID	Supplier_Country
Customer_LastName	Order_Type	Supplier_Name
Birth_Date	Product_ID	Supplier_ID
Customer_Address	Quantity	
...	...	

25

Without a Common Variable: Step 1

Merge **orion.customer** and **work.order_fact** by **Customer_ID**.

```
proc sort data=orion.order_fact
          out=work.order_fact;
   by Customer_ID;
   where year(Order_Date)=2007;
run;

data CustOrd;
   merge orion.customer(in=cust)
         work.order_fact(in=order);
   by Customer_ID;
   if cust=1 and order=1;
   keep Customer_ID Customer_Name Quantity
        Total_Retail_Price Product_ID;
run;
```

orion.customer is in order by **Customer_ID**

28

p209d03

Without a Common Variable: Step 2

Merge the results of step 1, **CustOrd**, with **orion.product_dim** by **Product_ID**.

```
proc sort data=CustOrd;
   by Product_ID;
run;

data CustOrdProd;
   merge CustOrd(in=ord)
         orion.product_dim(in=prod);
   by Product_ID;
   if ord=1 and prod=1;
   Supplier=catx(' ',Supplier_Country,Supplier_ID);
   keep Customer_Name Quantity
        Total_Retail_Price Product_Name Supplier;
run;
```

Product_dim is in order by **Product_ID**

29

p209d03

Performing a Match-Merge on Data Sets That Lack a Common Variable

p209d03

This demonstration illustrates how perform a match-merge on three data sets: **orion.customer**, **orion.order_fact**, and **orion.product_dim**.

1. Submit step 1 to sort **orion.order_fact** by **Customer_ID**, create **work.order_fact**, and match-merge **orion.customer** with the newly created data set **work.order_fact**.

```
*** Step 1 ****************************************************;
proc sort data=orion.order_fact
          out=work.order_fact;
   by Customer_ID;
   where year(Order_Date)=2007;
run;

data custord;
   merge orion.customer(in=cust)
         work.order_fact(in=order);
   by Customer_ID;
   if cust=1 and order=1;
   keep Customer_ID Customer_Name Quantity
        Total_Retail_Price Product_ID;
run;
```

2. Examine the output data set, **work.custord**. Notice that it contains only matches, with a total of 128 observations.

Partial PROC PRINT Output

Obs	Customer_ID	Customer_Name	Product_ID	Quantity	Total_Retail_ Price
1	5	Sandrina Stephano	230100500026	1	$247.50
2	5	Sandrina Stephano	240100100433	1	$3.00
3	5	Sandrina Stephano	240700300002	2	$43.98
4	5	Sandrina Stephano	230100500093	2	$265.60
5	5	Sandrina Stephano	230100600030	1	$86.30

3. Submit step 2 to sort **work.custord** by **Product_ID**. Match-merge **work.custord** with **orion.product_dim** by **Product_ID**.

```
*** Step 2 ****************************************************;
proc sort data=custord;
   by Product_ID;
run;

data custordprod;
   merge custord(in=ord)
         orion.product_dim(in=prod);
   by Product_ID;
   if ord=1 and prod=1;
   Supplier=catx(' ',Supplier_Country,Supplier_ID);
   keep Customer_Name Quantity
        Total_Retail_Price Product_Name Supplier;
run;
```

4. Examine the output data set, **work.custordprod**. It is in order by **Product_ID**.

Partial PROC PRINT Output

Obs	Customer_Name	Quantity	Total_Retail_ Price	Product_Name	Supplier
1	Najma Hicks	2	$92.00	Kid Basic Tracking Suit	US 3664
2	Najma Hicks	2	$39.00	Kid Children's T-Shirt	US 2963
3	Eyal Bloch	1	$102.10	Sports glasses Satin Alumin.	US 1303
4	Yan Kozlowski	1	$50.00	Big Guy Men's Fresh Soft Nylon Pants	US 1303
5	David Black	3	$68.40	Big Guy Men's T-Shirt	US 1303

5. Submit the PRINT procedure to display the first 15 observations in the newly merged data set, **work.custordprod**.

```
proc print data=custordprod(obs=15) noobs;
   var Customer_Name Quantity Total_Retail_Price
       Product_Name Supplier;
run;
```

Partial PROC PRINT Output

Customer_Name	Quantity	Total_Retail_ Price	Product_Name	Supplier
Najma Hicks	2	$92.00	Kid Basic Tracking Suit	US 3664
Najma Hicks	2	$39.00	Kid Children's T-Shirt	US 2963
Eyal Bloch	1	$102.10	Sports glasses Satin Alumin.	US 1303
Yan Kozlowski	1	$50.00	Big Guy Men's Fresh Soft Nylon Pants	US 1303
David Black	3	$68.40	Big Guy Men's T-Shirt	US 1303

Business Scenario: Rename BY Variable

Management requests a list of customers qualifying for bonus gifts. This requires an Excel workbook to be merged with a SAS data set.

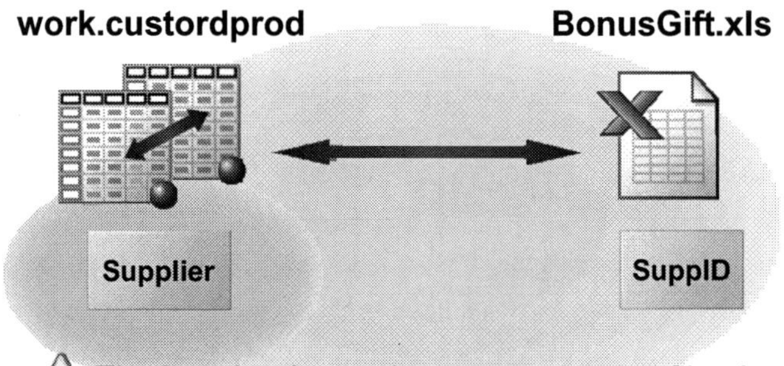

⚠ The key that is used to merge the two files is named differently.

32

Business Scenario: Rename BY Variable

You want to keep merged observations where the value of **Quantity** in **work.custordprod** is more than the value of **Quantity** in **BonusGift.xls**.

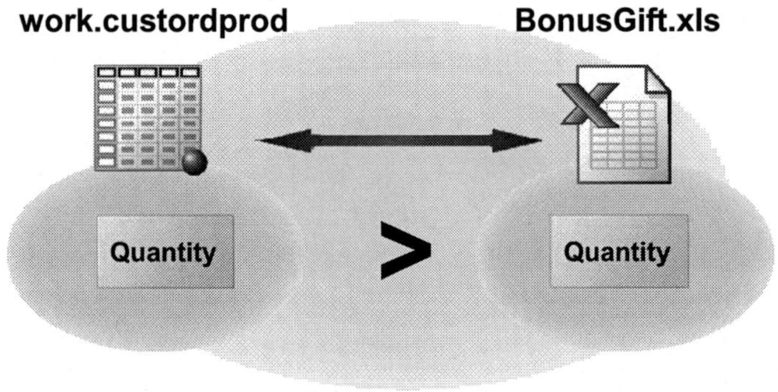

33

9.05 Quiz

Which statements access the **Supplier** worksheet in the Excel workbook correctly?

a.

```
libname bonus "BonusGift.xls";

proc print data=bonus.Supplier;
run;
```

b.

```
libname bonus "BonusGift.xls";

proc print data=bonus."Supplier$"n;
run;
```

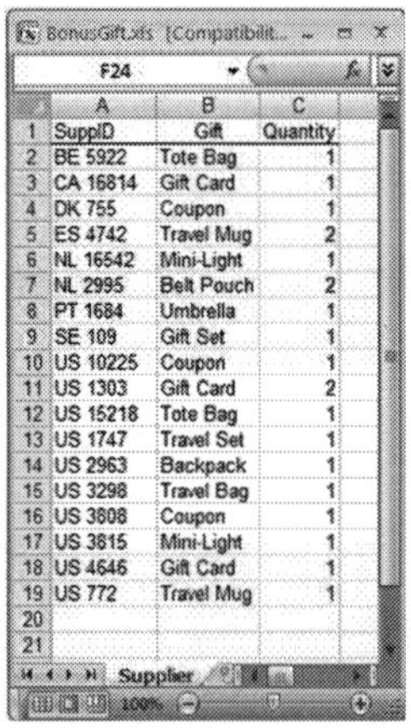

	A	B	C
1	SuppID	Gift	Quantity
2	BE 5922	Tote Bag	1
3	CA 16814	Gift Card	1
4	DK 755	Coupon	1
5	ES 4742	Travel Mug	2
6	NL 16542	Mini-Light	1
7	NL 2995	Belt Pouch	2
8	PT 1684	Umbrella	1
9	SE 109	Gift Set	1
10	US 10225	Coupon	1
11	US 1303	Gift Card	2
12	US 15218	Tote Bag	1
13	US 1747	Travel Set	1
14	US 2963	Backpack	1
15	US 3298	Travel Bag	1
16	US 3808	Coupon	1
17	US 3815	Mini-Light	1
18	US 4646	Gift Card	1
19	US 772	Travel Mug	1
20			
21			

Supplier

34

Create Gift List: Solution

Access the Excel workbook, specify the worksheet to use, and release the workbook after the DATA step.

```
libname bonus "&path\BonusGift.xls";

data CustOrdProdGift;
   merge CustOrdProd(in=c)
         bonus.'Supplier$'n(in=s
                rename=(SuppID=Supplier
                    Quantity=Minimum));
   by Supplier;
   if c=1 and s=1 and Quantity > Minimum;
run;

libname bonus clear;
```

36 p209d04

Both SAS and Microsoft Office offer both 32-bit and 64-bit versions. Different SAS/ACCESS engines are needed based on matching and non-matching number of bits, also known as ***bitness***. If the bitness of both products is the same, use the default SAS/ACCESS Excel engine. If the bitness differs, use the PC Files Server engine and specify PATH= in front of *workbook-name*.

Default Engine:

LIBNAME *libref* <engine> "*workbook-name*.xls" <*options*>;

Example:

```
libname xyz "C:\myfiles\sales.xls";
```

PC Files Server:

LIBNAME libref **pcfiles path=**"*workbook-name*.xls" <*options*>**;**

Example:

```
libname xyz pcfiles path='C:\myfiles\sales.xls';
```

The table below summarizes the possible bit combinations and the appropriate engine to use for each.

SAS	Microsoft Office	SAS/ACCESS Engine
9.4	32-bit	PC Files Server
9.4	64-bit	Default
9.3 32-bit	32-bit	Default
9.3 32-bit	64-bit	PC Files Server
9.3 64-bit	32-bit	PC Files Server

9.3 64-bit	64-bit	Default
SAS 9.2 or earlier	32-bit	Default
SAS 9.2 or earlier	64-bit	PC Files Server

For more information, see the usage note "Installing SAS® 9.3 PC Files Server and using it to convert 32-bit Microsoft Office files to SAS® 64-bit files": **http://support.sas.com/kb/43/802.html**.

Create Gift List: Solution

Use the RENAME= data set option to ensure that the BY variable has the same name to use for merging.

```
libname bonus "&path\BonusGift.xls";

data CustOrdProdGift;
   merge CustOrdProd(in=c)
         bonus.'Supplier$'n(in=s
               rename=(SuppID=Supplier
                    Quantity=Minimum));
   by Supplier;
   if c=1 and s=1 and Quantity > Minimum;
run;

libname bonus clear;
```

37 p209d04

Create Gift List: Solution

Change the name of the **Quantity** variable from the Excel worksheet so that it can be used in a subsetting IF statement.

```
libname bonus "&path\BonusGift.xls";

data CustOrdProdGift;
   merge CustOrdProd(in=c)
         bonus.'Supplier$'n(in=s
               rename=(SuppID=Supplier
                    Quantity=Minimum));
   by Supplier;
   if c=1 and s=1 and Quantity > Minimum;
run;

libname bonus clear;
```

Quantity value from the CustOrdProd data set

renamed Quantity value from the 'Supplier$'n data set

38 p209d04

Create Gift List: Solution

Use the IN= option and a condition in the subsetting IF statement to keep only the matches.

```
libname bonus "&path\BonusGift.xls";

data CustOrdProdGift;
   merge CustOrdProd(in=c)
         bonus.'Supplier$'n(in=s
               rename=(SuppID=Supplier
                    Quantity=Minimum));
   by Supplier;
   if c=1 and s=1 and Quantity > Minimum;
run;

libname bonus clear;
```

39

p209d04

Create Gift List: Solution

Fifty-two gifts are sent to customers.

Partial SAS Log

```
207  libname bonus "&path\BonusGift.xls";
NOTE: Libref BONUS was successfully assigned as follows:
      Engine:        EXCEL
      Physical Name: BonusGift.xls
208
209  data CustOrdProdGift;
210     merge CustOrdProd(in=c)
211           bonus.'Supplier$'n(in=s
212              rename=(SuppID=Supplier
213                      Quantity=Minimum));
214     by Supplier;
215     if c=1 and s=1 and Quantity > Minimum;
216  run;

NOTE: There were 148 observations read from the data set WORK.CUSTORDPROD.
NOTE: There were 18 observations read from the data set BONUS.'Supplier$'n.
NOTE: The data set WORK.CUSTORDPRODGIFT has 52 observations and 7 variables.
NOTE: DATA statement used (Total process time):
      real time           0.04 seconds
      cpu time            0.03 seconds
```

40

Create Gift List: Output

Sort the data set by customer name before printing the list of customers and the gifts that they should receive.

```
proc sort data=CustOrdProdGift;
   by Customer_Name;
run;

proc print data=CustOrdProdGift;
   var Customer_Name Gift;
run;
```

41 p209d04

Create Gift List: Output

The output below shows the list of customers and gifts.

Partial PROC PRINT Output

```
Customer_Name          Gift

Alvan Goheen           Travel Mug
Angel Borwick          Belt Pouch
Cynthia Martinez       Travel Set
Cynthia Martinez       Gift Card
Cynthia Martinez       Travel Mug
Cynthia Mccluney       Tote Bag
Cynthia Mccluney       Tote Bag
Cynthia Mccluney       Gift Card
David Black            Backpack
Dericka Pockran        Coupon
Dericka Pockran        Travel Mug
Dericka Pockran        Travel Mug
```

42 p209d04

Exercises

If you restarted your SAS session since the last exercise, open and submit the **libname.sas** program found in the data folder.

Level 1

1. Performing a Match-Merge on Two Data Sets

The data set **orion.web_products** contains an observation for every product available for sale on Orion Star's wholesale website.

Partial **orion.web_products** (20 Total Observations)

Product_ID	Price	Product_Name
120400304333	114.36	Smasher Super Rq Ti 350 Tennis Racket
120400305288	53.26	Knife
120400305846	107.74	Big Guy Men's Air Deschutz Viii Shoes
120400308766	40.96	Big Guy Men's Packable Hiking Shorts
120400308849	12.23	Wood Box for 6 Balls

The data set **orion.web_orders** contains a list of orders made in a single day from the website. Each observation contains the product ID, the quantity ordered, and the customer's name.

Partial **orion.web_orders** (43 Total Observations)

Product_ID	Quantity	Customer
120400305288	16	Carglar Aydemir
120400305288	19	Sanelisiwe Collier
120400305846	13	Candy Kinsey
120400305846	13	Cynthia Martinez
120400305846	10	Rolf Robak

The two data sets are sorted by **Product_ID**.

a. Create ***three*** data sets:

- A data set named **revenue** contains the product code (**Product_ID**), the price (**Price**), the quantity sold (**Quantity**), the product name (**Product_Name**), the customer name (**Customer**), and the revenue generated from each sale (**Revenue**). **Revenue** is a new variable that is equal to **Price*Quantity**.
- A data set named **notsold** contains the product code (**Product_ID**), price (Price), and product name (**Product_Name**) for each product that was not sold.
- A data set named **invalidcode** contains the product code (**Product_ID**), quantity (**Quantity**), and customer name (**Customer**) for each observation in the **web_orders** data set that does not have a corresponding product code in the **web_products** data set.

b. Print the three data sets with appropriate titles. The data sets should contain 39, 7, and 4 observations, respectively.

Partial **work.revenue** (39 Observations)

Revenue from Orders

Product_ID	Price	Product_Name	Quantity	Customer	Revenue
120400305288	53.26	Knife	16	Carglar Aydemir	852.16
120400305288	53.26	Knife	19	Sanelisiwe Collier	1011.94
120400305846	107.74	Big Guy Men's Air Deschutz Viii Shoes	13	Candy Kinsey	1400.62
120400305846	107.74	Big Guy Men's Air Deschutz Viii Shoes	13	Cynthia Martinez	1400.62
120400305846	107.74	Big Guy Men's Air Deschutz Viii Shoes	10	Rolf Robak	1077.40

Partial **work.notsold** (7 Observations)

Products Not Ordered

Product_ID	Price	Product_Name
120400304333	114.36	Smasher Super Rq Ti 350 Tennis Racket
120400308849	12.23	Wood Box for 6 Balls
120400311211	69.16	Tipee Summer Sleeping Bag
120400317183	164.82	Smasher Rd Ti 70 Tennis Racket
120400329978	114.47	Tipee Twin Blue/Orange

Partial **work.invalidcode** (4 Observations)

Invalid Orders

Product_ID	Quantity	Customer
120400311465	13	Thomas Leitmann
120400312556	7	Robyn Klem
120400315078	23	Tonie Asmussen
120400326278	10	Theunis Brazier

Level 2

2. Handling Same-Named Variables and Different Data Types for BY Variables

The data set **orion.web_products2** contains an observation for every product available for sale on Orion Star's wholesale website.

Partial **orion.web_products2** (20 Total Observations)

Product_ID	Price	Name
120400304333	114.36	Smasher Super Rq Ti 350 Tennis Racket
120400305288	53.26	Knife
120400305846	107.74	Big Guy Men's Air Deschutz Viii Shoes
120400308766	40.96	Big Guy Men's Packable Hiking Shorts
120400308849	12.23	Wood Box for 6 Balls

The data set **orion.web_orders2** contains a list of orders made in a single day from the website. Each observation contains the product ID, the quantity ordered, and the customer's name.

Partial **orion.web_orders2** (43 Total Observations)

Product_ID	Quantity	Name
120400305288	16	Carglar Aydemir
120400305288	19	Sanelisiwe Collier
120400305846	13	Candy Kinsey
120400305846	13	Cynthia Martinez
120400305846	10	Rolf Robak

The two data sets are sorted by **Product_ID**. **Product_ID** is a numeric variable in **orion.web_products2** and a character variable with a length of 12 in **orion.web_orders2**.

a. Create a new data set, **web_converted**, from the **orion.web_products2** data set. Change the type of **Product_ID** to character. (Use the data set **web_converted** to merge with **orion.web_orders2** in the next step.)

Hint: Use the RENAME= data set option to change **Product_ID** to some other name, such as **nProduct_ID**, the LENGTH statement to declare a new character variable named **Product_ID**, and an assignment statement with a PUT function to explicitly convert the numeric value in **nProduct_ID** into a character value in **Product_ID**.

b. Create *three* new data sets:

- A data set named **revenue** contains the product code, the price, the quantity sold, the product name, the customer name and the revenue generated from each sale. **Revenue** is calculated as **Price*Quantity**.

  The **Name** variable in **web_converted** refers to the product name and the **Name** variable in **web_orders2** refers to the customer name. Give each variable an appropriate name in the **revenue** data set.

- A data set named **notsold** contains the product code, price, and product name for each product that was not sold.
- A data set named **invalidcode** contains the product code, quantity, and customer name for each observation in the **web_orders2** data set that does not have a corresponding product code in the **web_products2** data set.

c. Print the three data sets with appropriate titles. The data sets should contain 39, 7, and 4 observations, respectively. (The data sets you create might have different variable names than the ones shown here.)

Partial **work.revenue** (39 Observations)

Revenue from Orders

Product_ID	Price	Product_Name	Quantity	Customer	Revenue
120400305288	53.26	Knife	16	Carglar Aydemir	852.16
120400305288	53.26	Knife	19	Sanelisiwe Collier	1011.94
120400305846	107.74	Big Guy Men's Air Deschutz Viii Shoes	13	Candy Kinsey	1400.62
120400305846	107.74	Big Guy Men's Air Deschutz Viii Shoes	13	Cynthia Martinez	1400.62
120400305846	107.74	Big Guy Men's Air Deschutz Viii Shoes	10	Rolf Robak	1077.40

Partial **work.notsold** (7 Observations)

Products Not Ordered

Product_ID	Price	Name
120400304333	114.36	Smasher Super Rq Ti 350 Tennis Racket
120400308849	12.23	Wood Box for 6 Balls
120400311211	69.16	Tipee Summer Sleeping Bag
120400317183	164.82	Smasher Rd Ti 70 Tennis Racket
120400329978	114.47	Tipee Twin Blue/Orange

Listing of **invalidcode** (4 Observations)

Invalid Orders

Product_ID	Quantity	Name

```
120400311465        13      Thomas Leitmann
120400312556         7      Robyn Klem
120400315078        23      Tonie Asmussen
120400326278        10      Theunis Brazier
```

9.2 Solutions

Solutions to Exercises

1. Performing a Match-Merge on Two Data Sets

```
data revenue
   NotSold(keep=Price Product_ID Product_Name)
   InValidCode(Keep=Product_ID Quantity Customer);
   merge orion.web_products(in=InProduct)
         orion.web_orders(in=InOrders);
   by Product_ID;
   if InProduct and InOrders then do;
      Revenue=Quantity * Price;
      output revenue;
   end;
   else if InProduct and not InOrders then output notsold;
   else if not InProduct and InOrders then output invalidcode;
run;

title 'Revenue from Orders';
proc print data=revenue noobs;
run;

title 'Products Not Ordered';
proc print data=notsold noobs;
run;

title 'Invalid Orders';
proc print data=invalidcode noobs;
run;
title;
```

2. Handling Same-Named Variables and Different Data Types for BY Variables

```
data web_converted(drop=nProduct_ID);
   length Product_ID $ 12;
   set orion.web_products2(rename=(Product_ID=nProduct_ID));
   Product_ID=put(nProduct_ID,12.);
run;

data revenue
   NotSold(keep=Price Product_ID Product_Name)
   InValidCode(Keep=Product_ID Quantity Customer);
   merge web_converted(in=InConv rename=(Name=Product_Name))
         orion.web_orders2(in=InOrders rename=(Name=Customer));
   by Product_ID;
```

```
   if InConv and InOrders then do;
      Revenue=Quantity * Price;
      output revenue;
   end;
   else if InConv and not InOrders then output notsold;
   else if not InConv and InOrders then output invalidcode;
run;

title 'Revenue from Orders';
proc print data=revenue noobs;
run;

title 'Products Not Ordered';
proc print data=notsold noobs;
run;

title 'Invalid Orders';
proc print data=invalidcode noobs;
run;
title;
```

Solutions to Student Activities (Polls/Quizzes)

9.01 Multiple Choice Poll – Correct Answer

Which statement is true concerning match-merging?

a. The MERGE statement must refer to permanent data sets.

b. The variables in the BY statement can be in only one of the data sets.

c. Only two data sets can be specified in the MERGE statement.

(d.) When you use the MERGE statement with the BY statement, the data must be sorted or indexed on the BY variable.

5

9.02 Quiz – Correct Answer

Write the appropriate IF statement to create the desired data set that contains only non-matches.

```
data combine;
   merge products(in=InProd) costs(in=InCost);
   by ID;
   if InProd=0 or InCost=0;
run;
```

Products

Product	ID
XYZ Shoe	A123
ABC Coat	B456

+

Costs

ID	Cost
B456	59.99
C789	35.75

=

Combine

Product	ID	Cost
XYZ Shoe	A123	
	C789	35.75

10

9.03 Quiz – Correct Answer

What two temporary variables are created due to the BY statement?

```
data orders(keep=Customer_Name Quantity
                 Product_ID Total_Retail_Price)
     noorders(keep=Customer_Name Birth_Date);
   merge orion.customer
         work.order_fact(in=order);
   by Customer_ID;
   if order=1 then output orders;
   else output noorders;
run;
```

First.Customer_ID and Last.Customer_ID

18

9.04 Quiz – Correct Answer

Do the following data sets have a common variable?

No, these data sets do not share one common variable. Therefore, they cannot be combined in a single DATA step.

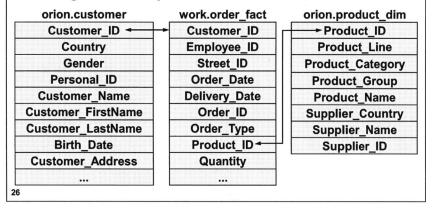

orion.customer	work.order_fact	orion.product_dim
Customer_ID	Customer_ID	Product_ID
Country	Employee_ID	Product_Line
Gender	Street_ID	Product_Category
Personal_ID	Order_Date	Product_Group
Customer_Name	Delivery_Date	Product_Name
Customer_FirstName	Order_ID	Supplier_Country
Customer_LastName	Order_Type	Supplier_Name
Birth_Date	Product_ID	Supplier_ID
Customer_Address	Quantity	
...	...	

26

9.05 Quiz – Correct Answer

Which statements access the **Supplier** worksheet in the Excel workbook correctly?

a.

```
libname bonus "BonusGift.xls";

proc print data=bonus.Supplier;
run;
```

(b.)

```
libname bonus "BonusGift.xls";

proc print data=bonus."Supplier$"n;
run;
```

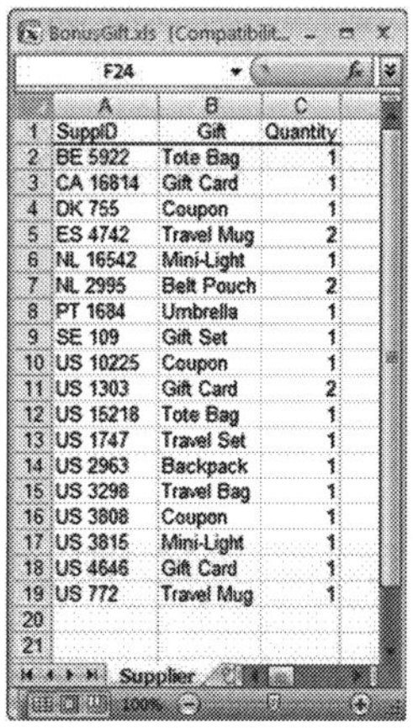

	A	B	C
1	SuppID	Gift	Quantity
2	BE 5922	Tote Bag	1
3	CA 16814	Gift Card	1
4	DK 755	Coupon	1
5	ES 4742	Travel Mug	2
6	NL 16542	Mini-Light	1
7	NL 2995	Belt Pouch	2
8	PT 1684	Umbrella	1
9	SE 109	Gift Set	1
10	US 10225	Coupon	1
11	US 1303	Gift Card	2
12	US 15218	Tote Bag	1
13	US 1747	Travel Set	1
14	US 2963	Backpack	1
15	US 3298	Travel Bag	1
16	US 3808	Coupon	1
17	US 3815	Mini-Light	1
18	US 4646	Gift Card	1
19	US 772	Travel Mug	1
20			
21			

35

Chapter 10 Creating and Maintaining Permanent Formats

10.1 Creating Permanent Formats **10-3**

Demonstration: Using a Control Data Set to Create a Format 10-11

Demonstration: Maintaining Permanent Formats 10-17

Exercises 10-18

10.2 Solutions **10-20**

Solutions to Exercises 10-20

Solutions to Student Activities (Polls/Quizzes) 10-24

10.1 Creating Permanent Formats

Objectives

- Create permanent formats.
- Access permanent formats.
- Create formats from SAS data sets.
- Maintain formats.

2

Business Scenario

Management has requested that country names, instead of country codes, be used in reports.

Country	Population	Country_ID
AU	20,000,000	160
CA	.	260
DE	80,000,000	394
IL	5,000,000	475

Country	Population	Country_ID
Australia	20,000,000	160
Canada	.	260
Germany	80,000,000	394
Israel	5,000,000	475

3

Creating a Format (Review)

Use PROC FORMAT to create the format.

```
proc format;
   value $country 'AU' = 'Australia'
                  'CA' = 'Canada'
                  'DE' = 'Germany'
                  'IL' = 'Israel'
                  'TR' = 'Turkey'
                  'US' = 'United States'
                  'ZA' = 'South Africa';
run;
```

4

Using a Control Data Set to Create a Format

Instead of entering all of the values in PROC FORMAT, you can create a format from a SAS data set that contains the code and value information.

Partial Listing of
orion.country

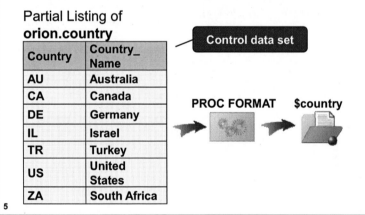

Country	Country_ Name
AU	Australia
CA	Canada
DE	Germany
IL	Israel
TR	Turkey
US	United States
ZA	South Africa

Control data set

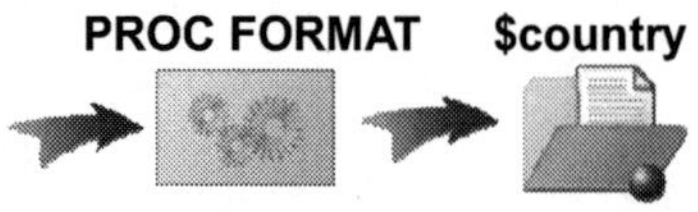

5

Using a Control Data Set to Create a Format

Use the CNTLIN= option to read the data and create the format.

```
proc format library=orion.MyFmts
            cntlin=orion.country;
run;
```

CNTLIN=*SAS-data-set*

⚠ The variables **FmtName**, **Start**, and **Label** are required in order to create a format from a CNTLIN data set.

6

Using a Control Data Set to Create a Format

Partial **country**

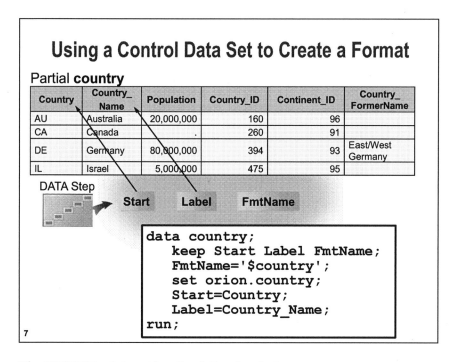

Country	Country_ Name	Population	Country_ID	Continent_ID	Country_ FormerName
AU	Australia	20,000,000	160	96	
CA	Canada	.	260	91	
DE	Germany	80,000,000	394	93	East/West Germany
IL	Israel	5,000,000	475	95	

DATA Step

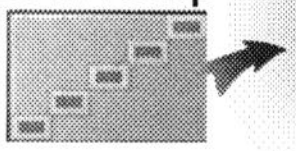

Start **Label** **FmtName**

```
data country;
   keep Start Label FmtName;
   FmtName='$country';
   set orion.country;
   Start=Country;
   Label=Country_Name;
run;
```

7

The CNTLIN= data set has the following features:

- assumes that the ending value of the format range is equal to the value of **Start** if no variable named **End** is found
- can be used to create new formats, as well as re-create existing formats
- must be grouped by **FmtName** if multiple formats are specified

FmtName

- can be up to 32 characters in length
- for character formats, must begin with a dollar sign ($), followed by a letter or underscore

- for numeric formats, must begin with a letter or underscore
- cannot end in a number
- cannot be the name of a SAS format.

Setup for the Poll

The following DATA steps both create a SAS data set named **country**.

p210d01

```
data country;
   keep Start Label FmtName;
   retain FmtName '$country';
   set orion.country(rename=(Country=Start
                             Country_Name=Label));
run;
```

p210d01a

```
data country;
   keep Start Label FmtName;
   FmtName='$country';
   set orion.country;
   Start=Country;
   Label=Country_Name;
run;
```

8

10.01 Multiple Choice Poll

Which program should be more efficient?

a. p210d01
b. p210d01a
c. They should be equally efficient.

9

Using a Control Data Set to Create a Format

Use the LIBRARY= option to control where the format is stored.

```
proc format library=orion.MyFmts
            cntlin=country;
run;
```

LIBRARY=*libref.catalog*

11

How Formats Are Stored

Formats are stored as SAS catalog entries.

- *SAS catalogs* are special SAS files that store many different types of information in smaller units called *entries*.
- A single SAS catalog can contain many different catalog entries.

Examples of SAS Catalogs

work.formats **orion.formats** **orion.MyFmts**

12

Catalog entries have four-level names: *libref.catalog.entry-name.type.*

The *type* for character formats is ***formatc***. The *type* for numeric formats is ***format***.

Where Formats Are Stored

Without the LIBRARY= option, formats are stored in the **work.formats** catalog and exist only for the duration of the SAS session.

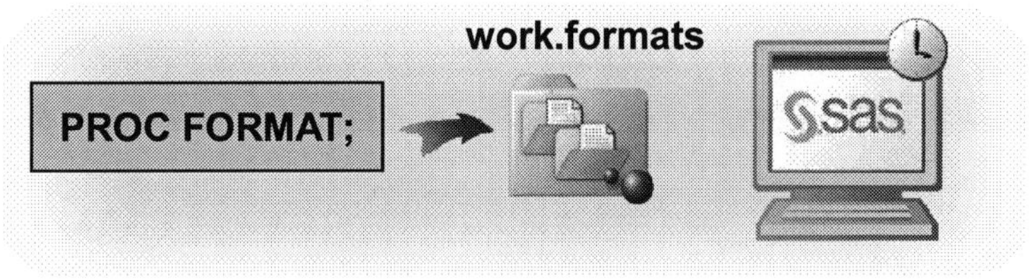

13

Where Formats Are Stored

If the LIBRARY= option specifies only a *libref*, formats are stored permanently in a catalog named **formats**, referenced by ***libref*.formats**.

```
proc format library=orion;
```

PROC FORMAT LIBRARY=*libref*;

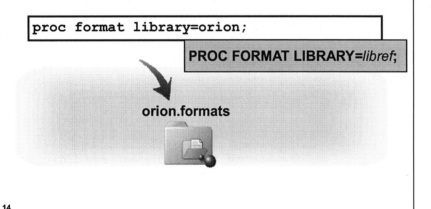

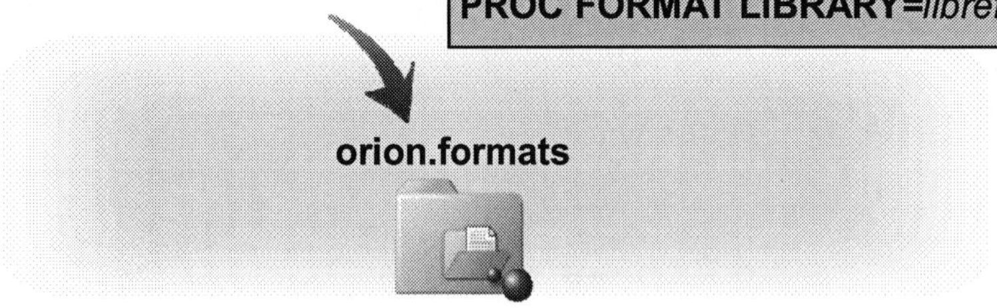

14

Where Formats Are Stored

If the LIBRARY= option specifies *libref.catalog*, formats are stored permanently in that catalog.

```
proc format library=orion.MyFmts;
```

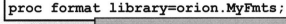

PROC FORMAT LIBRARY=*libref.catalog*;

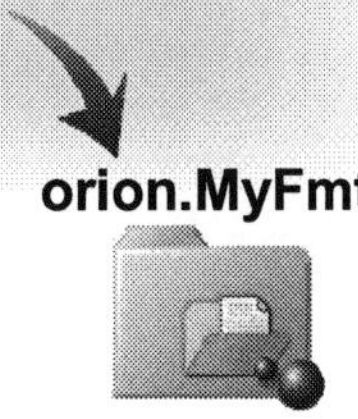

✎ Store frequently used formats in permanent catalogs.

15

Viewing Formats

You can use the SAS Explorer window to view formats stored in a catalog.

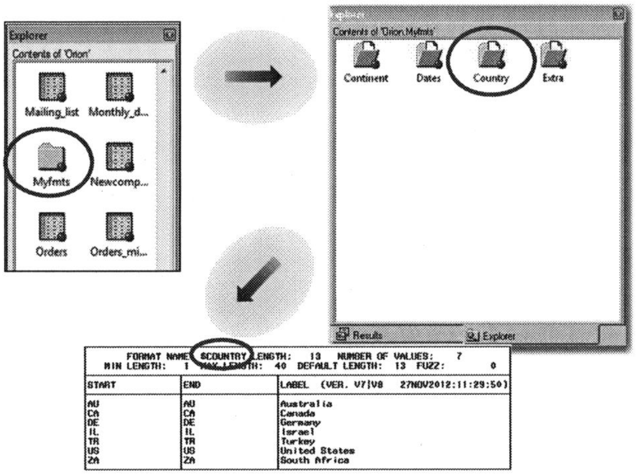

FORMAT NAME: $COUNTRY LENGTH: 13 NUMBER OF VALUES: 7
MIN LENGTH: 1 MAX LENGTH: 40 DEFAULT LENGTH: 13 FUZZ: 0

START	END	LABEL (VER. V7|V8 27NOV2012:11:29:50)
AU	AU	Australia
CA	CA	Canada
DE	DE	Germany
IL	IL	Israel
TR	TR	Turkey
US	US	United States
ZA	ZA	South Africa

16

CATALOG Procedure

The CATALOG procedure manages entries in SAS catalogs.

```
proc catalog cat=orion.MyFmts;
   contents;
run;
```

PROC CATALOG CATALOG=*libref.catalog*;
CONTENTS;

Contents of Catalog ORION.MYFMTS

#	Name	Type	Create Date	Modified Date
1	DATES	FORMAT	29Jan08:16:26:39	29Jan08:16:26:39
2	COUNTRY	FORMATC	29Jan08:16:33:30	29Jan08:16:33:30
3	COUNTRY_NAME	FORMATC	20Apr09:15:30:14	20Apr09:15:30:14
4	EXTRA	FORMATC	20Apr09:15:30:14	20Apr09:15:30:14

17

p210d01

Documenting Formats

You can use the FMTLIB option in the PROC FORMAT statement to document the format.

```
proc format library=orion.MyFmts fmtlib;
   select $country;
run;
```

FORMAT NAME: $COUNTRY LENGTH: 13 NUMBER OF VALUES: 7
MIN LENGTH: 1 MAX LENGTH: 40 DEFAULT LENGTH 13 FUZZ: 0

START	END	LABEL (VER. V7|V8 05MAY2009:12:34:42)
AU	AU	Australia
CA	CA	Canada
DE	DE	Germany
IL	IL	Israel
TR	TR	Turkey
US	US	United States
ZA	ZA	South Africa

18

p307d01

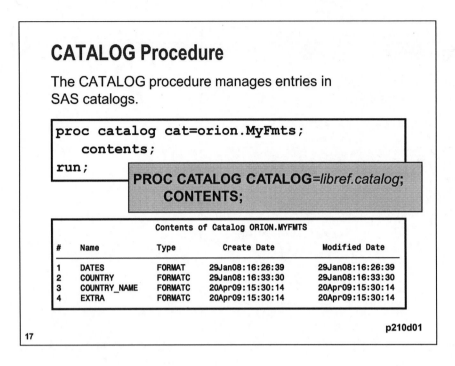

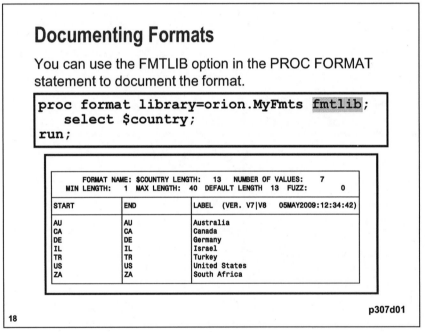

You can use either the SELECT or EXCLUDE statement to process specific formats rather than an entire catalog.

Nesting Formats

In the VALUE statement, you can specify that the format use a second format as the formatted value.

Enclose the format name in square brackets:

```
proc format library=orion.MyFmts;
   value $extra ' '='Unknown'
                  other=[$country30.];
run;
```

value=[existing-format]

19 p210d01

Avoid nesting formats for more than one level. The resource requirements can increase dramatically with each additional level.

Using a Control Data Set to Create a Format

p210d01

This demonstration illustrates how to create a permanent format from a SAS data set.

1. Submit step 1 to create a SAS data set that contains the format name, labels, and start values.

   a. The DATA step creates the control data set **country**.

   b. Use PROC PRINT to view the new data set.

```
/* Step 1 */

/* Make a CNTLIN data set containing */
/* the variables FMTNAME, START, and */
/* LABEL.                            */

data country;
   keep Start Label FmtName;
   retain FmtName '$country';
   set orion.country(rename=(Country=Start
                             Country_Name=Label));
run;

proc print data=country noobs;
   title 'Country';
run;
```

2. Submit Step 2 to use a SAS data set to create the permanent format.

   a. The first PROC FORMAT creates the format **$country**.

   b. Use PROC CATALOG to view the contents of the catalog **orion.formats**.

   c. The second PROC FORMAT augments **$country** by creating a label for missing values.

   d. Use PROC FORMAT with the FMTLIB option to document **$country** and **$extra**.

```
/* Step 2 */
/* Use the data set COUNTRY to        */
/* make the format $country.          */

proc format library=orion.MyFmts cntlin=country;
run;

proc catalog cat=orion.MyFmts;
   contents;
run;

/*******************************************************/
/* If there are missing country values, they can be    */
/* handled by creating the format $extra. This format  */
/* specifically sets missing values to the label       */
/* Unknown and uses the label of the $country          */
/* format for all other values. Notice that a length   */
/* of 30 is provided for the $country format.          */
/* The default would be 40.                            */
/*******************************************************/

proc format library=orion.MyFmts;
   value $extra    ' '='Unknown'
               other=[$country30.];
run;

proc format library=orion.MyFmts fmtlib;
   select $country $extra;
run;
```

Using Formats

When a format is referenced, SAS does the following:

- loads the format from the catalog entry into memory
- performs a binary search on values in the table to execute a lookup
- returns a single result for each lookup

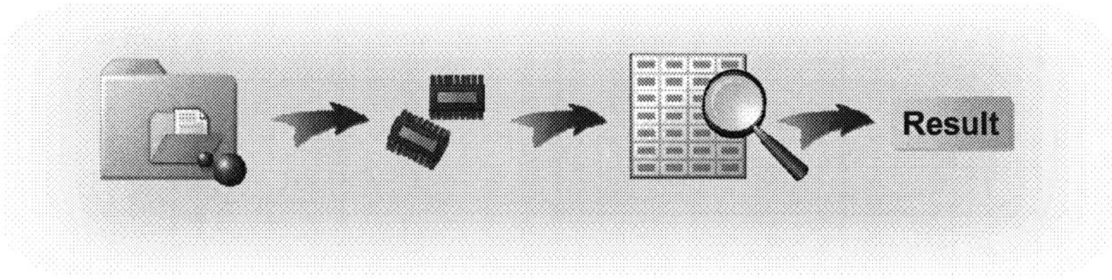

21

Using Formats

You can reference formats in any of the following:

- FORMAT statements
- FORMAT= options
- PUT statements
- PUT functions

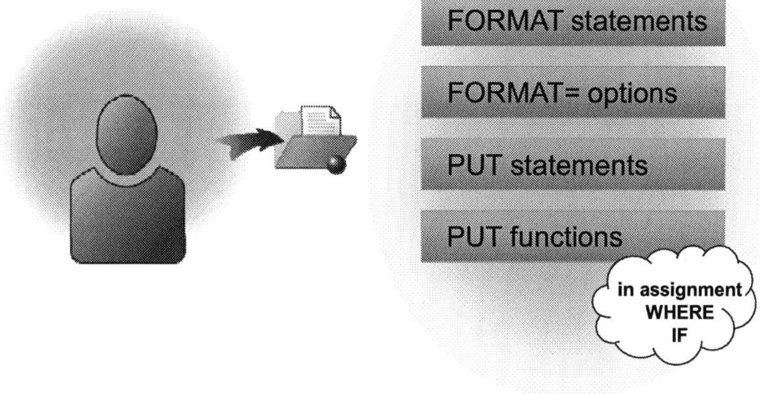

22

10.02 Quiz

Submit the program **p210a01**.

What error messages do you see in the SAS log?

```
data customers;
   set orion.customer;
   Country_Name=put(Country,$country.);
run;

proc freq data=orion.employee_addresses;
   tables Country;
   format Country $extra.;
run;
```

23

10.03 Quiz

1. Add the following OPTIONS statement to **p210a01** and resubmit the program. What is the result?

```
options nofmterr;
```

2. Replace the current OPTIONS statement with the following statement and resubmit the program. What is the result?

```
options fmterr fmtsearch=(orion orion.MyFmts);
```

25

Using the NOFMTERR System Option

By default, the FMTERR system option is in effect. If you use a format that SAS cannot load, SAS issues an error message and stops processing the step.

To prevent the default action, change the system option FMTERR to NOFMTERR.

```
OPTIONS FMTERR | NOFMTERR;
```

28

FMTERR	Specifies that when SAS cannot find a specified variable format, it generates an error message and does not enable default substitution to occur.
NOFMTERR	Replaces missing formats with the w. or $w. default format, issues a note, and continues processing.

Using the FMTSEARCH= System Option

To use permanent formats or to search multiple catalogs, use the FMTSEARCH= system option to identify the catalog(s) to be searched for the format(s).

General form of the FMTSEARCH= system option:

OPTIONS FMTSEARCH=(*item-1 item-2...item-n***);**

29

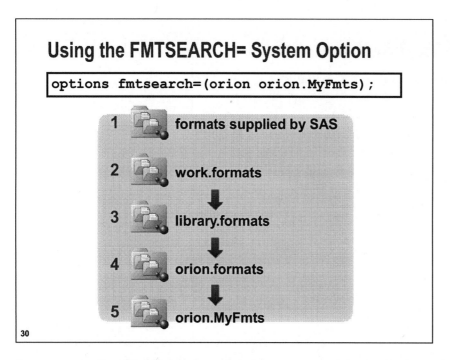

Using the FMTSEARCH= System Option

```
options fmtsearch=(orion orion.MyFmts);
```

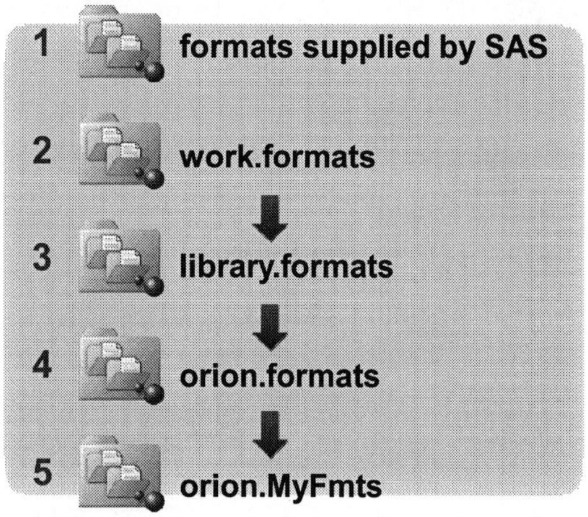

30

Because **orion** is a libref without a catalog name, **formats** is assumed to be the catalog name.

Formats supplied by SAS are always searched first. The **work.formats** catalog is always searched second, unless it appears in the FMTSEARCH list. If the **library** libref is assigned, the **library.formats** catalog is searched after **work.formats** and before anything else in the FMTSEARCH list, unless it appears in the list. To assign the **library** libref, use the code shown below:

```
libname library 'SAS-data-library-containing-format-catalog';
```

Maintaining Formats

To maintain formats, perform one of the following tasks:

- Edit the PROC FORMAT code that created the original format.
- Create a SAS data set from the format, edit the data set, and use the CNTLIN= option to re-create the format.

31

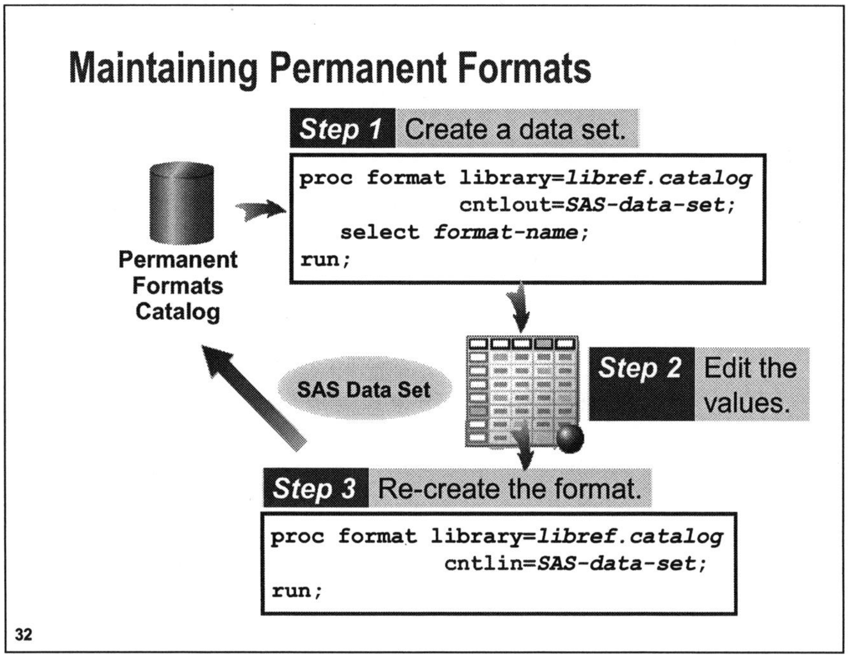

Maintaining Permanent Formats

p210d02

This demonstration illustrates how to maintain a permanent format from a SAS data set.

1. Submit step 1 to create a SAS data set from a permanent format.
2. Submit step 2 to concatenate the new country codes to **countryfmt**.
3. Submit step 3 to replace **$country** with the old and new formatted values.

```
/* Step 1 */
proc format library=orion.myfmts cntlout=countryfmt;
   select $country;
run;

proc print data=countryfmt;
run;

proc print data=orion.NewCodes;
run;

/* Step 2 */

data countryfmt;
   set countryfmt orion.NewCodes;
run;

/* Step 3 */
```

```
proc format library=work.myfmts cntlin=countryfmt fmtlib;
   select $country;
run;
```

Exercises

If you restarted your SAS session since the last exercise, open and submit the **libname.sas** program found in the data folder.

Level 1

1. Creating Formats with Values from a SAS Data Set

The data set **orion.continent** contains the **Continent_ID** and the **Continent_Name** variables.

Obs	Continent_ ID	Continent_Name
1	91	North America
2	93	Europe
3	94	Africa
4	95	Asia
5	96	Australia/Pacific

a. Create a CNTLIN data set named **continent** that reads the data from **orion.continent** and contains the variables **FmtName**, **Start**, and **Label**. The name of the format should be CONTINENT.

b. Use the CNTLIN= option to create a format from the **continent** data set and store the format in the **orion.MyFmts** catalog.

c. Open the program **p210e01c** and submit it. The program should execute successfully with no errors in the SAS log.

p210e01c

```
/*******************/
/* Part C          */
/* Use continent.  */
/*******************/

data countries;
   set orion.country;
   Continent_Name=put(Continent_ID, continent.);
run;

proc print data=countries(obs=10);
   title 'Continent Names';
run;
```

d. Open the program **p210e01d**.

p210e01d

```
/***********************************************/
/* When START and END are created using the    */
/* CNTLOUT= option, they are created as character*/
/***********************************************/


data continentfmt;
     set continentfmt orion.NewContinent;
run;
```

1) Before the DATA step, add a PROC FORMAT step with the CNTLOUT= option to create a control output data set named **continentfmt** from the CONTINENT format.

2) Submit the program to add new observations to the **continentfmt** data set.

3) Add another PROC FORMAT step with the CNTLIN= option to read the **continentfmt** data set and re-create the CONTINENT format. Use the FMTLIB option in this PROC FORMAT step to ensure that the new values were added to the format CONTINENT.

Level 2

2. Creating Formats with Inclusive Ranges from a SAS Data Set

The data set **orion.ages** contains three variables: **First_Age**, **Last_Age**, and **Description**.

Partial **orion.ages**

Obs	First_ Age	Last_Age	Description
1	15	30	15-30 years
2	30	45	31-45 years
3	45	60	46-60 years
4	60	75	61-75 years

a. Create a format from the **orion.ages** data set and store it permanently in the **orion.MyFmts** catalog. Use the appropriate option to view the values in the format.

b. Write a DATA step to create a data set named **sales** that reads the **Employee_ID** and **Birth_Date** variables from the **orion.sales** data set. Create a new variable named **Age** that is the employee's age as of the current date, and another new variable named **Age_Cat** that is the value of the variable **Age** using the AGE format. The YRDIF format with the AGE basis calculates the exact age of the employee with decimal places.

c. Print the first five observations of the **sales** data set to confirm that the new variables were created correctly.

PROC PRINT Output (as of July 18, 2012)

Sales Data Set

Obs	Employee_ID	Birth_ Date	Age	Age_Cat

1	120102	11AUG1973	38	31-45 years
2	120103	22JAN1953	59	46-60 years
3	120121	02AUG1948	63	61-75 years
4	120122	27JUL1958	53	46-60 years
5	120123	28SEP1968	43	31-45 years

Challenge

3. Creating Formats with Exclusive Ranges from a SAS Data Set

The data set **orion.ages_mod** contains three variables: **First_Age**, **Last_Age**, and **Description**.

Partial **orion.ages_mod**

Obs	First_ Age	Last_Age	Description
1	15	30	15-29 years
2	30	45	30-44 years
3	45	60	45-59 years
4	60	75	60-75 years

a. Create a format named AGES_MOD from the **orion.ages_mod** data set and store it permanently in the **orion.MyFmts** catalog. Use the appropriate option to view the values in the format.

The value of the **Last_Age** variable is not to be included in the **Description** variable. Use SAS Help or SAS OnlineDoc to investigate the **EEXCL** variable that is required to get the correct results for this exercise.

b. Write a DATA step to create a data set named **sales** that reads the **Employee_ID** and **Birth_Date** variables from the **orion.sales** data set. Create a new variable named **Age** that is the employee's age as of the current date, and another new variable named **Age_Cat** that is the value of the variable **Age** using the AGES_MOD format. One possible solution for calculating **Age** is to use the YRDIF function with the AGE basis.

c. Print the first five observations of the **sales** data set to confirm that the new variables were created correctly.

PROC PRINT Output (as of July 18, 2012)

Sales Data Set

Obs	Employee_ID	Birth_ Date	Age	Age_Cat
1	120102	11AUG1973	38	30-44 years
2	120103	22JAN1953	59	45-59 years
3	120121	02AUG1948	63	60-75 years
4	120122	27JUL1958	53	45-59 years
5	120123	28SEP1968	43	30-44 years

10.2 Solutions

Solutions to Exercises

1. Creating Formats with Values from a SAS Data Set

a. Create a CNTLIN data set named **continent** that reads the data from **orion.continent** and contains the variables **FmtName**, **Start**, and **Label**. The name of the format should be CONTINENT.

p210s01

```
/*********************/
/* Part A            */
/* Make continent    */
/*********************/

data continent;
   keep Start Label FmtName;
   retain FmtName 'continent';
   set orion.continent(rename=(Continent_ID=Start
                               Continent_Name=Label));
run;

proc print data=continent(obs=10) noobs;
   title 'Continent';
run;
```

b. Use the CNTLIN= option to create a format from the **continent** data set and store the format in the **orion.MyFmts** catalog.

p210s01

```
/***********************************/
/* Part B                          */
/* Use continent to create format. */
/***********************************/

proc format library=orion.MyFmts cntlin=continent fmtlib;
   select continent;
   title 'Continent format';
run;
```

c. Open the program **p210e01c** and submit it. The program should execute successfully with no errors in the SAS log.

d. Open the program **p210e01d**.

1) Before the PROC SQL step, add a PROC FORMAT step with the CNTLOUT= option to create a control output data set named **continentfmt** from the CONTINENT format.

p307s01

```
/********************/
/* Part D           */
/* Update Continent.*/
/********************/

proc format library=orion.MyFmts cntlout=continentfmt;
   select continent;
run;
```

2) Submit the program to add new observations to the **continentfmt** data set.

3) Add another PROC FORMAT step with the CNTLIN= option to read the **continentfmt** data set and re-create the CONTINENT format. Use the FMTLIB option in this PROC FORMAT step to ensure that the new values are added to the CONTINENT format.

p210s01

```
proc format library=orion.MyFmts cntlin=continentfmt
            fmtlib;
   select continent;
run;
```

2. Creating Formats with Inclusive Ranges from a SAS Data Set

a. Create a format from the **orion.ages** data set and store it permanently in the **orion.MyFmts** catalog. Use the appropriate option to view the values in the format.

p210s02

```
data ages;
   set orion.ages (rename=(First_Age=Start Last_Age=End
                           Description=Label));
   retain FmtName 'ages';
run;

proc format library=orion.MyFmts fmtlib cntlin=ages;
   select ages;
run;
```

b. Write a DATA step to create a data set named **sales** that reads the **Employee_ID** and **Birth_Date** variables from the **orion.sales** data set. Create a new variable named **Age** that is the employee's age as of the current date, and another new variable named **Age_Cat** that is the value of the variable **Age** using the AGE format.

p210s02

```
data sales;
   set orion.sales(keep=Employee_ID Birth_Date);
   Age=int(yrdif(Birth_Date, today(), 'AGE'));
   Age_Cat=put(Age, ages.);
run;
```

c. Print the first five observations of the **sales** data set to confirm that the new variables were created correctly.

p210s02

```
proc print data=sales(obs=5);
   format Birth_Date date9.;
   title 'Sales Data Set';
run;
```

3. Creating Formats with Exclusive Ranges from a SAS Data Set

a. Create a format named **ages_mod** from the **orion.ages_mod** data set and store it permanently in the **orion.MyFmts** catalog. Use the appropriate option to view the values in the format.

p210s03

```
data ages_mod;
```

```
   set orion.ages_mod(rename=(First_Age=Start Last_Age=End
                              Description=Label));
   retain fmtname 'ages_mod';
   EEXCL='Y';
run;

proc format library=orion.MyFmts fmtlib cntlin=ages_mod;
   select ages_mod;
run;
```

b. Write a DATA step to create a data set named **sales** that reads the **Employee_ID** and **Birth_Date** variables from the **orion.sales** data set. Create a new variable named **Age** that is the employee's age as of the current date, and another new variable named **Age_Cat** that is the value of the variable **Age** using the AGES_MOD format.

p210s03

```
options fmtsearch=(orion.MyFmts);

data sales;
   set orion.sales(keep=Employee_ID Birth_Date);
   Age=int(yrdif(Birth_Date, today(), 'AGE'));
   Age_Cat=put(Age, ages_mod.);
run;
```

c. Print the first five observations of the **sales** data set to confirm that the new variables were created correctly.

p210s03

```
proc print data=sales(obs=5);
   format birth_date date9.;
   title 'Sales Data Set';
run;
```

Solutions to Student Activities (Polls/Quizzes)

10.01 Multiple Choice Poll – Correct Answer

Which program should be more efficient?

a. p210d01 (circled)
b. p210d01a
c. They should be equally efficient.

- **The RETAIN statement assigns an initial value at compilation time.**
- **The RENAME= option renames the variables in the new data set at compilation time.**

10

10.02 Quiz – Correct Answer

Submit the program **p210a01**.

What error messages do you see in the SAS log?

```
477  data customers;
478     set orion.customer;
479     Country_Name=put(Country,$country.);
                                 ---------
                                 48
ERROR 48-59: The format $COUNTRY was not found or could not be loaded.

480  run;

NOTE: The SAS System stopped processing this step because of errors.
WARNING: The data set WORK.CUSTOMERS may be incomplete.  When this step was stopped there were
         0 observations and 13 variables.
WARNING: Data set WORK.CUSTOMERS was not replaced because this step was stopped.
NOTE: DATA statement used (Total process time):
      real time           0.00 seconds
      cpu time            0.00 seconds

481
482  proc freq data=orion.employee_addresses;
483     tables Country;
484     format Country $extra.;
ERROR: The format $EXTRA was not found or could not be loaded.
485  run;

NOTE: The SAS System stopped processing this step because of errors.
NOTE: PROCEDURE FREQ used (Total process time):
      real time           0.10 seconds
      cpu time            0.00 seconds
```

24

10.03 Quiz – Correct Answer

1. Add the following OPTIONS statement to **p307a01** and resubmit the program. What is the result?

```
options nofmterr;
```

All of the procedure steps were executed with no warnings or errors in the SAS log. The user-defined formats were *not* applied.

26

10.03 Quiz – Correct Answer

2. Replace the current OPTIONS statement with the following statement and resubmit the program. What is the result?

```
options fmterr fmtsearch=(orion orion.MyFmts);
```

All of the procedure steps were executed with no warnings or errors in the SAS log. The user-defined formats *were* applied.

27

Chapter 11 Other SAS® Languages

11.1 An Overview of Other Languages **11-3**

11.2 Using the SQL Procedure **11-5**

Exercises 11-19

11.3 The SAS Macro Language **11-23**

Exercises 11-33

11.4 Solutions **11-35**

Solutions to Exercises 11-35

Solutions to Student Activities (Polls/Quizzes) 11-37

11.1 An Overview of Other Languages

Objectives

- Describe other languages available in SAS.

3

Other SAS Languages

The languages that are available in SAS include the following:

- the SAS language
- SQL
- macro
- SCL
- SAS/C

The focus has been on the SAS language.

This chapter introduces SQL and the macro language.

4

Why Learn SQL?

SQL (Structured Query Language) is a standardized language used by many software products.

The SQL procedure in SAS

- can be used to retrieve, join, and update data in tables
- can perform more efficient join operations than DATA step merges in some cases
- can replace the need for multiple DATA and PROC steps with one query.

5

Why Learn Macro?

The SAS macro language permits code substitution as well as automatic code generation and execution.

Macro programming makes more efficient use of a SAS programmer's time by

- simplifying program maintenance
- generating flexible, customizable code
- executing code iteratively.

6

11.2 Using the SQL Procedure

Objectives

- Explain the purpose and syntax of the SQL procedure.
- Use the SQL procedure to query a SAS data set.
- Use the SQL procedure to create a SAS data set.
- Use the SQL procedure to join SAS data sets.

8

Business Scenario

The director of sales at Orion Star wants a report listing employee IDs, titles, and salaries for his direct reports. The employee data is stored in the **orion.sales_mgmt** table.

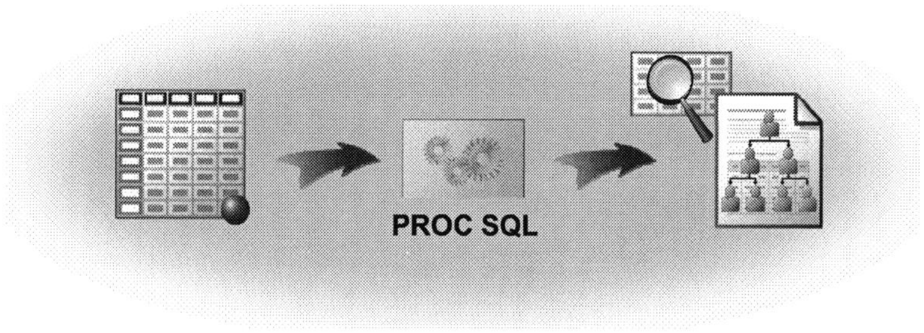

Use a PROC SQL query to examine the table and create a report.

p211d01

9

SQL Procedure

The SQL procedure enables you to write ANSI standard SQL queries in a SAS program.

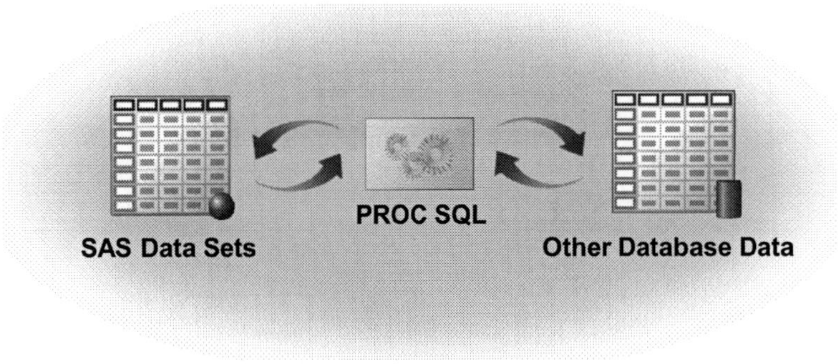

This section focuses on accessing SAS data sets.

10

With PROC SQL, you can access other DBMS tables with the appropriate SAS/ACCESS product license.

SQL Procedure

The following table shows SAS terms and the equivalent SQL terminology:

SAS Term	SQL Term
Data Set	Table
Observation	Row
Variable	Column

When using SQL to access a table, remember that you are accessing a SAS data set.

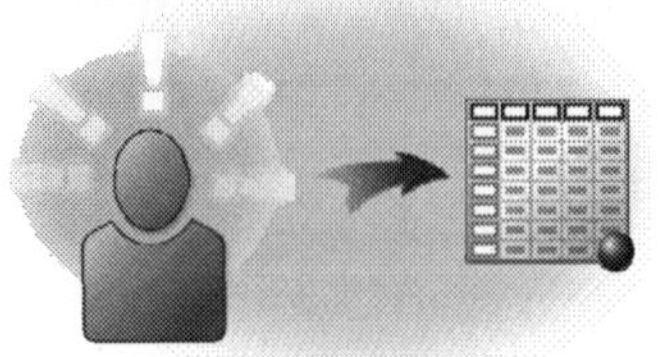

11

11.01 Multiple Choice Poll

Which of the following best describes your experience level with the SQL procedure?

a. more than one year
b. six months to one year
c. less than six months
d. I have seen SQL code but not written any.
e. no experience with SQL

12

SQL Procedure: Syntax Overview

The PROC SQL statement signals the start of an SQL procedure.

The QUIT statement ends an SQL procedure. A RUN statement is not needed because the query is executed when the semicolon is reached.

PROC SQL;

```
options ls=80;
proc sql;
select *
   from orion.sales_mgmt;
quit;
```

QUIT;

13

If the QUIT statement is omitted, the SQL procedure remains in memory to process subsequent queries. A QUIT statement or the start of another step terminates the SQL procedure and removes it from memory.

SQL Procedure: Syntax Overview

An SQL SELECT statement (also called a *query*) is submitted to query SAS tables. A query contains smaller building blocks named *clauses*.

SELECT *

```
options ls=80;
proc sql;
select *
   from orion.sales_mgmt;
quit;
```

The SELECT clause identifies columns to include in the query result. To select all columns, use an asterisk in place of the column names.

14

Query Results

The output includes all rows and all columns from **orion.sales_mgmt**.

```
                                                                   Employee
                   Start                                             Annual
  Employee ID       Date    End Date  Employee Job Title             Salary
           Employee                  Employee
 Employee     Birth    Employee   Termination    Manager for
 Gender        Date   Hire Date          Date       Employee
 ---------------------------------------------------------------------------
       121143  01JUL2001  31DEC9999  Senior Sales Manager           $95,090
 M        26NOV1973  01JUL2001              .         121142

       121144  01NOV1995  31DEC9999  Sales Manager                  $83,505
 F        28JUN1968  01NOV1995              .         121142

       121145  01APR1980  31DEC9999  Sales Manager                  $84,260
 M        22NOV1953  01APR1980              .         121142

       121147  01SEP1991  31DEC9999  Secretary II                   $29,145
 F        28MAY1973  01SEP1991              .         121142
```

15

FROM Clause

Columns listed in the SELECT statement are separated by commas. There is no comma following the last column in the list.

SELECT *object-item<, ...object-item>*

```
options ls=80;
proc sql;
select job_title, salary
   from orion.sales_mgmt;
quit;
```

FROM *from-list ...*

The FROM clause identifies the SAS table or tables from which to read.

16

11.02 Quiz

Open and submit **p211a01**. The query displays all variables in the **orion.sales_mgmt** table. Modify the SELECT statement to display only the **Employee_ID**, **Job_Title**, and **Salary** columns.

```
proc sql;
select *
   from orion.sales_mgmt;
quit;
```

17 **p211a01**

Output: A Simple SQL Query

By default a query generates a report. It does not create a table.

PROC SQL Output

Employee ID	Employee Job Title	Employee Annual Salary
121143	Senior Sales Manager	$95,090
121144	Sales Manager	$83,505
121145	Sales Manager	$84,260
121147	Secretary II	$29,145

What if you want to use the results to create a data set?

19

CREATE TABLE Statement

The CREATE TABLE statement creates an output data set or SAS table. The results are not displayed in the Output window.

CREATE TABLE *table-name* **AS...**

```
proc sql;
create table direct_reports as
select employee_id, job_title, salary
   from orion.sales_mgmt;
quit;
```

Partial SAS Log

```
38   proc sql;
39   create table direct_reports as
40   select employee_id, job_title, salary
41      from orion.sales_mgmt;
NOTE: Table WORK.DIRECT_REPORTS created, with 4 rows and 3 columns.
42   quit;
```

p211d02

20

Displaying the SAS Table Using an SQL Query

Use an SQL query to display the new table. Notice that the PROC SQL output does not identify rows by number.

```
proc sql;
select *
   from direct_reports;
quit;
```

PROC SQL Output

Employee ID	Employee Job Title	Employee Annual Salary
121143	Senior Sales Manager	$95,090
121144	Sales Manager	$83,505
121145	Sales Manager	$84,260
121147	Secretary II	$29,145

21

p211d02

Displaying the SAS Table Using an SQL Query

Use an SQL query to display the table. The NUMBER option includes a column of row numbers similar to the Obs column generated by the PRINT procedure.

```
proc sql number;
select *
   from direct_reports;
quit;
```

PROC SQL Output

Row	Employee ID	Employee Job Title	Employee Annual Salary
1	121143	Senior Sales Manager	$95,090
2	121144	Sales Manager	$83,505
3	121145	Sales Manager	$84,260
4	121147	Secretary II	$29,145

22

p211d02

Displaying the SAS Table Using PROC PRINT

You can use the PRINT procedure to display the new table, because it is a SAS data set.

```
proc print data=direct_reports;
run;
```

PROC PRINT Output

Obs	Employee_ID	Job_Title	Salary
1	121143	Senior Sales Manager	$95,090
2	121144	Sales Manager	$83,505
3	121145	Sales Manager	$84,260
4	121147	Secretary II	$29,145

23

p211d02

Business Scenario

The director wants employee names added to the previous report. The names are not in the **orion.sales_mgmt** table, but they are in **orion.employee_addresses**.

orion.employee_addresses **orion.sales_mgmt**

Employee ID	*Employee_Name*	Employee Job Title	Employee Annual Salary
121143		Senior Sales Manager	$95,090
121144		Sales Manager	$83,505
121145		Sales Manager	$84,260
121147		Secretary II	$29,145

25

Using PROC SQL to Join Tables

The **Employee_ID** column appears in both tables, so it must be qualified to identify which variable is selected.

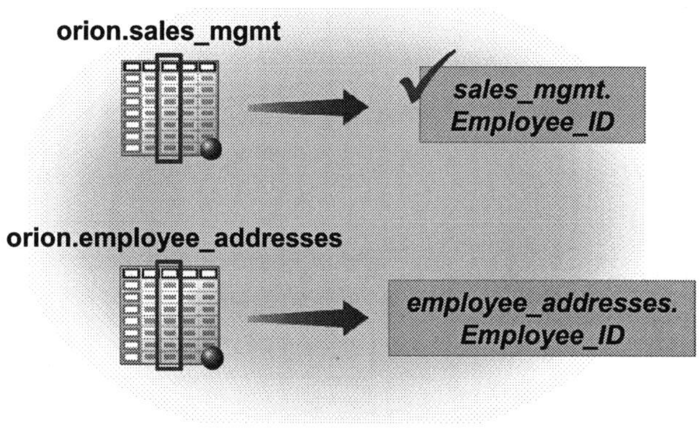

26

Using PROC SQL to Join Tables

To qualify the column, use the table name as a prefix when the column is referenced.

```
proc sql number;
select sales_mgmt.Employee_ID,
       Employee_Name,
       Job_Title,
       Salary
   from orion.sales_mgmt,
        orion.employee_addresses;
quit;
```

27 p211d03

Using PROC SQL to Join Tables

To join two or more SAS tables, list them in the FROM clause separated by commas.

```
proc sql number;
select sales_mgmt.Employee_ID,
       Employee_Name,
       Job_Title,
       Salary
   from orion.sales_mgmt,
        orion.employee_addresses;
quit;
```

FROM *SAS-table-1, SAS-table-2...*

28

11.03 Quiz

Open **p211a02,** submit the program, and view the output. It joins **orion.sales_mgmt** (4 rows total) and **orion.employee_addresses** (424 rows) to obtain the names of the director's four direct reports.

```
proc sql number;
select sales_mgmt.Employee_ID,
       Employee_Name,
       Job_Title,
       Salary
   from orion.sales_mgmt,
        orion.employee_addresses;
quit;
```

Does the output show the names of the four direct reports as desired?

29 **p211a02**

Cartesian Product

Each row in **orion.sales_mgmt** is combined with every row in **orion.employee_addresses**.

Partial **orion.sales_mgmt**

121143	Senior Sales Manager	$95,090
121144	Sales Manager	$83,505
121145	Sales Manager	$84,260

Partial **orion.employee_addresses**

121044	Abbott, Ray
120145	Aisbitt, Sandy
120761	Akinfolarin, Tameaka
120656	Amos, Salley

Partial Output

1	121143	Abbott, Ray	Senior Sales Manager	$95,090
2	121143	Aisbitt, Sandy	Senior Sales Manager	$95,090
3	121143	Akinfolarin, Tameaka	Senior Sales Manager	$95,090
4	121143	Amos, Salley	Senior Sales Manager	$95,090

31

Conceptually, when two tables are specified in a join, each row of the first table is matched with every row of the second table to produce a *Cartesian product*, which is stored in an internal or intermediate table. The number of rows in the intermediate table is equal to the product of the number of rows in each of the source tables. The intermediate table becomes the input to the rest of the query, although some of its rows might be eliminated by the WHERE clause.

Joining on a Common Variable

Obtaining the desired output requires matching the values of **Employee_ID** in both tables. This is referred to as an *inner join.*

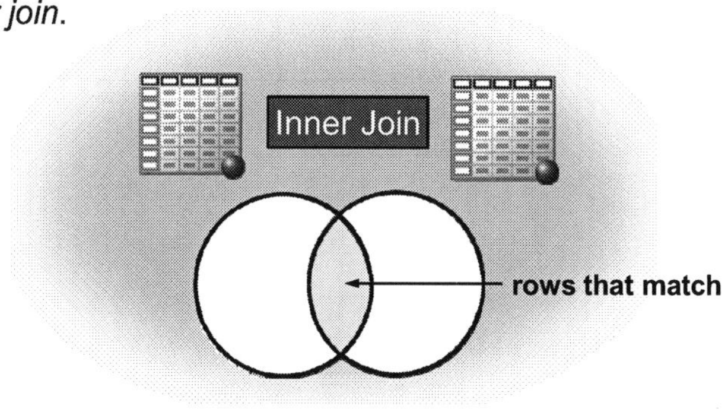

Employee_ID from **orion.sales_mgmt** =
Employee_ID from **orion.employee_addresses**

32

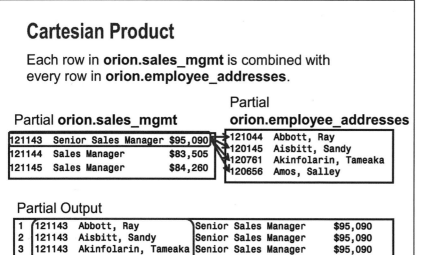

Joining on a Common Variable

A WHERE clause is used to specify the join criteria and possibly other subsetting criteria. When the conditions are met, the rows are displayed in the output.

```
proc sql;
select sales_mgmt.Employee_ID,
       Employee_Name,
       Job_Title,
       Salary
   from orion.sales_mgmt,
        orion.employee_addresses
   where sales_mgmt.Employee_ID =
         employee_addresses.Employee_ID;
quit;
```

WHERE *join-condition(s)*
<AND *other subsetting conditions*>

p211d04

33

A WHERE clause can use logical operators to include join conditions as well as other subsetting conditions.

```
where sales_mgmt.employee_id=employee_addresses.employee_id
      and Salary > 900000;
```

Output: Joining on a Common Variable

PROC SQL Output

Employee ID	Employee_Name	Employee Job Title	Employee Annual Salary
121144	Capachietti, Renee	Sales Manager	$83,505
121143	Favaron, Louis	Senior Sales Manager	$95,090
121145	Lansberry, Dennis	Sales Manager	$84,260
121147	Sneed, Christine	Secretary II	$29,145

34

An inner join is equivalent to a DATA step merge in which both data sets contribute to the merge and include matching observations. The following program is an equivalent process using the SORT procedure and a DATA step:

```
proc sort data=orion.staff out=staff;
   by employee_id;
run;
proc sort data=orion.employee_addresses out=addresses;
   by employee_id;
run;

data sqlEquiv (keep=employee_id job_title salary employee_name);
     merge staff (in=inStaff) addresses (in=inAddr);
   by employee_id;
   if instaff and inaddr;
run;

proc print data=sqlEquiv;
run;
```

11.04 Quiz

The **orion.customer** and **orion.country** tables both have a column named **Country** that contains a country abbreviation. Open **p211a03** and add a WHERE clause to join the tables based on matching values of **Country**.

```
proc sql;
select Customer_ID, Customer_Name,
       Customer.Country, Country_Name
   from orion.customer,
        orion.country
   where [                              ]
     ;
quit;
```

35

p211a03

Assigning an Alias for a SAS Table

You can specify an alias for a SAS table. The alias can replace the table name in a query. An alias can be any valid SAS name.

```
proc sql;
select s.Employee_ID,Employee_Name,
       Job_Title,Salary
   from orion.sales_mgmt as s,
        orion.employee_addresses as a
   where s.Employee_ID=a.Employee_ID;
quit;
```

FROM *SAS-table-1 <AS> alias-1,*
SAS-table-2 <AS> alias-2 ...

37 p211d05

Output: Assigning an Alias for a SAS Table

PROC SQL Output

Employee ID	Employee_Name	Employee Job Title	Employee Annual Salary
121144	Capachietti, Renee	Sales Manager	$83,505
121143	Favaron, Louis	Senior Sales Manager	$95,090
121145	Lansberry, Dennis	Sales Manager	$84,260
121147	Sneed, Christine	Secretary II	$29,145

38 p211d05

Advantages of PROC SQL and the DATA Step

With the SQL procedure, you can do the following:
Join tables and produce a report in one step without creating a SAS data set
Join tables without presorting the data
Use complex matching criteria

With the DATA step, you can do the following:
Create multiple data sets
Direct output to data sets based on data set contributors
Use First. and Last. processing
Use DO loops and arrays
Perform complex data manipulation

39

The SELECT statement syntax shows the clauses allowed and the order in which they must be written.

```
SELECT <DISTINCT> object-item <, ...object-item>
      <INTO macro-variable-specification<, ... macro-variable- specification>>
      FROM from-list
      <WHERE sql-expression>
      <GROUP BY group-by-item<, ... group-by-item>>
      <HAVING sql-expression>
      <ORDER BY order-by-item<, ... order-by-item>>;
```

Exercises

> If you restarted your SAS session since the last exercise, open and submit the **libname.sas** program found in the data folder.

Level 1

1. Modifying an Inner Join

An existing PROC SQL inner join combines information from the **orion.discount** and **orion.product_dim** tables on the matching product IDs.

- The table **orion.discount** contains discount information.
- The table **orion.product_dim** contains product descriptions.
- Both tables have a column named **Product_ID**.

a. Open and submit the program **p211e01**. Examine the output.

Partial PROC SQL Output

Product Name	Supplier Country	Start Date
Osprey Girl's Tights	US	01DEC2011
Big Guy Men's Woven Warm Up	US	01JUL2011
Woman's Foxhole Jacket	US	01JUL2011
Armadillo Road Dmx Men's Running Shoes	CA	01JUN2011
...		
Amber Cc	CA	01DEC2011

b. Modify this program as follows:

- Display the columns **Product_ID**, **Product_Name**, **Start_Date**, **End_Date**, and **Discount** as shown below.
- Modify the WHERE clause so that only rows with **Discount** greater than or equal to 60% are returned.

Hint: Add an AND to the WHERE clause to put in the condition for **Discount**. Also, remember to qualify any columns that appear in both tables.

Partial PROC SQL Output

Product ID	Product Name	Start Date	End Date	Discount as Percent of Normal Retail Sales Price
220100100309	Big Guy Men's Woven Warm Up	01JUL2011	31JUL2011	60%
220100100536	Woman's Foxhole Jacket	01JUL2011	31JUL2011	60%
220100700023	Armadillo Road Dmx Men's Running Shoes	01JUN2011	30JUN2011	70%
220100700024	Armadillo Road Dmx Women's Running Shoes	01JUL2011	31JUL2011	60%
...				
240700400002	Stephens Shirt	01JUN2011	30JUN2011	70%

Level 2

2. Coding a PROC SQL Inner Join

- The table **orion.order_fact** contains a group of orders.
- The table **orion.product_dim** contains descriptions of products.
- Both tables have a column named **Product_ID**.

Partial **orion.order_fact** (617 Total Rows, 12 Total Columns)

Product_ID	Order_ID	Quantity
220101300017	1230058123	1
230100500026	1230080101	1
240600100080	1230106883	1
240600100010	1230147441	2
240200200039	1230315085	3

Partial **orion.product_dim** (481 Total Rows, 8 Total Columns)

Product_ID	Product_Name
210200100009	Kids Sweat Round Neck,Large Logo
210200100017	Sweatshirt Children's O-Neck
210200200022	Sunfit Slow Swimming Trunks
210200200023	Sunfit Stockton Swimming Trunks Jr.
210200300006	Fleece Cuff Pant Kid'S

Write a PROC SQL inner join to combine information from these tables.

- Use the column **Product_ID** to match rows.
- Display columns **Order_ID**, **Product_ID**, **Product_Name**, and **Quantity** in the results.
- Add an appropriate title.

Partial PROC SQL Output

Detail Information for Ordered Products and Quantities

Order ID	Product ID	Product Name	Quantity Ordered
1243960910	210200100009	Kids Sweat Round Neck,Large Logo	2
1234198497	210200100017	Sweatshirt Children's O-Neck	1
1235926178	210200200022	Sunfit Slow Swimming Trunks	2
1240886449	210200200023	Sunfit Stockton Swimming Trunks Jr.	1
1242149082	210200300006	Fleece Cuff Pant Kid'S	1
1237789102	210200300007	Hsc Dutch Player Shirt Junior	1
1236701935	210200300052	Tony's Cut & Sew T-Shirt	2
1233920786	210200400020	Kids Baby Edge Max Shoes	1
1233920786	210200400070	Tony's Children's Deschutz (Bg) Shoes	1
1241086052	210200500002	Children's Mitten	3

Challenge

3. Comparing PROC SQL Inner Joins and Outer Joins

- The table **orion.order_fact** contains a group of orders.
- The table **orion.employee_addresses** contains personal information for employees.
- Both tables have a column named **Employee_ID**.

a. Write a PROC SQL inner join in order to combine information from these tables.

- Join the tables based on the column **Employee_ID**.
- Use the alternative syntax featuring the ON clause to code this inner join.
- Display the columns **Employee_Name**, **City**, and **Order_Date** in the results.
- Order the results based on **Order_Date**.
- Create a table named **work.matches** from the query results.
- Display the new table with an appropriate title.

✎ Consult SAS Help for information about using the ORDER BY clause.

Partial PROC PRINT output (324 Total Rows)

Matches from the Order and Address Tables

Obs	Employee_Name	City	Order_ Date
1	Washington, Donald	Miami-Dade	11JAN2007
2	Simms, Doungkamol	Melbourne	28JAN2007
3	Shannan, Sian	Sydney	27FEB2007
4	Carhide, Jacqulin	San Diego	15MAR2007
5	Chantharasy, Judy	Melbourne	22MAR2007
6	Shannan, Sian	Sydney	25MAR2007

b. Change the inner join that you wrote in part **a** so that you include all rows from **orion.order_fact** and matching rows from **orion.employee_addresses**.

- Create a table named **work.allorders** from the query results.
- Display the new table with an appropriate title.

Consult SAS Help for information about using a left join.

Partial PROC PRINT Output (617 total rows)

Order Dates, with Employee Information when Available

Obs	Employee_Name	City	Order_ Date
1	Washington, Donald	Miami-Dade	11JAN2007
2			15JAN2007
3			20JAN2007
4	Simms, Doungkamol	Melbourne	28JAN2007
5	Shannan, Sian	Sydney	27FEB2007
6			02MAR2007
7			03MAR2007
8			03MAR2007

11.3 The SAS Macro Language

Objectives

- State the purpose of the macro facility.
- Describe the two types of macro variables.
- Create and use macro variables.
- Display the values of macro variables in the SAS log.

43

Purpose of the Macro Facility

The *macro facility* is a text-processing facility that supports symbolic substitution within SAS code.

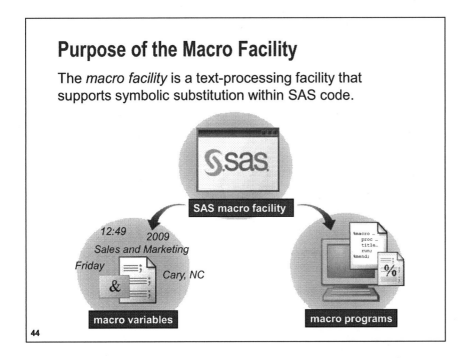

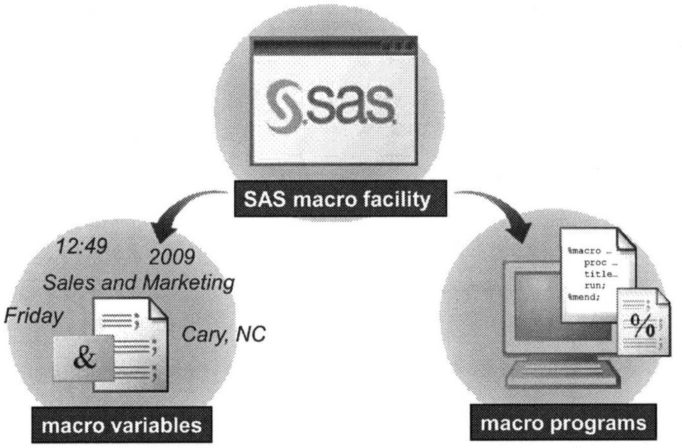

44

Types of Macro Variables

There are two types of macro variables.

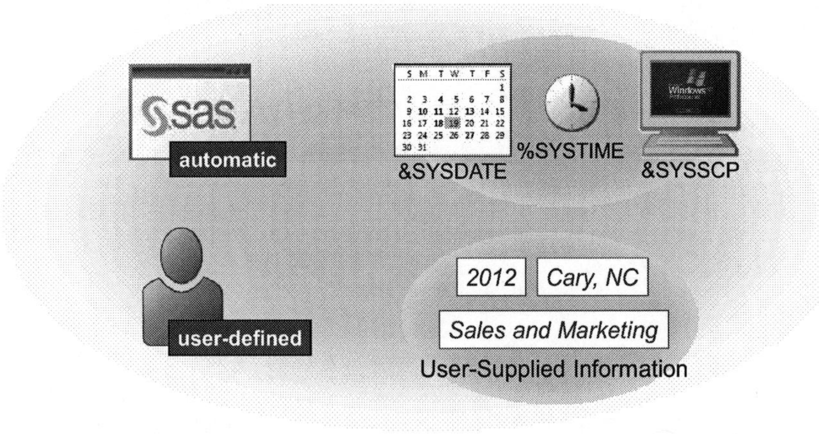

45

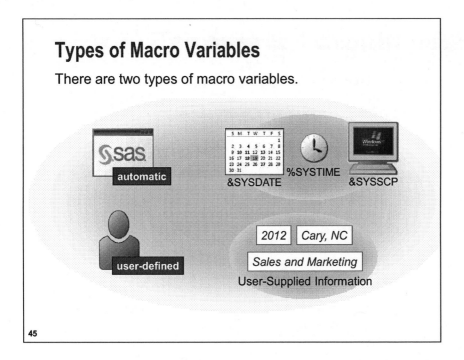

System-Defined Automatic Macro Variables

Automatic macro variables are set at SAS invocation and are always available. These include the following:

Name	Description
SYSDATE	Date of SAS invocation (DATE7.)
SYSDATE9	Date of SAS invocation (DATE9.)
SYSDAY	Day of the week of SAS invocation
SYSTIME	Time of SAS invocation
SYSSCP	Abbreviation for the operating system: OS, WIN, HP 64, and so on
SYSVER	Release of SAS software being used

To refer to a macro variable, use *&macro-variable-name*.

46

Using Automatic Macro Variables

Automatic macro variables can be used to avoid hardcoding values.

```
proc print data=orion.customer_type noobs;
title "Listing of Customer_Type Data Set";
footnote1 "Created &systime &sysday, &sysdate9";
footnote2 "on the &sysscp System Using Release &sysver";
run;
```

❶ ❷ ❸ ❹ ❺

Prior to compilation, the macro variable references are replaced with the values of the corresponding macro variables.

```
proc print data=orion.customer_type noobs;
title "Listing of Customer_Type Data Set";
footnote1 "Created 12:22 Tuesday, 14FEB2012";
footnote2 "on the WIN System Using Release 9.3";
run;
```

47

p211d06

...

Output: Using Automatic Macro Variables

Partial PROC PRINT Output

```
                         Listing of Customer_Type Data Set

Customer_                                    Customer_
 Type_ID      Customer_Type                   Group_ID     Customer_Group

  1010   Orion Club members inactive             10   Orion Club members
  1020   Orion Club members low activity         10   Orion Club members
  1030   Orion  Club members medium activity     10   Orion Club members
  1040   Orion  Club members high activity       10   Orion Club members
  2010   Orion Club Gold members low activity    20   Orion Club Gold members
  2020   Orion Club Gold members medium activity 20   Orion Club Gold members
  2030   Orion Club Gold members high activity   20   Orion Club Gold members
  3010   Internet/Catalog Customers              30   Internet/Catalog Customers

                         ❶      ❷      ❸
                       Created 12:22 Tuesday, 14FEB2012
                       on the WIN System Using Release 9.3
                              ❹                ❺
```

48

Using %PUT to Display Macro Variables

The %PUT statement displays the names and values of all automatic macro variables.

```
%put _automatic_;
```

Partial SAS Log

```
1     %put _automatic_;
AUTOMATIC AFDSID 0
AUTOMATIC AFDSNAME
AUTOMATIC AFLIB
AUTOMATIC AFSTR1
AUTOMATIC AFSTR2
AUTOMATIC FSPBDV
AUTOMATIC SYSBUFFR
AUTOMATIC SYSCC 0
AUTOMATIC SYSCHARWIDTH 1
AUTOMATIC SYSCMD
AUTOMATIC SYSDATE 25JAN08
AUTOMATIC SYSDATE9 25JAN2008
```

49

11.05 Quiz

Submit a %PUT statement to display the values of all automatic macro variables.

What are the values of the **SYSVER** and **SYSSCP** macro variables?

50

Using User-Defined Macro Variables

A developer manually changes the year values each time that the following program is submitted. Use user-defined macro variables to simplify program maintenance.

```
proc print data=orion.order_fact;
   where year(order_date)=2006;
   title "Orders for 2006";
run;
proc means data=orion.order_fact mean;
   where year(order_date)=2006;
   class order_type;
   var total_retail_price;
   title "Average Retail Prices for 2006";
   title2 "by Order_Type";
run;
```

53

p211d07

Creating and Using a Macro Variable

Use a %LET statement to create a user-defined macro variable, **year**, and a macro variable reference, **&year**, to obtain the value of the macro variable.

%LET *variable=value;*

```
%let year=2006;
proc print data=orion.order_fact;
   where year(order_date)= &year;
   title "Orders for &year";
run;
proc means data=orion.order_fact mean;
   where year(order_date)= &year;
   class order_type;
   var total_retail_price;
   title "Average Retail Prices for &year";
   title2 "by Order_Type";
run;
```

54

p211d08

...

Resulting Code: After Symbolic Substitution

The macro variable references are resolved prior to compilation. The references are replaced with the corresponding text value. The resulting code is sent to the compiler.

```
proc print data=orion.order_fact;
   where year(order_date)= 2006;
   title "Orders for 2006";
run;
proc means data=orion.order_fact mean;
   where year(order_date)= 2006;
   class order_type;
   var total_retail_price;
   title "Average Retail Prices for 2006";
   title2 "by Order_Type";
run;
```

55

Examples of the %LET Statement

```
%let year=2006;

%let city=Dallas, TX;
```

Name	Value
year	2006
city	Dallas, TX

56

11.06 Quiz

Complete the rest of the table.

```
%let year=2006;

%let city=Dallas, TX;

%let fname=     Marie    ;

%let name=" Marie Hudson ";

%let total=10+2;
```

Name	Value
year	2006
city	Dallas, TX

57

11.07 Quiz

Examine the program below. What change (or changes) must be made to generate reports for 2007?

```
%let year=2006;
proc print data=orion.order_fact;
   where year(order_date)= &year;
   title "Orders for &year";
run;
proc means data=orion.order_fact mean;
   where year(order_date)= &year;
   class order_type;
   var total_retail_price;
   title "Average Retail Prices for &year";
   title2 "by Order_Type";
run;
```

59 p211a04

Displaying Macro Variable Values in the Log

Enable the SYMBOLGEN system option to write a message to the SAS log each time that a macro variable is resolved.

OPTIONS SYMBOLGEN;

```
options symbolgen;
%let year=2006;
proc means data=orion.order_fact mean;
   where year(order_date)=&year;
   class order_type;
   var total_retail_price;
   title "Average Retail Prices for &year";
   title2 "by Order_Type";
run;
```

The default option is NOSYMBOLGEN.

61 p211d09

Displaying Macro Variable Values

A message is written to the SAS log each time that a macro variable is resolved.

```
59   options symbolgen;
60   %let year=2006;
61   proc means data=orion.order_fact mean;
62      where year(order_date)=&year;
SYMBOLGEN:  Macro variable YEAR resolves to 2006
63      class order_type;
64      var total_retail_price;
SYMBOLGEN:  Macro variable YEAR resolves to 2006
65      title "Average Retail Prices for &year Orders";
66      title2 "by Order_Type";
67   run;
```

62

Substitution within a SAS Literal

Suppose you need to reference a macro variable within a SAS literal.

```
%let site=Melbourne;
proc print data=orion.employee_addresses;
   where City="&site";
   var Employee_ID Employee_Name;
   title 'Employees from &site';
run;
```

Will this program create this output?

Partial PROC PRINT Output

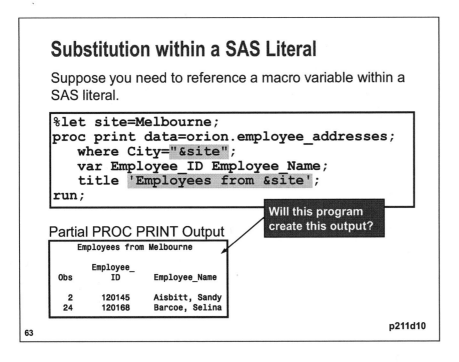

```
      Employees from Melbourne

          Employee_
 Obs         ID        Employee_Name

   2       120145      Aisbitt, Sandy
  24       120168      Barcoe, Selina
```

63

p211d10

Substitution within a SAS Literal

Double quotation marks enable macro variable resolution and single quotation marks prevent macro variable resolution.

```
%let site=Melbourne;
proc print data=orion.employee_addresses;
   where City="&site";
   var Employee_ID Employee_Name;
   title 'Employees from &site';
run;
NOTE: There were 41 observations read from the data set
ORION.EMPLOYEE_ADDRESSES.
      WHERE City='Melbourne';
```

site resolved in double quotation marks.

```
      Employees from &site

          Employee_
 Obs         ID        Employee_Name

   2       120145      Aisbitt, Sandy
  24       120168      Barcoe, Selina
```

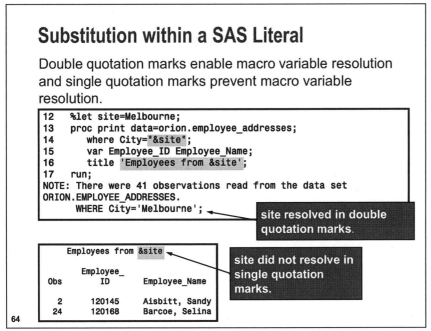

site did not resolve in single quotation marks.

64

Substitution within a SAS Literal

There is no SYMBOLGEN message for the second reference to **site** because it is not resolved.

```
options symbolgen;
%let site=Melbourne;
proc print data=orion.employee_addresses;
   where City="&site";
SYMBOLGEN:  Macro variable SITE resolves to Melbourne
   var Employee_ID Employee_Name;
   title 'Employees from &site';
run;

NOTE: There were 41 observations read from the data set
ORION.EMPLOYEE_ADDRESSES.
      WHERE City='Melbourne';
```

65

p211d11

Using Macro Variables within a SAS Literal

If the code requires quotation marks, the macro variable reference should be enclosed in double quotation marks.

```
%let site=Melbourne;
proc print data=orion.employee_addresses;
   where City="&site";
   var Employee_ID Employee_Name;
   title "Employees from &site";
run;
```

Partial PROC PRINT Output

```
        Employees from Melbourne

            Employee_
 Obs           ID         Employee_Name

   2        120145        Aisbitt, Sandy
  24        120168        Barcoe, Selina
```

66

p211d11

Using %PUT to Display Macro Variables

Remember, you can use the %PUT statement to display the names and values of all automatic macro variables.

Partial SAS Log

```
1    %put _automatic_;
AUTOMATIC AFDSID 0
AUTOMATIC AFDSNAME
AUTOMATIC AFLIB
AUTOMATIC AFSTR1
AUTOMATIC AFSTR2
```

Suppose you want to display the names and values of only the user-defined macro variables in the SAS log?

67

Using %PUT to Display Macro Variables

To display the names and values of all user-defined macro variables, use this form of the %PUT statement:

```
%put _user_;
```

Partial SAS Log

```
136  %put _user_;
GLOBAL SITE Melbourne
GLOBAL YEAR 2007
```

To display both user-defined and automatic macro variables, use this form of the %PUT statement:

```
%put _all_;
```

Partial SAS Log

```
136  %put _user_;
GLOBAL SITE Melbourne
GLOBAL YEAR 2007
AUTOMATIC AFDSID 0
AUTOMATIC AFDSNAME
AUTOMATIC AFLIB
```

68

Exercises

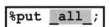

If you restarted your SAS session since the last exercise, open and submit the **libname.sas** program found in the data folder.

Level 1

4. Replacing a Hardcoded Value with a Macro Variable

a. Modify the program **p211e04** to display only customers in Germany.

- Open the file **p211e04**.
- Submit the program.
- Modify the program by creating a macro variable named **location** and use it in place of the hardcoded value, **DE**. (DE is the country code for Germany.)
- Submit the program and verify your results.

Partial PROC PRINT Output (10 Total Observations)

```
                     Customers in DE

Obs     Customer_ID    Customer_Name           Gender

  3               9    Cornelia Krahl            F
  5              11    Elke Wallstab             F
  7              13    Markus Sepke              M
  8              16    Ulrich Heyde              M
 11              19    Oliver S. Füßling         M
```

b. Change the value of **location** to **ZA** to display customers in South Africa and resubmit the program. (ZA is the country code for South Africa.) Verify your results.

PROC PRINT Output

```
                     Customers in ZA

Obs     Customer_ID    Customer_Name            Gender

 53            2550    Sanelisiwe Collier         F
 54            2618    Theunis Brazier            M
 56            2806    Raedene Van Den Berg       F
 57            3959    Rita Lotz                  F
```

Level 2

5. Creating and Using a Macro Variable

a. Generate a report showing a list of all employees earning at least a designated minimum salary.

- Write a program to create a macro variable, **minSal**, and set its value to represent a minimum salary of $60,000.
- Use the **orion.employee_payroll** data set and the PRINT procedure to generate the report below.
  - Format **birth_date**, **employee_hire_date**, and **employee_term_date** with the DATE9. format.
  - Add an appropriate title and verify your results.

Partial PROC PRINT Output (34 Total Observations)

Employees Earning at Least $60000

Obs	Employee_ID	Employee_ Gender	Salary	Birth_ Date	Employee_ Hire_Date	Employee_ Term_Date	Marital_ Status	Dependents
1	120101	M	163040	18AUG1980	01JUL2007	.	S	0
2	120102	M	108255	11AUG1973	01JUN1993	.	O	2
3	120103	M	87975	22JAN1953	01JAN1978	.	M	1
99	120259	M	433800	25JAN1968	01SEP1993	.	M	1
100	120260	F	207885	02DEC1968	01NOV1988	.	M	2

b. Modify the previous solution to display employees who earn at least $100,000. Verify your results.

PROC PRINT Output (9 Total Observations)

Employees Earning at Least $100000

Obs	Employee_ID	Employee_ Gender	Salary	Birth_ Date	Employee_ Hire_Date	Employee_ Term_Date	Marital_ Status	Dependents
1	120101	M	163040	18AUG1980	01JUL2007	.	S	0
2	120102	M	108255	11AUG1973	01JUN1993	.	O	2
99	120259	M	433800	25JAN1968	01SEP1993	.	M	1
100	120260	F	207885	02DEC1968	01NOV1988	.	M	2
101	120261	M	243190	21FEB1973	01AUG1991	.	O	1

11.4 Solutions

Solutions to Exercises

1. **Modifying an Inner Join**

```
proc sql;
select d.Product_ID, Product_Name, Start_Date, End_Date, Discount
   from orion.discount as d, orion.product_dim as p
   where d.Product_ID=p.Product_ID and Discount >= .6;
quit;
```

2. **Coding a PROC SQL Inner Join**

```
title 'Detail Information for Ordered Products and Quantities';
proc sql;
select Order_ID, o.Product_ID, Product_Name, Quantity
   from orion.order_fact as o, orion.product_dim as p
   where o.Product_ID=p.Product_ID;
quit;
title;
```

Alternate Solution

```
title 'Detail Information for Ordered Products and Quantities';
proc sql;
select Order_ID, o.Product_ID, Product_Name, Quantity
   from orion.order_fact as o
```

```
      INNER JOIN
   orion.product_dim as p
   on o.Product_ID=p.Product_ID;
quit;
title;
```

3. **Comparing PROC SQL Inner Joins and Outer Joins**

```
proc sql;
create table work.matches as
select Employee_Name, City, Order_Date
   from orion.Order_fact as o
      INNER JOIN
   orion.Employee_addresses as a
   on a.Employee_ID=o.Employee_ID
   order by Order_Date;
quit;

title 'Matches from the Order and Address Tables';
proc print data=work.matches;
run;
title;

proc sql;
create table work.allorders as
select Employee_Name, City, Order_Date
   from orion.Order_fact as o
      LEFT JOIN
   orion.Employee_addresses as a
   on a.Employee_ID=o.Employee_ID
   order by Order_Date;
quit;

title 'Order Dates, with Employee Information when Available';
proc print data=work.allorders;
run;
title;
```

4. **Replacing a Hardcoded Value with a Macro Variable**

```
%let location=DE;
title "Customers in &location";
proc print data=orion.customer;
   var customer_id customer_name gender;
   where country="&location";
run;

%let location=ZA;
title "Customers in &location";
proc print data=orion.customer;
   var customer_id customer_name gender;
   where country="&location";
run;
```

5. **Creating and Using a Macro Variable**

```
%let minSal=60000;
title "Employees Earning at Least $&minSal";
proc print data=orion.employee_payroll;
   where salary >= &minSal;
run;

%let minSal=100000;
title "Employees Earning at Least $&minSal";
proc print data=orion.employee_payroll;
   where salary >= &minSal;
run;
```

Solutions to Student Activities (Polls/Quizzes)

11.02 Quiz – Correct Answer

Modify the SELECT statement to display **Employee_ID**, **Job_Title**, and **Salary**. **List the columns in the desired order in the SELECT clause.**

```
libname orion "SAS-data-library";
proc sql;
select employee_id, job_title, salary
   from orion.sales_mgmt;
quit;
```

Employee ID	Employee Job Title	Employee Annual Salary
121143	Senior Sales Manager	$95,090
121144	Sales Manager	$83,505
121145	Sales Manager	$84,260
121147	Secretary II	$29,145

18

p211a01s

11.03 Quiz – Correct Answer

No, the output contains many more rows than expected.

```
  /* SQL query to join two SAS tables */
proc sql number;
select sales_mgmt.Employee_ID,
       Employee_Name,
       Job_Title,
       Salary
   from orion.sales_mgmt,
        orion.employee_addresses;
NOTE: The execution of this query involves performing one or more
      Cartesian product joins that cannot be optimized.
quit;
```

A Cartesian product was created.
The result contains 1696 rows (4 * 424).

30

11.04 Quiz – Correct Answer

The **orion.customer** and **orion.country** tables both have a column named **Country** that contains a country abbreviation. Open **p211a03** and add a WHERE clause to join the tables based on matching values of **Country**.

```
proc sql;
select Customer_ID, Customer_Name,
       Customer.Country, Ccountry_Name
   from orion.customer,
        orion.country
   where customer.Country=country.Country
     ;
quit;
```

36

p211a03s

11.05 Quiz – Correct Answer

Submit a %PUT statement to display the values of all automatic macro variables.

```
%put _automatic_;
```

What are the values of the **SYSVER** and **SYSSCP** macro variables?

Answers vary, but for many installations, the value of SYSVER is *9.3* and the value of SYSSCP is *WIN*.

51

11.06 Quiz – Correct Answer

Complete the rest of the table.

```
%let year=2006;

%let city=Dallas, TX;

%let fname=      Marie    ;

%let name=" Marie Hudson ";

%let total=10+2;
```

Name	Value
year	2006
city	Dallas, TX
fname	**Marie**
name	**" Marie Hudson "**
total	**10+2**

58

11.07 Quiz – Correct Answer

Examine the program below. What change (or changes) must be made to generate reports for 2007? **Change the value assigned in the %LET statement.**

```
%let year=2007;
proc print data=orion.order_fact;
   where year(order_date)= &year;
   title "Orders for &year";
run;
proc means data=orion.order_fact mean;
   where year(order_date)= &year;
   class order_type;
   var total_retail_price;
   title "Average Retail Prices for &year";
   title2 "by Order_Type";
run;
```

60

p211a04s

Chapter 12 Learning More

12.1 Introduction..12-3

12.1 Introduction

Objectives

- Identify the areas of support that SAS offers.
- Identify the next steps after the completion of this course.

2

Customer Support

SAS provides a variety of resources to help customers.

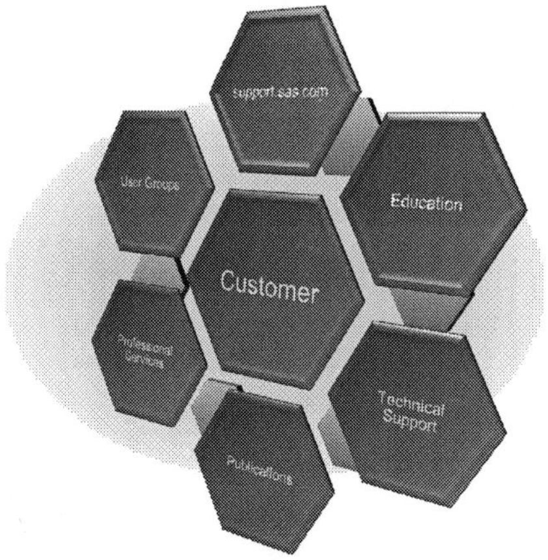

http://support.sas.com/resourcekit/

3

Education

SAS Education provides comprehensive training, including

- more than 200 course offerings
- world-class instructors
- multiple delivery methods
- worldwide training centers.

http://support.sas.com/training/

4

SAS Global Certification Program

SAS Education also provides

- globally recognized certifications
- preparation materials
- practice exams.

http://support.sas.com/certify/

5

Networking

Social media channels and user group organizations enable you to

- interact with other SAS users and SAS staff
- learn new programming tips and tricks
- get exclusive discounts.

For training-specific information:

http://support.sas.com/training/socialmedia

6

Icons are from top left to right, and then bottom left to right:

Twitter, RSS, Myspace, You Tube, Facebook, Technorati, and sasCommunity.org

SAS Books

SAS Books offers a complete selection of publications, including

- eBooks
- CD-ROM
- hard-copy books
- books written by outside authors.

http://support.sas.com/bookstore/

1-800-727-3228

7

Beyond This Course

To grow your SAS skills, remember to activate the ***extended learning page*** for this course.

Individual learning software licenses are available through SAS® OnDemand for Professionals: Enterprise Guide.

http://support.sas.com/learn/ondemand/professionals

8

Next Steps

To learn more about this:	Enroll in this course:
How to use SQL to manipulate and merge data files	SAS® SQL 1: Essentials
How to write SAS programs that are reusable, dynamic, and easily maintained	SAS® Macro Language 1: Essentials
DATA step programming techniques and comparing the efficiencies of different techniques	SAS® Programming 3: Advanced Techniques and Efficiencies
Creating reports using the REPORT and TABULATE procedures, plus the Output Delivery System (ODS)	SAS® Report Writing 1: Using Procedures and ODS
Performing statistical analysis using SAS/STAT software	Statistics 1: Introduction to ANOVA, Regression, and Logistic Regression
Preparing for the Base Certification Exam	SAS® Certification Review: Base Programming for SAS®9

9